WHAT IS SELF?

Also by Bernadette Roberts:

The Experience of No-Self
The Path to No-Self

WHAT IS SELF?

*A Study of the Spiritual Journey
in Terms of Consciousness*

Bernadette Roberts

Mary Botsford Goens

Austin, Texas

Library of Congress Catalog Card Number 89-91249
ISBN: 0-9623993-0-2

Sixth Printing
Printed in the United States of America

ACKNOWLEDGEMENTS

Without the help of family and friends this book could not have been written or published. In the order of the book's various stages I wish to thank the following people. First, the community of St. Benedict's Monastery, Snowmass, Colorado. Due to their generosity this book took shape in their barn room in the early months of 1985. Being able to share in their monastic life, however, was the best gift of all.

Next in order is my sister Marjorie and her husband, Dewey. Without their help I would not have a roof over my head. Due to a financial disaster in the early 1980's my children and I were left penniless. After 1983 no writing was possible. Because of this I finally accepted my sister's offer of accommodations in 1985, and here I remain. For this and much more I am forever indebted to Marjorie and her husband.

Finally, my meeting in 1988 with Dr. Mary Goens at a workshop at Esalen Institute brought everything to a head. I have no way of accounting for Mary's offer to publish the first printing of this book or her dedication to the project. After all, she has nothing to gain —and may even stand to lose. Her getting nothing for her trouble, however, reminds me of our first encounter. People in the workshop were articulating their immediate goals; Mary said, "I am wondering if it is ever possible to reach a point where there is no self in anything we do." I think this statement is a fitting explanation of how this book came to be published. As a product of selfless enterprise, I dedicate this book to God and to Mary. To both, I am eternally grateful.

CONTENTS

CONTENTS

INTRODUCTION

After writing the account of my journey,[1] I began a third book in order to present a complete overview of the psychological-spiritual journey from beginning to end. Without the opportunity to complete this work, however, I wrote several shorter pieces in immediate response to those who had read the books in print, but had misunderstood the true "no-self experience" and its place in the journey. The present book, *What Is Self?*, consists of three of these shorter pieces. While this writing cannot compensate for a more thorough and detailed study of the journey, I hope that it will help to resolve some of the immediate questions and misunderstandings that have arisen because of the previous works.

From the beginning, the sole purpose of my writing has been to put into the contemplative literature an entire stage and final event (the no-self event) that presently is not there. Despite objections to the contrary, this particular stage and final event have not been accounted for in our contemplative literature, East or West. To search a hundred or more classics in the field and find only a few

---

[1] *The Path To No-Self* covers a period of twenty years and begins with the account of the Dark Night of the Spirit (falling away of the ego-center) that culminates in the unitive state. After this the journey moves up to the point at which the unitive state and true self (not the ego) falls away. The second book, *The Experience of No-Self*, begins with this latter experience (falling away of the unitive state and true self) and covers a period of two years. (Shambhala Publications, 1985 and 1984 respectively.)

hidden suggestions of such an event is not sufficient. My affirming that it is not in the literature, however, has been the cause of some ridicule. The impression is that I am illiterate, have no formal knowledge of the path, or am totally ignorant of the available classics. The whole problem is that until we come upon this final event we do not know it is missing from the literature; thus we have no way of knowing what, specifically, to look for. In other words, until we know first hand or by experience exactly what to look for, we are not in a position to judge whether or not this event is in the literature.

This does not mean that millions of people have not come upon the no-self event; indeed, sooner or later everyone will do so. All it means is that an accurate, distinguishable or clarifying account is not in the literature. The challenge of providing such an account is what my writing is about. Attesting to the difficulty of this challenge is the fact that my first two books failed in this matter, so here, now, is a third attempt. I might add, the fact this book was not acceptable to a trade publisher further demonstrates the difficulty of putting the no-self event into the literature. It may be that for centuries our various censors have eliminated any event they did not understand or which they thought too upsetting to their clientele. I can only speculate about this.

In general, our contemplative maps of the journey come to an end with the discovery of the true self and its oneness with the divine. This unitive state—known by various terms in different traditions—follows the falling away or transcendence of the ego (self-center) and entails a radical change or transformation of consciousness. Beyond this, however, our maps do not go. But this unitive or transcendental state is not the end of the journey. It may be the end of the ego-self, but by no means is it the end of self— either the true self or the phenomenal self. For this, we have much further to go.

This is saying that our completed journey consists of two very different endings: first, the falling away of the ego or self-center and, second, the much later falling away of the true self and divine-center (and consequently the phenomenal self). In one of my earlier books I referred to these two different endings as the "two major move- ments" of the journey. While this may not have been the best wording, the reference was nevertheless the same—first, no-ego; second, no-self. Nowhere does our contemplative literature make this specific distinction; instead, it speaks of only *one* major move- ment or ending, which ending is always indicative of a unitive state no matter how variously it has been described. The final event, however, is the falling away of the unitive state; in fact, the whole purpose of the unitive state or stage is to bring us to the final no-unitive or no-self event. It is imperative, then, to make a clear distinction between first getting to the egoless unitive state and from here going forward to the eventual falling away of this same egoless unitive state. To make this distinction as clear as possible and leave no doubts or questions is what this book attempts to do.

The true no-self event or falling away of the unitive state is bound to alter our traditional maps and paradigms of the journey. It not only pushes our previous boundaries by presenting us with a totally new view of self or consciousness, but it necessitates a change in our usual perspective and understanding of the completed journey. The major change is that the unitive state of oneness is no longer regarded as the ultimate goal but, instead, is seen as the mid-point of the passage and a state that moves on to a more final end. This means that a long portion of the journey, between arriving at the unitive state and its eventual falling away, must now be accounted for. It means that the subtle, largely unconscious movement between the beginning and end of the unitive state has yet to be considered and described.

As matters stand now, however, it seems that the very idea that the unitive state eventually falls away strikes the mind as incomprehensible, unbelievable—impossible in fact. For this reason the no-self event has been variously misinterpreted as: (1) the "no-ego" event, (2) a mistaken interpretation of an experience, (3) a misunderstanding of the traditional path, (4) a semantic error or improper use and definition of terms, (5) a kind of mulish pride and prejudice on the part of the author. The list of misinterpretations goes on. At bottom, however, the whole problem is that, by its very nature, self or consciousness is incapable of conceiving its own nonexistence. It cannot possibly imagine any kind of life without itself because that which could imagine such a life IS self. So the true difficulty of understanding the no-self event is not one of semantics; rather, it is consciousness' (psyche or self's) own inability to go beyond itself; it is impossible. It is also a problem of understanding the true nature of self or consciousness, the nature of its movement and the final cessation of this movement. In some ways it is also a problem of belief. We cannot believe experiences we have not had or are unable to conceive or imagine; much less can we believe any experience we cannot find verified and described in our traditional literature. But our literature, as I have said, is almost exclusively concerned with how to get to the egoless unitive state. It says nothing about the next twenty or thirty years in the marketplace and how this state works to make possible the eventual falling away of all self and its unitive state. To account for this vital and necessary stage in the marketplace—between the beginning and end of the unitive state—is another purpose of my writing.

The following pages are divided into three parts. Each part answers the question "What is Self?" from a slightly different perspective, though always in terms of experience. What I know about the true nature of self has not been derived from any theory, speculation or academic study, but solely from experience or what has been learned for having made the journey. If the reader lacks similar experiences or cannot recognize a given perspective, then it is inevitable that much of this writing can only be given an academic understanding. In lieu of experiences there seems to be no other choice in the matter.

Part I presents an overview of the journey with particular emphasis on its major milestones or turning points. As a shortened version of a larger work in progress, however, this part is not intended to be a detailed or thorough account of the journey. Beginning with the structure and function of consciousness we will follow the self-experience (which IS consciousness) as it changes in the course of the journey. Viewing our psychological-spiritual journey as a passage through self or consciousness, this overview illustrates how self or consciousness works to bring man to his ultimate destiny.

Part II, "Three Views of Consciousness," was written primarily for those who mistook my view of self or consciousness for that of either Carl Jung or orthodox Hinduism. Since these two views are essentially different from mine—and even different from one another—it was hoped that by putting these views side by side their differences would become obvious. The purpose of this format is not to put down the beliefs and experiences of any individual or group of people; rather, the use of contrast is simply a way of presenting an alternative view or perspective.

Recently someone asked if there was anything beyond no-self or if this was the ultimate goal of the journey. The question is important because no-self is by no means the ultimate goal or final revelation of the journey. Rather, the no-self event is the necessary means for coming upon final Truth—Truth, however, as it lies beyond all self or consciousness. Part III, "The Christian Passage," is a brief account of what I learned of this Truth for having made the passage. We cannot treat the subject of God and self apart from one another; not only does one necessitate the revelation of the other, but the deepest or furthest experience of which self or consciousness is capable IS God. What is more, in proportion as God increases, self decreases. Thus the gradual revelation of the true nature of self is by its decreasing or absence which, at the same time, is the further or increasing revelation of the true nature of God—for the Christian, God's Trinitarian nature. So there is no way we can disconnect the eventual falling away of self from the revelation of God. They are, as it were, two sides of the same event.

Part III is what I learned of Christ both in the course of the journey and, more especially, when it was finished. The second chapter of this section is an account of the major turning points in my journey wherein the truth and reality of Christ were gradually revealed. I think this account is the clue to a true understanding of the eventual falling away of self. Outside the Christian context I do not see how it would be possible to have a true understanding of the no-self event, or of how and why it comes about. Apart from Christ's death such an event might be viewed as nothing but an incomprehensible tragedy.

Now I think enough has been said to give the reader a general idea of what this book is about. If the content and purpose of this writing seems to be in total contradiction to the reader's beliefs and expectations regarding self and the journey, then he or she is advised to read no further. Those who do read further are advised to keep in mind that the Christian path is the only one I ever lived; thus what I know of other religious traditions and psychological paradigms is solely by way of reading and discussion with others. So, although I speak of Hinduism, Buddhism and the psychology of Carl Jung, I have never had their particular experiences or shared their perspectives. I trust readers will allow for this just as they allow for those who, never having lived the Christian contemplative path, nevertheless continue to give us their views on it.

PART I
WHAT IS SELF?

PART I: WHAT IS SELF?

Definition of Terms

No one knows the true nature of self as long as he is living it, or is it. The true nature of self can be disclosed only when it falls away and becomes known in retrospect, by its absence or what was. As it turns out, self is first and foremost an unconscious experience and only secondarily a conscious experience. Thus the self we know is the conscious-self, and the self we do not know is the unconscious-self; together these constitute the entire human dimension of knowing, feeling and experiencing. In essence, self is what it means to be human. As a dynamic but non-eternal experience it is in passage, a passage that is our life. Thus we might say that what self or consciousness IS, is a passage through human existence. With the falling away of self, it becomes possible to get an overview of this passage along with its major milestones. From this particular perspective we will be discussing the experience that we consciously know as self, but unconsciously cannot recognize until it is gone.

Before we begin, however, it should be pointed out that beyond the human dimension of knowing and experiencing lie other dimensions of existence: animal, plant, mineral, elemental, as well as the dimension of ultimate Truth, the divine—Absolute, God, or whatever we wish to call the alpha and omega of all possible levels of existence. What keeps human beings locked within the centrality of their own experience is self or consciousness; while man knows *about* other dimensions of existence he cannot experience these dimensions because consciousness precludes his doing so. Thus no one, for example, can know the immediate experience of a bird or a lump of sugar. In order to BE a bird or a lump of sugar there could be no human experience, and thus there would be no one to give us a report. Consciousness then precludes the experience of other dimensions of existence, and it does so in order to make the human experience possible. If consciousness had not come into existence, the limit of experience would be that of the animal; if the animal or purely sensory experience had not come into existence, the dimension of experience would have remained that of the plant; and without the plant, existence would be purely elemental, and so on, back to the ultimate source or beginning. The point is that consciousness is only one dimension or level of existence and this dimension is our unique human way of knowing, feeling and experiencing.

Because the terms "self" and "consciousness" express the same experiences and because nothing can be said of one that cannot be said of the other, we use these terms interchangeably and affirm that the true nature of self IS consciousness. The study of self, therefore, is equally the study of consciousness. But since we cannot use two interchangeable terms to define one another, we must derive our definition of self or consciousness from the experiences that give rise to these terms in the first place. As everyone's most immediate knowing ("I exist," for example), self or consciousness is first of all an experience and only secondarily a word or an idea that expresses this experience. Thus if there were no experiences to back up the terms "self" or "consciousness" (and all their subsidiary expressions: I, me, you, etc.), these terms could not have arisen. It is solely by *experience* that we know self or consciousness; as a mere word, concept or theory held in the mind, we can never know it.

In these pages we use the term "consciousness" (or "awareness") to include the entire system of consciousness with its various levels of experience from the unconscious to God-consciousness. By "consciousness" or "self" we mean the whole of the psyche, which, in Jungian terms, includes the conscious ego and unconscious self. In Eastern terminology it includes the "true Self," "Atman," or "Pure Consciousness," at least as I see it. All of these experiences fall within the experiential boundaries of self or consciousness. To realize an abiding oneness with the divine is the highest potential of self or consciousness; in this case the deepest experience of self

IS the experience of the divine. But this realization or awareness is not outside the boundaries of self or consciousness. Throughout these pages the word "consciousness" always includes both the conscious and unconscious levels of consciousness. Although we will be going into the primary experiences that constitute the self-experience, our first interest is to find out what makes this experience possible in the first place.

Consciousness and the Senses

Although we say that man is unique by reason of consciousness and not by reason of the senses—which belong to the animals as well—the problem with excluding the senses from man's unique way of knowing is that as long as consciousness remains, man never experiences "pure" sensory perception (as the animals do). This is because these two systems, consciousness and the senses, are intimately connected and function as a unit or singular whole. Thus from the day we are born (or conceived even) the development of consciousness depends on the simultaneous development of the senses. Despite this developmental priority or dependency (of consciousness on the senses) we cannot equate the human sensory system with that of the animal whose sensory system has no potential for functioning in conjunction with consciousness. This means that the human sensory system is unique to man and must not be equated with the sensory system of the animal. Where the human sensory system has the potential for functioning in conjunction with consciousness, the animal sensory system has no such potential because no consciousness is present. To say that animals are not conscious beings frequently raises objections. These objections, however, are based on the fact that consciousness is incapable of experiencing *pure* sensory perception—which is knowing without consciousness—and thus it underrates, because it does not understand, any way of knowing other than its own.

For the most part it rarely occurs to anyone that the human sensory system can function without consciousness. Usually people believe it is the other way around—namely, that consciousness can function without the senses. This latter belief, however, is based on the notion that consciousness is eternal or an immortal soul perhaps, but in truth, matters are actually the reverse. Man, like the animal, can function without consciousness, but neither man nor animal can function without the senses. Thus while it is quite possible for man to go on living and functioning without consciousness, once the senses cease to function the result is a purely vegetative mode of existence. While plants can thrive in such a dimension of existence, neither man nor animal can do so. The whole point is that as long as consciousness remains, it functions in conjunction with the senses and does not allow for "pure" sensory knowing. Thus we must keep in mind that apart from consciousness or separate from it, the senses have their own way-of-knowing and partake of a dimension of existence not available to consciousness.

Although it is not our intention to go into the nature of "pure" sensory knowing, it is important to note that once consciousness falls away sensory knowing turns out to be quite different from what we had previously believed it to be. Where we thought the senses had been responsible for discriminating the particular and singular, and believed that consciousness and the intellect posited the universal or whole, it turns out to be the other way around. The senses do not know, and cannot focus on, the particular or singular; it is nowhere in their power to do so. Consciousness alone has this focusing and discriminating power. Thus by themselves the senses cannot discriminate the singular or particular, and without the singular there is also no plural, no parts and wholes, no one-and-the-many. Sensory knowing is not derived by reflection, intuition, feeling or any such experience; instead, whatever is to be known is simply "there"—quite flatly with no thought or feeling. The senses merely apprehend "what is" with none of the distinctions, discriminations and labeling that are so indicative of the function of consciousness. As it turns out then, consciousness is a discriminator, discriminating the particular and multiple, the knower and known, subject and object. Its dimension is entirely relative, while the senses are non-discriminating and non-relative, knowing neither parts nor whole. Also, pure sensory knowing is neither a different type of consciousness nor a different level of the same; rather, it is a totally different system or way of knowing—virtually a different dimension of existence. Pure sensory knowing bears no resemblance to the knowing, experiencing dimension of consciousness. Obviously there are more ways of knowing than that of consciousness.

Similar to the senses, consciousness is a physiological function integrated with the total body-mind functioning. From this integration man derives an unconscious subjective sense of physical form, or experiences himself as a discrete, separate entity or being. In the absence of consciousness, however, the experience and awareness of physical form dissolves, resulting in the unusual experience of bodilessness, a condition to which man would have to acclimate if consciousness were permanently to fall away. So form as it is experienced by consciousness is quite different from form experienced by the senses alone—and different as well from Form known in the absolute sense of the term. Thus when we have occasion to say that "form is void," we are not speaking from the experience of consciousness and its way of knowing (or even its way of not knowing); rather, this statement is made first of all from the experience of "pure" sensory knowing. Then ultimately, when we have realized that void IS absolute, this statement is made from the perspective of absolute knowing. For now, however, we wish only to emphasize that for mankind sensory knowing as it lies beyond consciousness is not the same as the animals' sensory knowing. The movement beyond consciousness is a forward step for man, not a backward step into the animal dimension of existence. Our human passage to the divine is an irreversible forward movement; it cannot reverse itself or move backwards to any lesser dimension of existence.

The Function of Consciousness

The fact that man is not always conscious of his own awareness (self-conscious, that is) attests to the rootedness of self-awareness in the unconscious. This rootedness is responsible for the continuity of self-consciousness across all levels of consciousness, including the level we call "unitive" or "God-consciousness." There could be no self-awareness if this awareness were not, first of all, unconscious. As someone once noted, nothing rises to the conscious level that is not first on the unconscious level of consciousness. This fact tells us that self-awareness on the conscious level is not sufficient to account for self or consciousness, and that we must look to a deeper level if we are to find the true source and origin of self-awareness.

This deeper level, of course, is everything we call the "unconscious," a level we often think of in terms of content and storage, or mysterious energies and powers—in a word, everything we do not know about ourselves on the conscious level. But far more important, on this unconscious level consciousness functions automatically, spontaneously, almost mechanically and beyond our conscious control. Also on this level, consciousness as a physiological function connects with other physiological functions and is integrated with the total body-mind. This integration is such that changes in either the function of consciousness or in any bodily function is reciprocally experienced by the body and consciousness alike. Sometimes we forget this fact and believe, instead, that consciousness or self is somehow separate from the body, suspended in it, or can exist apart from the body. If this were so, consciousness could never be integrated with body-mind functioning or affect our lives in any way, which is obviously not the case.

The great importance of the unconscious is that it is the root level of physiological functioning for the whole system of the psyche or consciousness. On this physiological level consciousness is the reflexive mechanism of the mind (or brain), which is the mind's ability to bend on itself in order to know itself—know its own functions, experiences, thoughts and content. *The act of bending on itself IS the act of self-awareness—the mind's own awareness of itself.* Because of this bending action we have the subject-object poles of consciousness, which is the mind knowing itself as object to itself. Thus subject and object are the same, the same mind knowing itself. Self-knowledge then is the subject-objectified or subject-as-object, and all "self" words are expressions of this reflexive act, expressions of the mind's own experience of itself. Although the word "self" can become a mere concept or content of the mind, the spontaneous origin of all self words are the experiential expressions of the reflexive mechanism of the mind. Everything else that can be said of self is secondary to the act or function which IS self-awareness on the unconscious level. Thus the reflexive act of the mind is what the knowing-self IS; self is not the result of a reflexive act; rather, self IS this act.

Because the reflexive mechanism or act of self- awareness is an autonomous mechanism; it is not under conscious control—we cannot stop or start it, or alter it in any way. Thus on a totally unconscious level, self-awareness goes on whether we are conscious of it or not. Only when we become aware of our own awareness (self-conscious, that is) do we move to the conscious level of consciousness, which is a "reflective" level (as opposed to the unconscious or "reflexive" level). Unlike the unconscious, we have some control over the conscious or reflective level. Here we can deliberately reflect on ourselves, look within (introspection), or remain in the state of simple self-awareness—there are various levels of reflectivity. In simple terms, self-awareness exists on both the conscious and unconscious levels of consciousness, and thus *all consciousness is self-consciousness.*

The self-awareness we know most about is the experience of the reflective or conscious level of consciousness; the self-awareness we know little about or may not know at all, is the experience of the unconscious level of consciousness—virtually the level of its physiological functioning. This tells us that even if we could do away with reflective self-awareness (conscious level of the psyche), we still could not do away with reflexive (unconscious) self-awareness. As a physiological function the reflexive mechanism underlies all levels of consciousness; thus to do away with one level would be to do away with all levels—which, of course, would be the end of all consciousness. This means that if consciousness (self) ceased to function, it would have to cease across all levels because, at its physiological root level, consciousness functions on an all-or-none basis. The mind does not "half bend" on itself.

Because self or consciousness is first and foremost a physiological function, nothing short of the cessation of this function could account for any state or condition we call "no-self" or "no-consciousness." Thus if the reflexive mechanism of the mind were to cease functioning it would cease across all levels of consciousness, from the conscious to the unconscious as well as God-consciousness. So long as the reflexive mechanism persists, however, self persists because this mechanism IS consciousness; it IS the mysterious unconscious self. The reflexive mechanism is not a function that may or may not give rise to the experience of self; rather, on the unconscious level, self IS this function. When we consider all the experiences and content to which this mechanism gives rise, we become so wrapped up in these secondary aspects of self or consciousness that we sometimes forget its physiological roots. Even though most of our passage through consciousness consists of dealing with its various experiences and content, our present interest is to focus on the true nature of self prior to all secondary experiences and content.

It is not difficult to see why the deepest self is virtually an unknown, or why we constantly experience its profound unconscious mystery. Because its deepest nature and experience is unknown some people identify self or consciousness as the mystery of the divine, or identify it AS the divine. Indeed, we do this without knowing. Thus, for example, we believe our experiences OF the divine to BE the divine when, in fact, what we experience is the unconscious responding to the divine. We might compare this to the experience of being stuck with a needle—our experience is our response to the needle, which means the experience is only ourself; it is not the needle's experience. We do not know the needle's experience or its particular dimension of existence; in fact, we do not know if the needle experiences anything at all. So too, when we experience the divine, the experience is our response to the divine, which means the experience is only ourself—our unconscious self. Our response (the effect), however, is not the divine's experience, just as it was not the needle's experience. We do not know the divine's experience or dimension of existence. While the divine (or needle) may be the cause of our experience, the experience itself is the effect. Thus no matter how divine our experiences may appear to be, we cannot justify the leap that claims our experience IS the divine or the divine's own experience. We have to admit that all we can know and experience of the divine—and the universe for that matter—is limited to our human dimension of knowing and experiencing and that this limited way of knowing and experiencing is the boundary of consciousness.

Although we say that experiences of the divine are virtually experiences of ourselves—the unconscious self as it touches upon the divine—this does not mean that consciousness is totally separate from the divine. On the contrary, so long as anything lasts, nothing is separate from the divine. The divine is the unknown of matter itself—not matter, however, as it is known and experienced by consciousness or the intellect and senses. But if consciousness as a structure and function is not divine, it is also not separate from the unknown divine substance from which it is formed. That which is truly divine about man and the universe is beyond any particular form, structure or function, and therefore beyond anything we can point to. Though consciousness has its own unique experience of the divine, the divine is beyond the knowing, experiencing dimension of consciousness.

The Knowing Self

So far we have mentioned only the reflexive mechanism of the mind, which is the "knowing self" and one of the two experiential dimensions that make up self or consciousness. The other dimension is the "feeling self," which is equally mysterious and rooted in the unconscious. Although the knowing self and the feeling self are two different experiences, they nevertheless function together to form the inseparable wholeness of self or consciousness. This functional unity is such that if there were no feeling self there also would be no knowing self, and vice versa; we cannot have one without the other.

We have already said that the mind bending on itself is responsible for all self-awareness. When the mind bends on itself what does it see? It sees itself, of course. As an automatic function, this seeing or self-awareness is first of all unconscious and only secondarily conscious. The developmental process is the movement from one level of awareness to another while the reflexive mechanism remains stable throughout. Because the mind bends on itself it sees or is aware of itself; thus we have the knowing experience "This is I," "I am myself," and so on. Self is not a socially learned or conditioned experience; it is not a mistake or an illusion. Rather, self or consciousness is a concrete function of the human brain; without it, man would not be man.

If we can understand the reflexive mechanism and how it works we can see that the mind knows itself solely as object to itself. This is a reflexive type of knowing in which the subject-self is no different from the object-self; either way the mind bends, it bends on itself. There are not two selves, of course, one an object and the other a subject. On the contrary, if the object-self changes, it is only because the subject-self changes. In the course of our journey, then, it is not the reflexive mechanism that changes; rather, it is the level of self-awareness that changes. Thus we can know ourselves on a superficial level (through the eyes of others, for example) or we can know ourselves to the depths of realizing we are not separate from the divine. What makes these changes in depth possible is the stability of the autonomous reflexive mechanism.

So we have to keep in mind that the reflexive mechanism underlies all levels of consciousness and self-knowing, and that its physiological roots constitute the unconscious or unknown aspect of self or psyche. It is not possible, however, to discover the true depth of these unconscious roots until the reflexive mechanism has permanently ceased to function. Thus to the very end of the journey, the final boundary of consciousness remains totally unconscious and unknown. When the reflexive mechanism has permanently ceased to function, however, the true unconscious nature of this mechanism becomes known—known by its absence.

The Feeling Self

Like the knowing self, the feeling self has profound roots in the unconscious, so profound that it could be said the feeling self predominates over the knowing self as man's primary experience of self. Off hand we tend to think of the feeling self as the emotional or affective system, when in truth, the affective system is only the more conscious experience of the feeling self. What few people realize or suspect is that the root experience of the feeling self is the experience of life and being. Thus *the true feeling self IS the experience of "life" and "being,"* which together with the reflexive mechanism or knowing self composes the whole of consciousness and the entire self-experience. Sometimes we attribute the feeling of life and being to physical energy or to the experience of soul or spirit. At one point in our journey, when we have realized oneness with the divine, we may even attribute this experience to "divine Life" and "divine Being." For the most part, however, people simply take their experience of life for granted—so much so, they would probably not think to list it among their experiences. But however we interpret it, we can appreciate how difficult it is to articulate our subjective experience of life and being. Its mystery defies adequate expression and description, which testifies to its profound roots AS the unconscious itself.

Although the experience of life and being seems to pervade the entire body-mind and to defy a specific bodily location, for the perceptive it seems to have a point of origin in a mysterious non-physical space within ourselves, *a space we regard as the center of consciousness.* Much has been said and written of this life-center. Under various names and headings we find this subjective phenomenon mentioned in the various literatures of the world, from philosophies and religious traditions on down to modern psychology. This feeling center (which IS the feeling self) has various experiential levels from the physical to the divine. How we see or experience it has to do with our level of spiritual and psychological maturity. Many people regard this mysterious center as the seat or origin of consciousness. While this is ultimately true, as a matter of developmental priority and experience, however, we cannot say which came first, the knowing or the feeling self. These are basically two sides of the same coin, which coin is the whole of consciousness.

Although it is not our intention to go into the various experiences that derive from the feeling center—energies, emotions, passions and other subtle feelings—it is important to point out that the "will" is, itself, the deepest experience of the feeling-self or center of consciousness. Thus in experience the will IS the experience of simple "being." We are not always clear on the experience of will because as a volitional faculty it can move in either of two directions—toward or away from something. This movement is actually the experience of "desire," which is a movement of the will, but not the will in its more profound immovable state. In other words, the will is simple energy or being, while its movement in either direction is desire. Perhaps the most simple expression of the deepest experience of will is "feeling-being." It is when the will moves, however, that we have desire, wanting, grasping. If all *movement* of the will were to cease—as in a desireless state—the will would nevertheless remain as the simple experience of being. Purely as a volitional faculty, however, the will or feeling self is its own "to be or not to be," meaning that self can either surrender its life and being to the divine from which it arises or it can keep it solely for itself. Though we are not free to choose existence—it is too late for that—HOW we are "to be" in this world is our choice. Underlying human freedom is the fact man exists by no power of his own, and so, too, by no power of his own can he cease to exist.

The human passage might be compared to a moving sidewalk that is carrying man to his ultimate destiny. The choice is either to tune-in and go with this movement or to spend our lives going against it. Either way we cannot get off or stop the movement, because the passage takes its own course and will be completed whether we wish to go with it or not. Thus the quality of life is our choice, but not life itself. The will as it exists primarily for itself is the "ego," and though it is the immature feeling self, it is not the "true" feeling self. The ego suffers and becomes anxious or has a tantrum when it does not get what it wants, whereas the true self, as the simple quiet experience of "being," is a joy. Having attained everything in its deepest divine center, it wants for nothing. Thus *"being" is the will prior to its movement in any direction,* a will that finds no lasting peace until it rests in its divine center. The point to keep in mind is that the will or feeling self is not a thinking or intellectual faculty, but instead is the experience of "feeling being" or "feeling life." Without a thorough account of the will, no description of consciousness or self can be complete. This feeling self together with the knowing self IS the whole of consciousness and each one's experience of personal selfhood and existence. Man has no greater certitude than this—that he exists.

Unity of Consciousness

To explain the unity of consciousness we might compare its structure to an inverted triangle. The subject-object poles (reflexive mechanism of the mind) form the base of the triangle which leads downward to converge at a one-pointed center. Without the base there can be no center, and without a center there can be no base. What posits a center is the reflexive mechanism of the mind looking into itself, an *unconscious* "look" which carries awareness down or within to a "point" where subject and object converge and come together in the simple experience of life and being. This center is the true focal point of the mind or reflexive mechanism (the knowing self) which, while it is initially an unconscious center, with maturity becomes the conscious center as well. As the immature center, the feeling self is the "ego." As the more mature center, it is what Carl Jung called the true "Self." But beyond even the deepest unconscious Self lies the divine. That which experiences the divine IS the unconscious Self, but when this Self—the experiencer and its experience—falls away, the divine turns out to be non-experiential by comparison. In other words, the divine is beyond all possible human experiences, which means that self or consciousness' highest experience of the divine is no experience at all.

Carl Jung suggested that the true unconscious center (Self) might coincide with the body's center of physical gravity. This suggestion makes sense when we consider that man's upright position in space is due to the body's experience of consciousness. Unconsciously the human body has a feeling of being centered, not in the brain, but in the body's mid-section—similar to the Japanese *hara*. This unconscious center is also responsible for man's experience of physical form or sense of being a discrete entity. Beyond this even, this center is the primary cause of all bodily awareness. Still, we should keep in mind that the reflexive mechanism of the mind is responsible for centering the whole experience of "life" and "being." Without this centering we could not speak of life and being in terms of "source" or "origin." So the center of consciousness is an energy, an energy unique to consciousness alone. This energy is not responsible for sensory or vegetative life; rather, it is solely responsible for conscious life. This energy IS consciousness; it IS the feeling self and the center of consciousness.

Similar to a machine that needs a specific fuel to function, the reflexive mechanism needs a specific energy to function. If there were no fuel there would be no function. If there were no function there would be no fuel—one cannot exist without the other. One way to imagine the function of consciousness is to think of it as similar to an electric typewriter, where the knowing-self is the reflexive mechanism, and the feeling-self is the fuel or energy that runs the mechanism. The keys are the senses that respond to external stimuli; the touch of a key triggers the reflexive mechanism, which instantly leaves its subjective stamp on the paper (the mind). *This reflexive action is a spontaneous discrimination whereby every sensory impression bears a subjective stamp, whether we are conscious of it or not.* These subjective impressions constitute the content of consciousness. But what would happen if the motor of the typewriter were turned off or had no fuel? Although the keys (the senses) would remain, when they were touched, nothing would happen. Because the reflexive mechanism no longer works, no subjective stamp is possible—that is, no discriminating, no content, and no self. This is what would happen if the reflexive mechanism or knowing self ceased for lack of energy to fuel it. This example gives us some idea of the unitary structure and function of consciousness, and of the impossibility of living with half a consciousness—that is, with only the reflexive mechanism (the knowing-self), or with only the central energy (feeling-self). Consciousness either functions as a whole or it does not function at all. We may not always experience this wholeness or unity of consciousness, yet it is always there whether we are aware of it or not.

Summary of the System of Consciousness

Altogether the feeling self is the center of consciousness; it is the experience of life, being and undifferentiated will. It is all the experiential energies, powers, emotions and feelings that arise from this center. The feeling-knowing self is not only the feeling and knowing OF self; rather, feeling and knowing IS self, self prior even to the feeling and knowing OF self. This means that it makes no difference if, at this moment, we feel nothing and are not aware of ourselves, because self or consciousness is still present *as the unconscious* prior to any conscious awareness or particular feeling. When, however, something rises to the conscious level, then we are aware of self, and it is this self we usually know, while the unconscious self we usually do not know. Everything we know and feel of self is, therefore, secondary to the unconscious act or function of the mind bending on itself, and secondary as well to the unconscious (largely taken for granted) experience of life and being.

Without the reflexive mechanism of the mind there could be no self at all. The reflexive mechanism is the mind's ability to bend on itself, and in doing so the mind sees and knows ITSELF. If the mind could not see or know itself, there would be no self experience and there would be no self to speak of because the term could not have arisen. At things stand, however, this bending action creates the subject-object poles of consciousness. If it were not for self-as-object there could be no knowledge of self-as-subject—no subject at all, in fact.

Some people hold that the mind itself, without a reflexive mechanism, is the true self or subject. As they see it, if we could just stop the mind's reflexive activity we would come upon a self beyond the subject-object self. Now the only way this notion or theory could be tested or verified would be to stop the reflexive mechanism and see if any self or self-experience remained, or see if some "other" self was revealed. The problem of verifying this theory, of course, is stopping the reflexive mechanism: who or what is going to stop it? Can self actually stop itself? At best, meditative silence can still the conscious self or *still deliberate* self-awareness; it cannot put an end to the knowing self or reflexive mechanism of the mind. While meditative silence can set the stage for the revelation of the true Self, this revelation is still Self. The point is that self cannot get rid of itself or cause its own cessation. Neither the reflexive mechanism (knowing self) nor the feeling center can ever bring about its own extinction. If such an event should happen (the cause being totally beyond self) there is no self or self-experience remaining, and no revelation of some "other" self. Those who say otherwise have never come upon the cessation of the true Self.

What we usually know about the autonomous reflexive mechanism is primarily its superficial experience—the conscious self, that is. The reason for this is that from birth we have unconsciously taken the self-experience for granted. Because of this we cannot begin to imagine what it would be like to live without some form of self-awareness or sense of self. Indeed, the very idea might strike us as unthinkable—which it is. Even if we tried to catch self (or self-awareness) in the act, we could not do this because we ARE this act. This fact constitutes the unique mystery of human existence, which is the same unique mystery of the whole self-experience. Only when the reflexive mechanism ceases to function can it be known that *all consciousness is reflexive and thus, all consciousness is self-consciousness.* Without the reflexive mechanism of the mind there is no awareness of self because there is no self to be aware of, and no self to BE awareness. If the mind is not bending on itself, there is no "itself."

What we usual find in our search for the true self is the profound feeling self, not the knowing self. The feeling self is not reflexive and thus it is non-dual. As the singular feeling of life and being, the feeling self is incapable of a subject-object dichotomy—such as the knowing self. It is this feeling self we usually regard as the stable true self. We have to remember, however, that the feeling self cannot stand apart from the knowing self or exist solely in its own right; a feeler without a knower is unthinkable. We might add that the surprise of the falling away of all self or consciousness is not the cessation of the reflexive mechanism; rather, it is the falling away of the feeling self. Somehow we expected the singular non-dual experience of life and being to be more eternal than the reflexive mechanism of the mind, but such is not the case.

But before we can discuss the true no-self event, we must first discuss a prior event—the falling away of the ego-self and the transforming process this event initiates. It is only after this event that we come upon the egoless condition generally known as unitive or transcendental consciousness, God-consciousness or whatever our preferred terminology. While this egoless or unitive condition is the mature condition of man in this world, it is not his final condition or destiny. The purpose of the egoless state is to get us to yet a further goal or end, which is no-self or no-union. Thus the egoless unitive condition is not the end of the journey; instead, it is the vehicle or condition for getting us there.

We cannot come upon mature existence or right living until we first come to the egoless unitive condition. Only the true unitive Self is able to live fully and fearlessly in the world—or in the ordinary marketplace. It is only after the true Self has been lived to the fullest extent of its potential that it ultimately falls away. Self or consciousness falls away because its purpose and potential for full human existence has been completed—finished. With its completion man moves to his final divine destiny.

Once again, the prevalent mistaken notion to dispel is that the egoless state is the end of the journey or the ultimate goal to be attained. There is far more to self or consciousness than the ego-self. What is urgently needed in order to understand the completed journey is a clear distinction between ego and self, and a clear distinction between the falling away of the ego and the much later falling away of self in its egoless unitive condition. These are two totally different events or experiences separated by years of living out the unitive condition in the marketplace to its ultimate end. Where our contemplative literature speaks of only ONE major event or goal (the falling away, transcendence, cessation or transformation of the ego, however we care to consider it), it does not address the much further event: the falling away of all self or consciousness along with its egoless unitive condition. Without this second event we do not have a complete map of the human journey. So long as we speak of only one major event (no-ego) we have only half the picture, which half brings us to the mid-point of our passage. To have the complete picture we need to understand the true nature of self or consciousness and make a clear distinction between the falling away of the self-center or "ego," and the much later falling away of the "true Self" and the divine center. So let us move on to discuss the ego, its falling away and the transforming process that culminates in the transcendental or unitive state.[2]

---

[2]In the Christian context the term "unitive state" can have several meanings. First of all, it cannot apply to any transient experience of oneness with the divine because this does not constitute a permanent state. The term "transforming union" is the cocoon stage that immediately follows the falling away of the ego-self; obviously it is a stage of transformation. Once the

The Ego

The term "ego" articulates a specific experience. Its best articulation might be this: the ego is what we feel when self-will is crossed, blocked or otherwise thwarted. It is the psychological pain that underlies all tantrum behaviors—anger, hitting back, revenge, anxiety and much more. It is the cause of true psychological and spiritual suffering and always symptomatic of an imbalanced, immature psyche. The ego is the interior movement we experience when we do not get what we want; it is also the experience of near uncontainable highs when we do get what we want. Obviously the ego is the experience of extremes—extreme feelings, that is—and for this reason it easily imbalances the whole psyche or consciousness. The ego is first and foremost the feeling self—it is not, primarily at least, the knowing self. Merely to know something exists—an object, a virtue, something good or bad—does not mean that we want it for ourselves. The ego springs alive only when we want something for ourselves and are determined to get it, possess it. This affirms that *the ego is the experience of self-will, a will turned solely on itself* that seeks its own fulfillment and benefit. When frustrated this egoic power or energy has given rise to all the evils in the world, yet the same ego in pursuit of goodness can give rise to great good in the world. Thus the ego is a particular self-energy or power that can go either way—negatively toward what is not good for self, positively toward what is good for self. If we believe that the divine is our highest good, then the ego (self-energy or self-will) goes in pursuit of the divine, and this pursuit is the ego's true, proper, developmental direction. The ego is, therefore,

---

butterfly emerges it is in a permanent state of "mystical union." In these pages "unitive state" is used in this sense of "mystical union." It applies to the butterfly's entire state of existence from its emergence from the cocoon to its death. While the caterpillar lives in the state of egoic consciousness, the butterfly lives in the state of unitive consciousness. This latter state is also what I call the "marketplace" stage of the journey. The caterpillar left the marketplace in search of oneness with the divine and thereafter entered the cocoon. Once it emerges from the cocoon, however, it returns to the marketplace—but as a butterfly. "Unitive state" then refers to the state following transformation; it is the ordinary life of the mature butterfly. What are known as "Espousals" and "Mystical Marriage" are basically transient experiences.

basically good; it is only bad when it goes against its own highest good.

Developmentally the ego is the original center of consciousness. What we call "egoic consciousness" is the totality of self or consciousness centered around its own central energy or self-will. If consciousness were represented as a circular piece of paper, this ego-energy would be its center. Initially this center is the feeling-self experienced as "I want," "I must have." There can be no underestimating the power and determination of the ego; it is no illusion or mistake. In fact, it is the most verifiable human experience that we know. Some people seem to believe that the ego is a mistake from the beginning, a mistake in that consciousness has failed to recognize the divine as its true center. But this belief is incorrect. We can both know and experience a divine center through the ego, even while the ego or our own self-center remains intact. Directly underlying this ego-center, then, is the divine. In this matter the function of consciousness is similar to a telescope where the center of consciousness is a peephole through which we glimpse the infinite—the divine beyond all consciousness. Because of this hole we can focus on the divine and even declare it to be the true center of consciousness. The divine, however, is EVERYWHERE; it is not the center of anything. Consciousness or self is what centers the divine and experiences it. When we speak of the divine as "within" or as a "center" we should ask ourselves, "Within what, the center of what?" The answer, of course, is "our self or consciousness." Without self or consciousness there would be no "within" and no "center."

As consciousness develops it becomes aware of the divine within, and with the whole force of its ego-energy or self-will it goes in pursuit of the divine—indeed, what other energy in man seeks Truth? The ego does not hide the divine; rather, initially at least, the ego is the feeling self that experiences the divine. We do not have to reach any particular age for this experience—children are good experiencers of the divine. The ego, then, is no hindrance to the divine; quite the opposite, the divine is an enormous help to the ego.

The greatest help in finding the center of consciousness is an interior experience of the divine (some form of presence or supernatural power). It is at this point or ego-center that the divine often reveals itself, and in doing so draws attention to the center. The divine revealing itself at the center virtually turns the will or feeling self in its direction, a direction deep within, underlying the self-center and away from the rest of self. In this way the divine sets up an attraction like a magnet that keeps consciousness singular and pointed in its direction. At first, staying aware of the center may entail a mental effort or some form of deliberate mindfulness, but with practice we become increasingly more centered and catch on to how this new awareness works in everyday life. This is how an experience of the divine brings about a shift in awareness and begins to move toward a definitive change of consciousness.

Initially there is the tendency to believe that self-awareness is primarily a mental process and, therefore, awareness of the divine is also a mental process. Thus many people making the spiritual journey start out by striving to keep the divine in mind at all times. But once we begin the passage in earnest we gradually discover that true self-awareness and true awareness of the divine are not mental at all. The first lesson we learn is that true awareness is not centered in the mind or in any mental process. Instead, it is centered at the point of the triangle we mentioned earlier: feeling-being, will or life-force, which is the feeling self prior to any movements that arise from this feeling center. This awareness is actually our experience of being prior to all reflective thoughts that arise in the mind regarding self—and the divine.

But no matter how numerous or blissful our experiences of the divine, there is no lasting satisfaction with transient experiences. What we want most of all is a permanent state of continuous awareness of the divine, awareness of an abiding oneness and union. Since by its very nature the thinking, remembering mind is incapable of such a feat, this abiding awareness must take place on the most profound level of the unconscious psyche or self, a level we cannot attain of our own accord because whatever we can do is limited solely to the conscious self. In other words, what we consciously experience and know of the divine (and as much as we know of ourselves) is obviously limited to the conscious self. By no activity of its own can the conscious self bring about an abiding awareness of oneness with the divine on an unconscious level; its own efforts can go only so far in this matter. Beyond a certain point, then, or at the limit of our own doing, the divine must take the initiative. Thus when some unknown critical point is reached, or when we have done all we can from our side of consciousness to attain this permanent awareness, the divine takes the initiative and breaks through the unconscious center of consciousness.

To understand the significance of this event in the context of the journey, it is important to note that prior to this breakthrough the ego (and the whole of egoic consciousness) was already enjoying an assurance of oneness and union with the divine. Indeed, at this stage people may even believe they have already attained an abiding union or oneness. This is why the sudden falling away of self's divine experiences is such a bewildering event. We do not know, of course, that the ego has fallen away, we only know this is retrospect; for the moment, all we know is that we no longer experience the divine. Since the self-center or ego had been that in ourselves which experienced the divine (as well as the experience itself), without the ego we are also without our experience of the divine. In other words, take away that which experienced the divine, and that which it experienced (the divine) goes with it. The self-center does not fall away, however, because it is bad or because it is a particular problem at this time; it falls away because it is not our deepest center. Underlying the self-center is the divine center; thus to come upon the divine without this medium, the self-center or ego must fall away.

No-Ego Experience

The divine's breaking through the center of consciousness shatters the ego like a hole made in the center of ourselves. To get some idea of this breakthrough we might again compare the psyche (consciousness) to a circular piece of paper where the original center was the ego. With this sudden breakthrough we now have an empty hole in the center of ourselves; instead of the ego or self-center, we now have a divine-center—the empty hole. The empty center is two things at once; it is the absence of self and the presence of the divine. There is no self-center anymore; there is only a divine-center. We might visualize this arrangement as a doughnut: consciousness or self is the bread that experiences an empty center in itself. From here on consciousness or self will be egoless. Obviously there has been a radical change of consciousness; there has been an upheaval to which we have no choice but to acclimate.

Many people see this change or upheaval as a process of transformation, but I see it as a process of acclimating to a divine center. Consciousness has not been changed into anything; rather, a chunk of consciousness or self has permanently fallen away. The divine increases as self decreases or falls away; this is the way it works. Self or consciousness is never transformed into the divine; it never "becomes" divine. If we knew the true nature of consciousness we would know this was impossible. The major problem with the notion of transformation is that it forever hangs on to some form of self and never lets it go. It perpetuates the notion that self gets better and better, more and more divine, when in truth, the divine increases in proportion as the self decreases or falls away. The notion of a divinized self only increases or inflates the self; for those who buy into this notion, the journey may well end it total disillusionment.

Off hand we would imagine that a permanent breakthrough of the divine into the unconscious would be a wonderful, blissful experience. But in fact it is a terrible experience; to unhinge self-will and everything to which it is attached is a shattering experience. What is more, this self-will, energy center or feeling-self, had been our primary sense of being in this world up to this point in the journey. Thus the whole of consciousness or self is affected and not just the center. But most important, with the shattering or falling away of the self-center, the ego's experiences of the divine go with it. The ego can no longer experience the divine because there is no ego anymore to experience the divine. The whole ground has been pulled out from under self; it can no longer turn on itself or have its own way—on its own ground or terms, that is. From here on self has a new ground or center of being to which it must now acclimate or adjust.

The account of this event by Christian contemplatives is the sudden disappearance of the divine. The divine, of course, cannot disappear; so what, then, disappears? "That" which experienced the divine (to this point in the journey) disappears, and with it go not only its experiences of the divine, but seemingly, that which it experienced—the divine. This event is John of the Cross' "Dark Night of the Spirit" wherein consciousness or self feels bereft and empty of the divine and, consequently, bereft and empty of itself. The ego was already firmly attached to the divine; this attachment was the ego's deepest joy and sense of true life. Thus the falling away of the ego is actually experienced as the falling away of the divine or one's deepest sense of true life. The contemplative's primary concern is not a loss of self (ego), but his loss of the divine. The divine, of course, is never absent or lost; what is absent or lost is that aspect of the psyche which experienced the divine: the ego.

Without the ego we do not at first recognize the divine on its own ground, which ground seems only to be a great emptiness or void in ourselves. We keep looking for the divine on our own (ego) ground and cannot understand why it does not appear. We are in for a struggle here on every level of consciousness, and there will be no peace until all the energies, will, desires and feelings have been totally submitted to the divine—a dark, unrecognized silent void in ourselves. Submitting ourselves to this interior emptiness—virtually our own nothingness—is not easy; it requires an enormous faith. Indeed the entire acclimating process will stretch the human limits. From this point on we can no longer direct our own journey; we seem unable to pull ourselves up by the bootstraps or return to our previous comfortable state. The only thing we can really do is grin and bear it—suffer. In experience it may feel as if a hole were being burned through the center of our being.[3]

After many difficulties we eventually get to the bottom of the void and acclimate to this empty state of affairs—but then there really has been no other choice. Finally one day the inner darkness, nothingness or emptiness, is revealed AS the divine Ground—reveals itself to consciousness or self. Thus once we have adjusted to a radical change of consciousness, the divine openly reveals itself AS the deepest center of our being, a center that is IN ourselves but not OF ourselves. From here on the unconscious self opens upon the divine, opens upon a dimension beyond itself which, at the same time, seems to be an extension of itself. At one and the same time we both know and experience that the deepest experience of our own existence is no different than our experience of the divine's existence. In other words we can truly say that our deepest experience of life, being and existence IS our experience of the divine. These are not two separate experiences, my life and God's life, but one single experience of life and being.

At the same time we know the divine Ground to be the center or source of all that exists, not just ourselves; thus through the divine we realize in what way we are one with all that exists. The moment of this revelation is also the disclosure of the true self, a new self, and perhaps the only self we had ever come upon. In experience, the basic sense of the true self is a wholistic sense of unity and oneness that results from the realization (or disclosure) of the divine center of ourselves. The true self is the whole self or consciousness centered on a divine center instead of a self-center or ego. In a deeper sense, however, the true self is that aspect of our self or consciousness that is one with the divine; in essence, the true

---

[3]Needless to say I have no understanding of those religious paths that imply that the falling away of the ego is just a matter of dispelling a piece of mental ignorance or a false idea of ourselves. Looking East, I do not find there any experience comparable to the Dark Night of the Spirit: no account of a bottoming out of a self-center (ego), or of an acclimating (or transforming) ordeal, or of dire interior emptiness and void that ultimately turns out to be the divine—not the self.

self is an unknown. Thus the true self is that mysterious unknown in ourselves that both knows and experiences the divine unknown. In terms of consciousness, the true self is the unknown unconscious self as it touches upon and experiences the divine. If we visualize consciousness as a doughnut, the true self is the innermost rim of bread that touches upon the divine and thereby experiences the empty divine center.

We learn something else once the acclimating process is over: we had spent a lot of time trying to transform our conditional phenomenal self, a self, however, that is not even transformable. In other words, we had tried to transform the self we knew (naturally) which turns out to be the superficial impermanent self and not the "true self" or that which is truly one with the divine. In retrospect we may feel tricked in this matter or want to kick ourselves for having spent so much time and energy trying to perfect that which can never be perfect. While the impermanent phenomenal self is vastly improved without the ego, it is not destined for perfection or eternal life. Basically, the phenomenal self is just personality or idiosyncratic expression, which, in a totally silent state (one of no expression), is nowhere to be found.

This brings us to a consideration of the change in the structure and function of consciousness due to the no-ego event. In terms of what I know of its immediate happening, the first event of the falling away of the ego could best be articulated as a cloud of unknowing suddenly descending and shrouding the thinking mind. In John of the Cross' view the mind is dazed as if by a brilliant light, but what we immediately know for sure is that the mind has been altered in some mysterious way. As it turns out the mind never returns to its former way of knowing and seeing. The second event follows immediately on the first. The moment the mind deliberately looks into itself it sees a dark empty hole where formerly it had encountered the divine. This hole is both the absence of a self-center or ego as well as the positive presence of the divine-center. *The empty center is not consciousness, self, or ego;* rather, the empty center is the divine, and what experiences this hole or empty center is consciousness or self. Thus self or consciousness experiences the divine, but is not itself the divine. Some people refer to this empty center as the "true self" and affirm that "the true self is no self," meaning that the true self is no-ego-self, or that the "true self" is the divine center OF self. Obviously self or consciousness remains; what is missing is only the self-center or ego which, prior to its shattering, was the only self we knew. The opening up or bottoming out of the center of consciousness does not do away with the rest of consciousness or self; rather, this opening up is experienced by consciousness as a new level of awareness, virtually a new dimension of *its own* existence. This new awareness we call God-consciousness or Mystical Union—different traditions have different names for it.

This breakthrough has not altered the reflexive mechanism of the mind. The only difference now is that the mind no longer bends solely on itself or its own self-center (ego), but it now bends on a totally divine center—the void or empty center of self. This means that the unconscious *self and the divine are given (known) in the same single act of the mind bending on itself,* which act or function, as we have said, IS self or consciousness. Self-awareness goes right on; only now, instead of unconscious self-awareness, there is unconscious God-awareness (due to the divine hole in the center). The reflexive mechanism has not been changed or altered; rather, the center of consciousness has changed. Although this change affects the whole of consciousness or self, it does not do away with it; indeed, we could not speak of a "true self" unless the mind continued to bend on itself and its divine center.

Having to bend on an empty unknown center radically affects the mind, virtually forcing it to adjust to a different dimension of knowing. The mind no longer bends on the usual self-center or the divine it once knew; instead, it bends on an empty center and the divine it does not know. The mind's unconscious seeing of an empty void in itself is responsible for the phenomenon we know as the "third eye." This phenomenon is the result of the cloud of un-knowing—seeing nothing, as it were. Thus when the mind sees the divine it sees nothing; but once this nothing is revealed AS the divine, then we call this unknowing "true knowing." This particular phenomenon—the mind seeing nothing—initially impairs the ordinary function of the mind. Sometimes, however, it borders on ecstasy, or becomes ecstasy. Physiologically the third eye can be a painful and annoying experience, and one that may last for years. Because of this phenomenon some people feel they may be going off the deep end of their journey. A piece of good news, however, is that once the acclimation process is over—which may take years —this phenomenon is no longer a problem or is rarely noticed anymore. The experience of the third eye then is reflexive con-sciousness or the knowing-self having to adjust to seeing its own empty center—seeing nothingness first of all, and then eventually seeing this is the divine. Here the mind is adjusting to a new dimension of knowing, a dimension we call "unknowing."

Another point regarding this new state of affairs is that, because the change of consciousness has taken place on the unconscious or reflexive level, we may not always be aware of the divine at the conscious or reflective level. This is important to keep in mind because many people think that in this state they will be conscious of the divine at all times, which is neither true, necessary, or even possible. Continuous divine awareness is on a different level of experience than that of a reflecting, remembering or thinking mind. Rather, this experience is first and foremost on the singular level of our feeling of "life" and "being." With the replacement of the divine-center for the self-center, our deepest experience of life and being is also our experience of the divine—Divine life and being, as it were. Everything outside this center is seen as relatively superficial (the facade of life) and ultimately perishable. But what is outside this divine center? Self or consciousness, of course. Here some people like to distinguish two selves: the divine center they call the "true self" or "higher self," and self outside this center they call the "lower self" or conditional (non-eternal) "phenomenal self." Although this terminology may be convenient for the sake of communication, the truth of the matter is quite different. The true center of consciousness is not self. As noted before, the hole in the center of a paper is not the paper; so too, the empty divine center of self or consciousness is not self or consciousness. Self is that which is aware of its divine center, but it is not itself the center. To have a center—of anything—there must also be a circumference; one is only known relative to the other. Take away the center and there is no circumference, and vice versa. In the unitive state the divine is the center and self or consciousness is the circumference. Take away either one, self or the divine, center or circumference, and both disappear together.

If I had to put my finger on the major change of consciousness or what actually happens with the falling away of the ego, I would pinpoint the feeling self, specifically self-will or the experience of self-being. Following the divine breakthrough, the specific energy or power that IS self-will does not work anymore. At first this predicament is reminiscent of St. Paul's complaining about doing the things he did not wish to do and not doing the things he wished to do. It is as if our self-will had been immobilized and all our efforts come to naught. The inability to help ourselves or the sense of our own helplessness is quite overwhelming. But what really has happened here? Obviously the particular energy of self-will—that which craves, clings, grasps and becomes attached—has disappeared. Although the breakthrough of the divine into the unconscious releases great psychological energy, this energy is not ours to get hold of; if anything, it is ours to be wary of. What we have to seek is a center of no energy, a center of calm, stillness and peace; we must submit all experiential energies to this interior silence and emptiness. The true drama of the falling away of the ego is centered in the will, energy, or feeling-self.

It is not without insight or experience that the Christian tradition holds that union with the divine is a union or conformity of wills— self-will with divine-will. That the energy, power or will that IS consciousness is united to the power or will of the divine is quite true. By reason of this divine power we (self or consciousness) are created, held in existence, and ultimately return to the divine. The falling away of the ego is a major step in the return journey; from now on self or consciousness can never move against the divine or go against the proper direction of the journey. So it is true to say that in the unitive state we have no will of our own—that is, no will separate from the divine or no self-will that can go against the divine. As the journey moves forward we will see again and again how this works—it will strike us as marvelous. This union of wills, however, was not brought about by our own doing. It occurred because the divine broke into the unconscious to dissolve a specific energy, the energy of self-will, or that which could go contrary to the divine—the ego.

Once again, the ego-center does not fall away because it is false or bad; rather, it attaches itself to the divine and gives its all until there is no more to give. Once we give all, the divine takes all— even what we did not know we had to give. Another reason the self-center dissolves is that its steadfastness in goodness cannot be compared to the divine center. So long as the self-center remains it can still reverse itself and go in pursuit of what is less than its highest good or less than the divine. This is why its falling away is an irreversible event that forever excludes the possibility of going in pursuit of evil or turning back on the divine. The whole purpose or function of the unitive condition is to give man the divine assurance of an abiding union and oneness that can never be reversed. The certitude of this union is the essence of human freedom that gives rise to the courageous and fearless living out of this condition in the human adventure. The egoic state has no such certitude or attributes.

From this distance we can now look back and see that all the years we lived solely from this superficial level of egoic cons- ciousness were years of immaturity. Naturally there was no way of knowing this ahead of time; there is no way of recognizing the ego or egoic consciousness until it has fallen away. For this reason it is somewhat pointless to talk about the ego ahead of time; so long as we ARE it, we do not know this and therefore think it is something else. So, although there is a lot of talk about the ego, nobody knows what it is until it is not there anymore. Later it works the same way with the "true self": no one knows what it is so long as they are living it or are it. The nature of the "true self" (the unconscious self) and its oneness with the divine is only disclosed when it, too, eventually falls away and becomes known in retrospect.

Beyond Transformation: The Pathless Path

Once we have fully acclimated to a new consciousness, the journey moves on. The further we move beyond this change, the more we lose remembrance of how things were experienced in the egoic state. Once the newness of the unitive state fades into the background of life, so too its initial contrast with the former egoic condition fades from recall. Without the ego anymore we cannot effectively recapture or resurrect the old egoic feelings and way of knowing—it is impossible. Thus where the initial emergence into the unitive state had seemed so mystical and supernatural, once acclimation is complete, the unitive state becomes the most natural thing in the world. In other words, what initially seemed to be a higher, superior mystical consciousness, becomes a quite ordinary everyday consciousness. Indeed it is the only one we immediately know.

In itself this new consciousness is not spectacular; it is only in contrast with our former consciousness or self that we know it as a more mature state or level of consciousness. Thus with the distance of years, looking back over the whole transforming process it now appears to be nothing more than everyman's normal developmental process, a process of human maturation. What the ancient mystics had regarded as a supernatural boon is now seen as the true developmental path required of every human being. Still, when going through this transformation everyone continues to regard it as high mysticism consisting of out of the ordinary experiences; then too, without the divine it would not have happened in the first place, nor without the divine would we have made it through. But if it is certainly out of the ordinary for egoic consciousness, from the perspective of unitive consciousness, it is all in the ordinary course of things. Here we might recall the Buddhist saying: *samsara* is *nirvana* and *nirvana* is *samsara*, meaning that just as egoic consciousness was once our natural, ordinary state, so too unitive consciousness now becomes our natural, ordinary state. From the position of egoic consciousness, unitive consciousness always appears to be quite supernatural, mystical or *nirvanic,* but once we get there, it turns out to be utterly ordinary. Between the two, however, there are great differences: the difference between an immature and mature human being, the difference between two different types of consciousness, and the difference between two very different ways of living and being in the world.

The ordinariness of the transformed, egoless, unitive condition is important to emphasize and put forward. In our Western religious tradition there is no veneration of those who have come to unitive, transcendental or God-consciousness. Holiness and sanctity are not calculated in terms of any state of consciousness, but by the fruit it manifests—first and foremost, unconditional charity (love) or compassion. Charity or compassion is the hallmark of the unitive state because the absence of a self-center makes it a spontaneous choiceless requirement. The unitive state is the inability to put ourselves first. The very need and energy for doing so is not there any more; it cannot be done even if we try to do so. In fact, when we try to do so we discover it cannot be done.

The unitive state is not an end in itself; rather, its purpose is authentic human existence, for it is only by living a mature existence that we can make our way to a far greater end or destiny. We do not know this great end ahead of time (though we may have glimpses of it), nor can we come upon it until the unitive condition has been exhaustively exercised and tested in the marketplace. By "marketplace" I mean not only the ordinary un-mystical circumstances of life, but a life basically indistinguishable from those around us. The unitive state claims no superiority because we now see the same divine in others that we see in ourselves—so how are we better than anyone else? As for the phenomenal self, we know it is perishable anyway. Thus any claim to superiority would not be indicative of the true unitive state. Returning to the marketplace we claim nothing for ourselves and expect no recognition from others. Indeed, no one knows about our "mystical" experiences.

Until the unitive condition has been lived out in the marketplace to its ultimate ending, all we usually hear about are the ecstasies and agonies of the transforming process, the glories of the new state and its superiority over the egoic state. Without accounting for the marketplace stage, however, this gives us a lopsided and incomplete view of the purpose and end of the unitive state, a view which has led us to believe that the unitive state is the end of the passage and the final goal of human existence. The immediate purpose of the unitive state, however, is simply the ability to live the human condition in its most mature state, that is, live it from a divine center and not from a self-center. Having finally arrived at the mature human state the immediate goal is not to die—as if there were no further to go—but to live the human experience as fully as possible. Without exercising this maturity or having had it tried in the fire of the marketplace, the journey cannot go forward to its true end. This end, of course, is the ultimate cessation of the entire self-experience (all consciousness) along with its mature, egoless unitive state. The marketplace is the necessary preparation for such an event.

The egoless condition has been mistaken for the end of the journey for a number of reasons. One is that the final revelation of the divine center and true self has a definitive sense of ending as well as a sense of a new beginning. This end, of course, is the ending of the egoic state and the beginning of the unitive state. From this particular position we do not see anything further to be attained in this world; nothing else is wanting. With the divine we have everything; we are home free. So what do we do now? The path ahead is to live this egoless condition to its fullest unitive potential, a potential we cannot know until it has been lived. From the beginning of the unitive state to its ultimate ending there is a lot of living to be done. In fact, between its initial disclosure and its eventual falling away lies a discrete stage of the journey that has been all but ignored in the literature. But, then, until the unitive state is lived to its ultimate ending, we do not even know if it has an ending. After all, there can be no end to what has not first been lived.

To understand how this works let us imagine for a moment that a butterfly represents someone who has just emerged from the transforming process—the cocoon. He recognizes that he is totally changed and feels as free as the wind, yet he has no idea about the life ahead. Where the cocoon had been a secure path unto itself, here, now, there is no path ahead. What is he to do? Obviously he has never before experienced life as a butterfly; up to this point all he has known is the life of a caterpillar and its transforming process. Though he is very good about telling us how life goes up to the point of emerging as a butterfly, he cannot tell us a single thing about the mature life of a butterfly. Until and unless he lives his new condition in the ordinary world, all he can tell us is how he became a butterfly; he cannot tell us about the life of a butterfly. In fact, until it dies, all the data on the life of a butterfly is not in. The obvious point is that we cannot have the whole story on the egoless unitive state until it has been thoroughly lived in the marketplace and then fallen away. This ending or falling away of the unitive state is the true "no-self experience." For those who have only come to the unitive state, then, the pathless way ahead is nothing more spectacular than life in the ordinary marketplace.

Once we have acclimated to the unitive state the picture is this: consciousness is now permanently centered in, on, and around divine Being; it is one with itself, one with the divine, and through the divine, one with all that exists. The true knowing-feeling self is integrated and unified; the psyche or subjective self is whole and balanced with a depth and dimension of insight not available prior to the transforming process. Finally man is as he should be, poised and ready for mature human existence and authentic living, and all this for the first time in his life. In the old days it was the blissful, ecstatic experiences of the transforming process that were acclaimed and emphasized, but today it seems that the well balanced psyche is more highly prized. That the attainment of right living is more highly valued than blissful living tells us something about the direction modern consciousness is taking in this matter of ego transcendence.

With the revelation of the divine source or ground of being, our experience of the divine becomes no different than our deepest experience of life. We can say in truth, "the divine is my deepest experience of life and being," and affirm that true self-awareness is equally awareness of the divine. Perhaps the key term for the unitive experience is "being." Some years ago the advent of Existential philosophy suggested, to me at least, that more people had come to the mature transcendental state, or had realized pure being, than was generally expected. Even though they have not been regarded as mystics or contemplatives, most existentialists have understood being from a religious and experiential point of view. This may indicate a change or evolution in modern consciousness and its view of the transcendental state, a view that sees this experience in the philosophical terms of everyman's passage, not just the passage of a few mystics. In kind and numbers we underestimate those who have made the journey thus far, or those who have made the existential leap—transcended the ego, been through the ordeal of transformation, and realized true being as the condition of mature human existence.

The Critical Turning Point

The unitive state is as far as we can go with the *inward* journey. Once we come to the unitive state, the inward movement comes to an end; it is over, finished. We cannot go beyond the divine or innermost center of being—we cannot go deeper than the deepest. If we feel there is any deeper movement possible, or any greater depth to be realized, we have not yet come to the unitive state. The divine is that deepest point in ourselves where no movement is possible or where all movement comes to an end.

The fact that we cannot go beyond the deepest divine center indicates that this center marks the deepest vertical boundary of consciousness. Though we *know* the divine is infinite and without boundaries, *in experience* the divine center is actually a boundary, a boundary that IS consciousness. The very terms, "innermost," "deepest," "centermost" all indicate an experiential boundary beyond which consciousness cannot go—thus it cannot go beyond its divine center. We have to face the truth that consciousness can experience only so much of the divine, simply because it is not divine. It is an error to believe that the unitive or transcendental condition is limitless or that it has no boundaries. What remains to be revealed in the unitive state is how far the human limits have been expanded due to the unitive state, and how far man can actually push these new limits. Until this state is fully exercised and tested in the ordinary marketplace, its limits can never be known. In fact, until we push limits (any limit, for that matter) we can never know if limits exists, much less know what they are.

Apart from the revelation of the deepest divine center and true self, one way we know that the transforming process is over and that the butterfly is complete and ready to fly is that *none of its experiences, even its ecstasies, add a jot to its new condition.* Thus all the experiences and practices that were helpful in the transforming process become unnecessary, they bring about no change and take us no deeper than the deepest center. The butterfly that is truly complete knows without doubt or hesitation that he has gone as far in this life as it is possible to go at this time, hence the definite sense of ending. The question that now arises is how best to live this new life. For the completed butterfly there will arise the courage and fearlessness to put the past behind and fly into the unknown as the servant of all in order to exercise and test its new life under the most trying circumstances. Failure to take this leap or risk indicates that the butterfly is not complete and still clings to its secure position with all its experiences and practices. Here I think of a Buddhist saying that once we have reached the other shore we have no need to carry the raft around with us. The raft, of course, are all the practices, experiences and even the life style that were a part of crossing over from the old to the new life, or from the egoic to the unitive state. These are of no use any more, they add nothing to the unitive state and if we cling to them, they may even hold us back.

We must be clear, however, about what is meant by letting go the raft of our former practices. Once we find the pearl of great price the search is over; we no longer need the tools, maps and other paraphernalia that had been helpful to the quest. (The tools and maps, for example, might be silence, solitude, meditation, inspirational reading and much more). Not all practices, of course, are means to an end—some practices are actually ends in themselves. In my own tradition, for example, the Eucharist (the true presence of Christ) is not a means to anything, but an end in itself and the truth that has been realized. Also, much that was formerly a practice has become the permanent state of affairs. Thus charity or compassion is no longer something we practice, it is the deepest center of our being that arises automatically, spontaneously. We no longer need silence and solitude to practice awareness of the divine because this is our everyday consciousness. It is not that we deliberately let go our former practices; rather, with the pearl in hand, digging automatically ceases. Now we go out to share our find with others.

The reason for bringing this up is that some people have the mistaken notion that a "realizer" is one who no longer practices his religion—or has no religion anymore. But this makes no sense if we understand that all someone has realized is the ultimate Truth of his religion. Once we realize Truth, what do we do with it—give it up? This makes no sense. Once we realize Truth we live it and share it; we cannot throw it away. Anything that can be dismissed or thrown away is obviously not ultimate Truth. The "raft" then refers to those specific aids and interior ruses by which we crossed the river. Letting go simply refers to the realization that we no longer need these helps and securities; once on the "other shore" (the divine center), we have no need for anything, because now we have everything.

Between the beginning and the end of the unitive state, then, there is a long road to traverse, a road that few people realize is there. To get on this road, the choice is to fly or not to fly—to leave the raft behind or not to leave it behind. The piece of enlightenment on which this decision is based is what I call "the critical turning point." The occurrence or non-occurrence of this turning point may give us a clue to why some butterflies remain remote and secure on their branches for the rest of their lives and why others take to the pathless path and enter the ordinary marketplace.

Once the inward journey is over and a new life begins, several enlightening experiences occur which, while they add nothing to the
unitive state, nevertheless give insight into it. One of these is a
glimpse beyond the unitive state to a final divine condition (beatific
or heavenly, there is really no name for it) wherein the unitive state
is canceled like a candle dissolved in the sun. From our present
position this final condition appears incompatible with continued
earthly existence, impossible in fact. Because this experience is
beyond the unitive state, the obvious conclusion is that the unitive
state is transient, non-eternal and meant only for this life. At the
same time we learn that in the final condition there is no sense of
any self, not even unitive or God-consciousness; the final state
seems to be beyond all this. Permanent entrance into such a
marvelous condition, however, seems to be the ultimate death
experience. But since we do not seem destined to die right away,
the question arises of how best to live and exercise the present
unitive condition in the here and now.

Following these experiences is a further piece of enlightenment.
Seeing that the unitive state can be transcended only in death, and
since death does not seem imminent, there comes the need for a
deliberate, generous acceptance of the phenomenal self with all its
conditional experiences and situations.   There arises a great
determination to live this human condition as fully as it was divinely
intended to be. At the same time the choice to live the unitive
state to its fullest human capacity entails an element of sacrifice,
which is the deliberate forfeiture of all beatific or heavenly experiences. There are several reason why this deliberate forfeiture is
required in order to get on with the unitive life.

To begin with, these advanced experiences are only transient, and
thus there is the repeated return to the unitive state. From this we
conclude that this heavenly condition cannot become permanent
this side of the grave. Also, because the final condition cancels the
unitive state, we know these two states are incompatible; the
heavenly state totally overwhelms the unitive state. Such lofty
experiences pull in the opposite direction from any earthly involvement. They do not invigorate the psyche; rather, they tend to
dissolve it. The choice involved here is either to foster these
advanced experiences or to forfeit them—walk away if possible.
What matters is that we make the choice.

There is also the recognition that because these experiences add
nothing to the unitive state, they serve no real purpose in our
spiritual life. We do not need them, desire them or cling to them;
above all, we are cautious lest they become self serving instead of

God serving. We have come too far to be attached to our "experiences." To get on with life is what the unitive life is all about; it is not about transient beatific or heavenly experiences, however wonderful these may be.

But the most important reason for putting off these experiences and opting instead to enter the marketplace is the great love and generosity engendered by the unitive condition. This love is too great to be kept within or solely for one's self; rather, this love wants to move outward to embrace not only the whole of human existence, but all that exists. *Thus when the inward journey is over, the whole movement of the passage turns around and begins to move outward because of the expanding divine center and its all-inclusive love and generosity.* This love finds no outlet for its energies in the mere enjoyment of transient beatific experiences. In fact so great is this love, it would sacrifice heaven in order to prove and test its love for the divine in this world. There comes to mind St. Therese's dying words, "I will spend my heaven doing good on earth," meaning she would choose to do good on earth rather than enjoy the bliss of heaven. It should be remembered, however, that this choice or forfeiture is peculiar to this particular stage of the journey. We cannot forfeit any experiential state if it is not ours to surrender.

The turning point then is the choice between our heavenly experiences and the generous, full acceptance of our human condition. While I cannot speak for others in this matter, as a Christian I saw this turning point in the light of Christ's own choice. At one point Christ deliberately "put off" his divinity in order to "take on" our humanity, take on this impermanent conditional self or consciousness in order to be with us in the marketplace. This was a choice for humanity over heaven itself. By doing this, however, he could show us the way and lead us back with him to the heavenly state from which he came. Thus in light of Christ's forfeiture of the ultimate divine condition and his acceptance of the human condition, the Christian follows in the footsteps of Christ when he moves into the marketplace and a life of selfless giving. He knows without question that when his earthly mission is complete the divine will take all, but in the meantime he will give all.

Though I am not a Buddhist and cannot speak for their experiential path, I think this same turning point may be found in their own tradition—at least in that of the *Mahayanas*. My understanding is that until the practitioner becomes an enlightened *Bodhisattva* he is only aspiring to become one. He becomes a true *Bodhisattva* when he definitively sees or realizes the impermanence of self—not merely the egoic self, but the impermanence of even the enlightened *Bodhisattva* condition. It is only at this point (the turning point) the Buddhist can "put off" his nirvanic experiences and with his wealth of compassion go forth to "save all sentient beings." Certainly this is a movement outward to all life and to a life of selfless giving. This is not, of course, a forfeiture of the unitive state which cannot be forfeited any more than the butterfly can return to its larva stage. Rather, this going forth means putting behind the delightful and lofty nirvanic experiences which add nothing to the immediate enlightened condition. As long as we continue to exist in this world the expression of love and compassion is a million times greater than our transient experiences of another existence wherein this world is neither seen nor known.

The turning point, then, is when the whole movement of the journey turns around. In the beginning the movement was inward, but having come to the infinite divine center there is no further inward to go, and the movement turns around and begins to go outward. This outward expansion is virtually an expansion of divine love and our love for the divine. Few people realize or recognize that the inward journey has a definitive end, and that at one point man's psychological-spiritual journey becomes an outward movement. We have to be cautious, however, that there is no premature going outward or an untimely return to the marketplace. When this happens we have a case of the blind leading the blind. But the turning point is well marked; when we come to it we shall know it and there will be no doubts. As a milestone it is so critical that if it does not occur we go no further with the journey, which means we can never come to the end of the unitive state this side of the grave. Unless the true self (or egoless self) has lived to the fullest extent of its unitive potential, there can be no ending of self or consciousness while still in this world. The whole purpose of this state is to bring us to yet a further end, which end is the death of self and the divine—in Christian terms, Christ's own death. Perhaps the difference between those who move on and those who do not lies in the particular experiences we have been discussing. In simple terms, the turning point is the realization that even the unitive state is impermanent and that, until it permanently falls away in death, it must be fearlessly exercised in the here and now.

But before we can discuss the eventual falling away of the unitive self or consciousness, we must return to the butterfly that has irrevocably left behind all the securities of the cocoon and embarked on the pathless journey that lies ahead. Although the ego-self is now known in retrospect as what was, the "true self" is yet unknown. All we know at this point is that self is one with the divine and that its deepest true nature (the essence of self or "what" it is) is as mysterious and unknown as the divine itself. The unitive state is virtually the union of two unknowns. We are well acquainted with the everyday phenomenal or impermanent self, but the unknown aspect of consciousness that is one with the divine, we do not know. It is only by living out the unitive condition in the marketplace that the final true nature of self or consciousness is gradually, and then finally, disclosed. Thus beyond the turning point there begins the further disclosure of the unknown true self.

Beyond the Turning Point: Unmasking the True Self

As already noted, in the unitive state the phenomenal or impermanent self still remains. This particular self-experience, however, is very different than it was in the egoic state. To get some idea of what makes the difference, let us again imagine self or consciousness as a circular piece of paper. The edges of the paper respond to incoming data and this response heads inward for the self-center where, in the egoic state, it becomes stuck because there is no place else to go. In the unitive state, however, the ego center is gone; the empty hole in the center of the paper is the divine. Thus when a response comes to the empty center it stops because it can go no further. At this point or threshold of consciousness all responses meet up with the divine empty center where they dissolve or come to naught. In this way our feeling responses to events and circumstances never go beyond a certain *threshold*—the threshold of consciousness or self—at which point self or consciousness meets up with the divine empty center.

Due to the empty center, consciousness is well balanced; for without the ego-center consciousness is incapable of extremes. The empty center is as far as any feeling response can travel inward. When it reaches that point, it goes down the hole and disappears. It is important to point out, however, that ordinarily few of our responses go deep enough to experience this threshold of consciousness—in this case, threshold of the feeling self. In the egoic state we defend ourselves against the experience of extremes because it is the cause of psychological pain and suffering. In the unitive state, however, because of the empty center we have no fear of extremes; in fact, we welcome any challenge that enables us to experience the dissolution of our deepest feelings into the divine center. When there is insufficient challenge to allow for this experience we may even go out and seek it. There is no emotional protectionism in the unitive state; we have learned that a suffering self flows into the divine and dissolves in it. To experience this dissolution is a joy in itself; sometimes it strikes us as miraculous.

Because the superficial phenomenal self is everything we know and experience of self in the unitive state, we might define the phenomenal self as everything BUT the divine or empty center. What we call the "true self," on the other hand, is the unknown link between the divine and the phenomenal self. The phenomenal self-experience does not arise from the divine, but from the true self or that unknown aspect of consciousness that touches upon the divine and stands midway between the divine and the phenomenal self. While the true self is known to exist and be one with the divine, its true nature, essence, or "what" it is, is unknown. Merely to label this aspect of consciousness as the "unconscious self" or the "true self" does not tell us "what" it is; all it tells us is "that" it is. In terms of the paper with the empty center, the true self would be the inner threshold where the unconsciousness touches upon the divine, or where divine air (as it were) blows through conscious- ness. In experience this unitive center is experienced as a steady flame, a consuming flame of love. But whatever the essence of the unknown true self, we know that it gives rise to the known phenom- enal self. The nature of this unknown self is the true mystery of the unitive state. The divine is not a mystery, nor is the phenomenal self a mystery; both are clear cut in experience: the divine is immovable and does not arise, while the phenomenal self constantly arises from the unknown true self.

It is important to emphasize the difference between the divine and true self because one of the major challenges or hurdles to be overcome in the unitive state is the temptation to regard various experiential energies as the divine instead of the self, which is all they really are. We have to keep in mind that consciousness is the experience of energy, and that in the unitive state there is still the experience of various energies and feelings. The energies experi- enced in this state, however, are different from those experienced in the egoic state, different because they arise from the unconscious self and not from the ego self. Because these energies are new to us they seem to be quite extraordinary; we may even think they are from the divine, or are the divine. But they only arise from the unconscious self. In purely Jungian terms we might call these particular energies of the unitive state the archetypes of the collective unconscious. Where in the egoic state and in the transforming process we had to come to terms with the archetypes of the personal unconscious—our past, relationships, false images, the conscious self, our own person, in other words—here in the unitive state we must now confront and unmask the more subtle but powerful archetypes or energies of the unconscious self. These are energies or powers that could not be *consciously* confronted prior to the unitive state, because they are powers specific to the unitive state. Until we come to this state we are not aware of their existence. So one task of the unitive state is that we do not mistake these energies (or any experience of energy, for that matter) for the divine, but instead, see them as belonging solely to the unconscious self. This task may not be as easy as it sounds; to regard certain energies as supernatural can be a powerful temptation.

In the unitive state the unconscious or unknown true self lies so close to the divine that in a state of great silence it is often indistinguishable from the divine. But outside this silence there is the temptation to mistake the experiential powers of consciousness or self for the powers of the divine. The truth that must eventually be learned or disclosed is that the *divine is not an energy or power, and that none of our experiences of energy or power is divine.* Instead, these are powers of the unconscious self which, in its oneness with the divine, we are tempted to regard as the divine itself. The claim to possess supernatural powers in the unitive state is well-known and documented. People have regarded themselves as prophets, healers, saviors, and God knows what else. As Carl Jung noted, the possible masks the unconscious self can take (the archetypes of the collective unconscious, that is) are almost unlimited. They represent the various cultural views man has of a superior being, even though what is regarded as superior in one culture may not be seen as superior in another. Although an archetype is a self-image of some sort, more importantly it is an experiential energy, virtually the energy of consciousness or self. In the unitive state this energy can take on a particular self-image and play out a particular role, usually the role of someone with a special mission, message, or powers. None of this, of course, is the divine; rather, it is the unconscious self which is often mistaken for the divine.

Throughout this stage or state there will be many temptations to put on one of these divine or supernatural masks and play out the role. If we fall for one of these masks or believe self is something it is not, or if we forget how utterly conditional and impermanent it is, we forfeit going any further with the journey. It is imperative to stay with the true divine center which is a "stillpoint" and not an "energy-point," and to dismiss these arising energies or powers if we think they belong to the divine in any way. Of our own accord we cannot get rid of these energies. After all, consciousness cannot put an end to itself. Our task is simply to *see* that they are self and nothing but the self. If we cannot eventually make this distinction, we march off to our own dead-end, and the passage may well end in total delusion.

In this matter it is interesting to note that prior to his final enlightenment Buddha resisted all such powers and energies by remaining in the silent, energy-less, seemingly powerless stillpoint. This divine stillpoint is actually more powerful than all man calls power and energy, a simple stillpoint that does not move at all, but wins out over every movement, force and power that we know of. At one time Christ also put aside temptations to seize power and presume on the divine or declare himself divine. No one comes to the ending of the passage who has not had these particular temptations and unmasked them completely. When one mask fails, another appears which means we must eventually make our way through all the collective archetypes until there is none left, or until they become like variations on a single theme, which theme is self—the true self and a very real experiential energy.

In certain cases it may be difficult to distinguish the behaviors of someone in the unitive state who has fallen prey to one of the archetypes from someone who is still ego-bound and believes himself to be God's gift to mankind. They can both be unconsciously noxious when trying to impress their divine powers on others. There is a great difference between the two, however. For one, the ego-bound are not dealing with the energies of the collective unconscious. Instead they are simply overrun by them and are made their helpless puppets so to speak. The egoless (unitive) condition, on the other hand, is irreversible. Once the ego center is gone, it is gone forever; thus there can be no return to the egoic state whatever the temptations that follow. In this case, since there is no ego to be overrun or ego energies involved, these people have a handle on the energies of the collective unconscious and are not helpless puppets. Always they have the conscious choice either of keeping a distance between the unconscious and the divine or of letting go this distance and proclaiming these energies divine. The difference, then, is between the totally helpless medium (the ego-bound) and the deliberate medium who always has the choice to back out. A number of important factors are involved in discerning the difference between the two, but we cannot go into them here. Our purpose is only to point out the possible dangers of the unitive state and the major hurdles to be overcome at this stage of the journey.

Something else to remember is that in the unitive state the reflexive mechanism is still intact—the mind bending on itself is not free of an object-self or self-image. To be free of an object-self there would also have to be no subject-self. One is only relative to the other and neither is absolute. If freed of the subject-object self we would not be tempted to regard ourselves as divine because there would be no self to BE divine. Also, we must remember that the self-image in the unitive state is quite different from the self-image in the egoic state. Because (in the unitive state) the mind unconsciously bends on a divine center and not an ego center, the unconscious self-image is not separate from the divine. This fact can play into an archetypal role. Our task is to stay clear of these unconscious images or archetypes and adhere to the unknown instead. We have to see that all experiential energies, feelings or archetypes are admixed with self, and that the divine can never be an image, energy, concept, feeling or whatever. The nature of all such archetypes IS self and nothing but self; certainly they are not divine. In this matter the true contemplative is an agnostic adhering to the unknown, in contrast to the gnostic who falls for the known—the archetypes, that is.

Where our journey through transformation was the unmasking of the conscious self and the personal unconsciousness, the journey through the unitive state is the gradual unmasking of the unconscious self and the collective unconscious with its far more subtle energies, intuitive way of knowing, self-image, and so on. Though self or consciousness is always one with the divine, it must be continuously and clearly distinguished from it. Even if our religious belief-system affirms that self is not divine, it would make no difference. In some form or other these archetypes or temptations are common to every human being who comes to the unitive state. Self-knowledge on the conscious egoic level is not the same as self-knowledge on the unconscious unitive level, and it is the latter that is being disclosed in the living out of the unitive condition. The moment the nature of the true self is finally and ultimately revealed is the same moment of its permanent dissolution. Obviously there is far, far more to self or consciousness than the ego, and much further to go in the journey than merely the ego's transcendence or dissolution.

In terms of structure and function it is difficult to trace the gradual dissolution of consciousness beyond the no-ego experience. This is because it takes place on a level of consciousness beyond our conscious awareness—reminiscent of Christ's definition of perfect giving, "Your left hand must not know what your right hand is doing." In the unitive state selfless giving is so automatic there is virtually no other way of living, and in this living, self continually decreases. Returning to the hole in the center of the paper, let us imagine the divine empty center expanding outward—the hole becoming larger—so that the void of self increases as the divine void increases. The paper diminishes from the center outward (not in its circumference) because the divine flame is consuming self from within. In a life of egoless giving and living the self is becoming increasingly *selfless* (it is already egoless), which means the paper diminishes (falls away) with each act of egoless giving. A true act of egoless giving is when we give and there is no return to self whatsoever. We get nothing back, not even the joy of giving— we may even be kicked for our efforts to be helpful. This requires selfless giving to be carried to heroic proportions; the hallmark of such an act is the falling away of some deep sense of self.

Although we may experience or intuit a further dying to self, we do not understand it because it is taking place on an unconscious or unknown level of ourselves. Then too the knowing-feeling self is so much in the service of others it increasingly has no life to call its own, nothing reserved for self, nothing left but the divine. In large measure the self is worn away or worn down by a life of continuous selfless giving—giving to the divine, to others and to all life without fear, stint or measure. There is nothing easy about this, yet there is ever present an undauntable spirit and a deep joy that is never diminished. Imperceptibly the unitive state is coming to an end. But it can only come to an end when there is no more self to give and no potential left untapped, which means consciousness or self has been fulfilled and can go no further. When the hole in the paper has expanded so that only the barest rim or circumference remains, we are on the fine line between self and no-self, consciousness and no-consciousness. One more expanse from the center and the boundaries of self or consciousness give way forever.

One reason people do not see the need for any further death of self or consciousness beyond the unitive state is that in this state self is not a problem—it is egoless, one with the divine, loving, good in every respect—so why lose it? To begin with, no one in this state sets out to lose self; until we come to the fine line no one even suspects such a possibility. Even if we did, by our own effort we can never go beyond self or consciousness; self cannot do away with itself anymore than it created itself in the first place. Also, because the problematic self was the ego, and the true self is one with the divine, the very idea of losing the true self is little different from the idea of losing the divine—it is unthinkable in other words. Until it actually happens it IS unthinkable; self cannot imagine or conceive its own non-existence or any life without itself. This is impossible because that which thinks about no-self IS self. Due to the unconscious reflexive mechanism of the mind ever-bending on itself, consciousness virtually goes around and round; of its own accord it can never get out of itself. In the end, however, by a single stroke of the divine, self and the divine go down together, fall away in one piece—but then they were one anyway. This experience is not only the experience of no-self, but equally the experience of no-divine. The eventual falling away of self is not because it is bad, sinful, a problem, or anything of the kind; rather, it falls away because it is not eternal and because it has lived to the fullest extent of its human potential and can go no further.

Self also falls away because its existence and whole dimension of knowing and experiencing (even in the unitive state) is less than perfect, less than final. Once it falls away it is clearly seen that self or consciousness had been a veil over the divine, a medium of knowing and experiencing which, unknown to us, had been responsible for the illusion we spoke of earlier. This illusion is the belief that experience of the divine IS the divine. Although the deepest experience of which self is capable IS experience of the divine, this experience is not the divine. By contrast, self or consciousness' most authentic experience of the divine is no experience, a non-experience, we might say. This means that in the end our experience of the divine turns out to have been the experience of our own deepest self. So the final unknown illusion to fall away is the revelation *that all human experiences of the divine are only the unconscious self.* And if we take away all consciousness or self, all its divine experiences go with it. The divine as it exists beyond the unconscious true self can never be experienced by any self or consciousness because, quite simply, self or consciousness is not equal to it, not up to it. The ultimate illusion, then, is mistaking self for the divine or believing our experiences of the divine to BE the divine.

Ecstasy: The Vehicle of Crossing Over

One way to explain the change that takes place between the beginning and the end of the unitive state involves a discussion of the true nature of ecstasy, defined as the suspension of all consciousness from the unconscious to God-consciousness. Suspension means the temporary cessation of the reflexive mechanism and the fuel (specific energy) that propels it, along with all the experiences to which consciousness or self gives rise. Because ecstasy can be experienced at any stage of the journey it is not indicative of any particular stage along the way; yet if we are familiar with this experience we notice a change in the ecstatic state as the journey progresses. What changes is not the nature of ecstasy or the suspension of consciousness; rather, what changes is the consciousness that is suspended. When only the barest rim of our circular paper (consciousness) remains, we can see that there is very little consciousness left to be suspended. In the egoic state (the solid paper without an empty center) the cessation of consciousness is an overwhelmingly extraordinary experience, whereas when only a fine line or the barest rim of consciousness remains, ecstasy is not too different from our present state. Thus ecstasy is not such an extraordinary experience. The further along we are in the journey, the less unusual and more prolonged the experience becomes because we are better prepared to sustain it.

If there is any problem with ecstasy it arises from the fact that consciousness is so integrated with the senses that the suspension of consciousness also seems to be a suspension of the senses—which it is not, of course. It is because of the integration of consciousness and the senses, however, that sustained or permanent ecstasy appears incompatible with continued earthly existence. After all, if both consciousness and the senses go down and stay down, we would verge on a condition of physical death or lapse into a purely vegetative state. We read accounts of ecstatic mystics and contemplatives who have blacked out for periods of time and have no awareness of the world at all. What would become of them if they remained in this condition? Obviously they would die because the senses have closed down along with consciousness. But if the senses could remain perfectly functional or awake during ecstasy, the world of ordinary life could go on as usual, only without self or consciousness. So *perfect ecstasy is the ability of the senses to remain awake and perfectly functional in the absence of consciousness.* If this can be done—or if some event makes it possible—life can go on without self or consciousness.

Thus one of the imperceptible changes that takes place between the beginning and end of the unitive state is the increasing ability of the *senses to stand alone and not be affected by any change in consciousness or any change in the self-experience.* Learning to ignore all the various movements of self or consciousness—which means not going along with them, getting caught up in them, and seeing them for what they are—is one of the automatic lessons we learn in the unitive state.

Authentic ecstasy is not something we can bring about by our own efforts. The unconscious reflexive mechanism is not under conscious control; rather, it is beyond all the efforts and movements of the phenomenal self. While the energies, feelings, thoughts and reflexions of the phenomenal self may not be problematic in the unitive state, they are nevertheless movements of self or consciousness. Ecstasy is a more perfect condition than the unitive state because there is no self or consciousness in it, hence no possibility of any movement or self-awareness.

Once we see that all movement of self arises from the true unconscious self and not from the divine Ground, we have come a ways in the unitive stage. With this realization "pure sensory perception" becomes increasingly important and trustworthy; also, ecstasy or the suspension of consciousness becomes increasing more perfect, more natural and everyday—though not permanent. So the path that lies ahead once we come to the unitive state will ultimately bring about the separation of these two different systems—namely, consciousness and the senses. The purpose of this separation is to enable the senses to remain awake and functional once the system of consciousness has fallen away.

Whether it is recognized or not, ecstasy is the immediate vehicle or condition that ultimately moves over the line or goes beyond the boundaries of consciousness. Obviously, self or consciousness does not move over the line or go beyond the boundaries of self or consciousness. Until the senses have become fairly independent of consciousness, there can be no permanent suspension of consciousness or crossing over—beyond all self or consciousness, that is. Until the preparation is right, ecstasy keeps returning to self or consciousness. We might add that for some people, ecstasy has never suspended the senses or made them totally inoperable; for others, however, it seems the senses are greatly affected and made inoperable by the suspension of consciousness. I do not know why this is so, but from the literature it seems that for the visionaries, the senses are more greatly affected by ecstasy. But whatever the case, ecstasy might be used as a gauge of our journey from beginning to end. This gauge is the increasing ability to "bear the vision" as it were, without the senses going down or without everyday life and its normal behaviors coming to a standstill. The goal, then, is to keep the senses awake and able to respond even though consciousness or self has been suspended, or once it has ceased to function.

As already said, when we come to the point of perfect ecstasy there will no longer be a significant gap between the ecstatic state and our ordinary, everyday unitive consciousness. This means that the final dissolution of the fine line between the two (the unitive state and ecstasy) falls away without notice. This dissolution becomes noticeable when the usual return to unitive consciousness does not occur. Because we have no way of knowing ahead of time what lies beyond this line or what the permanency of such a state of existence (ecstasy) would be like, there may be an initial movement of fear at the idea of crossing over and never again returning. But what eventually casts out all fear is a lifetime spent with the divine, a lifetime of being finely attuned to its ways and doings, and years of testing self's absolute immovable trust in the divine. An entire life's journey of love and trust is now brought to bear on the single unknown moment of permanently crossing the line. The enormous preparation and variety of experiences needed to come to this moment can never be sufficiently stressed.

What is meant by the "fine line" between two different dimensions of existence is the difference between a *temporary* suspension of consciousness (ecstasy) and an irreversible *permanent* suspension, which is the end of all ecstasy and the beginning of the no-self dimension. In other words, as long as ecstasy is a transient experience, there is always a return to the unitive state, but the moment there is permanent suspension of self or consciousness, there can be no return. Instead, there begins the adjustment to a totally new dimension of existence, and one that could not have been imagined ahead of time. Ecstasy does not define the new dimension of existence or the no-self condition; rather, ecstasy is only the vehicle or the condition of crossing over to a new dimension of existence. Prior to this moment, ecstasy, as it was experienced during the passage, was only the gauge of readiness for eventually passing over a hitherto unknown line, a line we are not aware of until we are on top of it.

The moment consciousness is permanently, irreversibly suspended—with no possibility of return—is a moment unknown to consciousness; thus the moment of passing over is totally unknown. It is not an "experience." Once on the other side we can no longer speak of ecstasy; there is no ecstasy anymore because there is no consciousness to be suspended. Here begins a totally new dimension of existence, one that bears no comparison to the ecstatic experience. We should also add that no one—no entity or being, no self or consciousness—passes over the line. Passing over simply means that all experiences of self or consciousness have permanently ceased. On the other side nothing remains that could possibly be called "self" or "consciousness."

One final point. As noted earlier, when we first came to the unitive state we had glimpses or experiences of yet a further, more final state: beatific, heavenly, or whatever we might designate as the ultimate divine condition. At that time, however, we regarded this final condition as incompatible with continued earthly life. But once beyond the fine line, the former divine condition becomes possible this side of the grave or without death. The reason for this is that over a long period of time the dependency of consciousness on the senses decreases, until finally (when we come to the fine line), the senses are not appreciably affected when consciousness is suspended. This means there comes a point in the journey when the senses can remain perfectly functional and can go right on without consciousness or self. Thus the distance traversed between the beginning and the end of the unitive state entails an increasing separation between the senses and consciousness; all of which, of course, is a preparation for eventually living in a state wherein there is no self or no consciousness.

No-Self Experience

The falling away of self or consciousness is composed of two different experiences or events. The first is the permanent suspension of consciousness—the cessation of the reflexive mechanism or knowing-self. The second experience is the falling away of the center of consciousness, which is not merely the feeling self, but the divine center, which is our entire experience of life and being. This *latter event* is the true and definitive no-self experience. What the second event insures is the permanency of the first event. The center of consciousness was the fuel or energy of the reflexive mechanism, and without this fuel or energy there can be no return of the reflexive mechanism. No return of the knowing-feeling self, that is. No return to any self.

In order to convey an understanding of this event we refer once again to the circular piece of paper (consciousness). By the time we come to the end of the unitive state there is only the barest rim or circumference remaining—which we have called the "fine line." Within this slender boundary is the divine center. Though no small center, the divine is still *within* the boundaries of consciousness; this is the divine *within* self and immanent in all that exists. But the moment this rim, fine line or circumference, disappears, not only is there no paper remaining (no self or no consciousness) there is also no divine center remaining. When the paper disappears so does its empty center. Without the paper (or some type of vessel) there is no *within* or without, no center or circumference. Thus we can no longer speak of the divine as immanent and/or transcendent, nor can we speak of oneness or union, or of any unitive or transcendental condition. Nor is there any experience remaining of life, being, energy, will, emotion, form, and much more. These experiences ARE (or were) self or consciousness, and now they are no more. And since consciousness or self WAS the experience of the divine, without this mediumship all divine experiences are gone.

So the definitive no-self experience is not the suspension of consciousness or a permanent state of ecstasy; rather, *the definitive no-self experience is the sudden falling away (or "drop") of the divine center of consciousness along* with its profound mysterious experience of life and being. This event is the sole indicator that the boundaries of consciousness—the whole knowing-feeling self and one entire dimension of existence—have irreversibly fallen away or dissolved. No other experiential event articulates the total dissolution of self or consciousness. The no-self experience, then, is, first, the cessation or permanent suspension of the knowing-self and, second, the sudden falling away of the divine center along with the entire feeling-self and all its experiences.

The extraordinary and unsuspected aspect of the no-self experience is not the falling away of the phenomenal self-experience, which was inconsequential anyway; rather, it is the falling away of the divine and the experience of "life." It is as if the Ground of Being had been pulled out from under the entire self-experience. For many long years the unitive experience had been our deepest self-experience, thus its dissolution is not merely the falling away of a superficial, conditional little self-experience; rather, it is the falling away of the experience of divine life and being which, in the unitive state, IS self's deepest experience of existence. Though this event might have been called the "experience of no-divine," this would not be wholly true to the experience and definitely not true to its reality. In the unitive state the divine IS the deepest experience of self and the singular experience of being; thus to dissolve the experience of the divine is to dissolve the deepest experience of self. Calling this the "experience of no-self" is not a name or title given after the experience, it is not a mental deduction or an approximation; rather, "no-self" IS the experience. This is its exact nature and an exact statement of its truth. No other experience in the journey lends itself to such an accurate statement of truth.

Intellectually we know, of course, that the divine cannot fall away or disappear. But in experience the divine can indeed fall away or disappear—this experience is well documented, particularly in the Christian no-ego experience. What disappears, however, is the *experience* of the divine, not the divine. The experience falls away because it is not divine. As it turns out, the experience of the divine is only self or consciousness. Thus *the deepest unconscious true self IS the experience of the divine,* or the divine in experience. This experience, however, is NOT the divine. What falls away, then, in the no-self experience is not the divine, but the unconscious true self that all along we thought was the divine!

The shocking revelation of the no-self experience is just this: that all our experiences of the divine are only experiences of ourself, and that all along the divine as it existed beyond self or consciousness had been *non-experiential.* While the divine had been the cause of our experiences, the experiences themselves (the effects, that is) were not the divine. This means that consciousness or self is the medium by which man experiences the divine. By medium we do not mean that consciousness is a veil through which we see and experience the divine—as if self were on one side and the divine on the other. Rather, consciousness is the experience we ARE: man himself. In essence man is consciousness and consciousness is man; thus consciousness or self is the whole human experience, including experiences of the divine.

What man does not know is that consciousness is the boundary that defines the entire human dimension of knowing and experiencing and that self's deepest experience is the experience of the divine. The divine, however, is beyond the boundaries of human existence, having existed before man or consciousness came into being. Consciousness comes from the divine and returns to the divine, and in between is our human passage. In making this journey our experience of the divine is according to consciousness or on human grounds; thus everything we know of the divine is according to consciousness or self. The fact that all experiences of the divine are self and not the divine should be good news to those who make the journey in the darkness of naked faith—without divine experiences, that is. In the long run nothing is really gained by these experiences. They are unnecessary and may even be deceiving. In truth, as imperceptible grace, the divine works beyond our awareness or experience of it. A great secret revealed beyond self is that so long as self or consciousness remains, its most authentic, true and continuous experience of the divine is simple faith. Few people think of faith as an experience because it is so mysterious. And yet faith IS the divine, simple and clear.

The true no-self experience can never be grasped unless we first know the unitive experience. In the unitive state the experience of the divine is our deepest spiritual experience of life and being. If someone told us that this experience could fall away, most probably we would only think of death. Although this is indeed the only true death experience man will ever have, yet those in the unitive state expect this mysterious experience of life and being to go right on. That it does not do so is the shock of the whole event—we should probably say "aftershock" because the event is over before we know it.   The shock consists in the sudden realization that everything (every experience, awareness and knowledge) we thought was the divine, turns out to have been only our self.   It is the shock of realizing we had spent our whole life living the error of thinking we were NOT that which we experienced, or not that which we had been aware of.   The truth of self, however, is that the *experiencer is the experience and the experienced.*   This means we are not only our own experience, but equally everything that we experience.   Such a disclosure might well be followed by a sense of having been cheated or hoodwinked all our life.   Where we had truly believed that the divine experienced within ourselves had been the divine, now suddenly it is clearly known to have been only ourself—our deepest true self.   While recognition of this error is not a happy realization, it is also not unhappy, for now, at least, there is no deception remaining; the unknown self, the great deceiver, is gone.   The paradox of the no-self event is that the falling away of self or consciousness is also its revelation, the revelation of its true nature. This revelation consists in nothing other than the absence of the entire self experience—that is, the whole dimension of knowing, feeling, experiencing.   This is no small event or revelation when we consider that what has fallen away is as mysterious and deeply rooted as the divine itself.   Beyond this event, however, there begins the gradual revelation of the true nature of the divine as it exists beyond all self or consciousness.

The first question that arises following this event is "What remains when there is no self and no divine?"   Discovering the true nature of "what remains" is virtually the journey from death to resurrection, or the journey from God to Godhead in Christian terms.   Right off, it is obvious that the body and senses remain— which seems easy enough to account for—yet knowing the *true nature* of the body and senses is another matter entirely.   The revelation of the true nature of the body is the revelation of the resurrection and the true nature of Christ's mystical body.   This revelation (true nature of the physical body), however, can never be accounted for in any terms available to consciousness (and the intellect), because its true nature is beyond consciousness.   Thus neither our intuitive nor scientific minds can grasp or articulate its true nature or, for that matter, the particular knowing available to the senses without consciousness.   While the ultimate truth of the body is beyond all our usual notions and experiences of it, the resurrection reveals that the eternal body outlasts all the experiences we call "soul" or "spirit." Consciousness had been responsible for these experiences, and without consciousness there is no experience of "within-ness," or of any soul or spirit dwelling "within" the body. The notion of a soul or spirit independent of the body, which leaves the body at death, is not true. As for the specific energy of life and being—the inner flame—that suddenly drops away in the no-self event; it vanishes like a bubble into divine air. When there is no fuel (self) left to consume, the divine flame goes out.

Beyond consciousness, the ultimate Truth of the divine is that it is neither immanent (within anything) nor transcendent (beyond anything), but IS everything that eternally exists. What the divine is NOT, however, is the structure, function or energy of anything. The energy that is consciousness or self is but one of many functions of matter, which function is not divine. As said before, what lies beyond the death of self or consciousness is the resurrection with its revelation of the true nature of the body or true nature of matter. To understand this revelation, however, it is important to distinguish between the scientific notion of matter and the true nature of matter. What I call the true nature of matter is "eternal form," eternal form that cannot be grasped by the senses, intellect or consciousness. Another way to articulate eternal form is to say that what consciousness regarded as matter turns out to be spirit; and what consciousness regarded as spirit turns out to be matter. Solely in terms of consciousness this means that the mystery of matter IS spirit, and the mystery of spirit IS matter. Consciousness was responsible for this dichotomy or distinction, but beyond consciousness no such distinction exists.

The question often asked regarding no-self is, "Who, beyond self or consciousness, knows the divine"? But if there is no self or "who," the question cannot be answered because it cannot be asked in the first place. The question presupposes an answer in the same terms or in the same dimension in which the question is asked—the dimension of self or consciousness, that is. Beyond the dimension of self, however, the question cannot and does not arise. Such a question can only arise within the dimension of consciousness, where consciousness or self is its own answer, of course. The type of "knowing" that lies beyond self or consciousness cannot be known, defined, articulated or identified in any terms of consciousness and its intellect. Whatever can be grasped by consciousness can find some form of articulation, but what cannot be grasped by consciousness cannot be articulated. For this reason the "knowing" that exists beyond consciousness and which most characterizes the no-self condition, cannot be accounted for at all. About the only thing that can be said is that it has no resemblance to either the knowing or unknowing of consciousness. I call this mysterious knowing the "cloud of knowing" to distinguish it from the "cloud of *unknowing*" or the type of unknown-knowing peculiar to the unitive state. The "cloud of knowing" is different because there is no "unknowing" about it.

To help understand the falling away of self it is helpful to make a distinction between God and Godhead, where *God* is the Absolute known to and experienced by consciousness, and *Godhead* is the Absolute as it lies beyond all self or consciousness and can never be experienced by it. The difference between God and Godhead is very great, and consciousness cannot bridge this difference; in truth, the span between the two is a great void. What it takes to bridge this void and come to the dimension of Godhead necessitates the death of God—the death of consciousness or self and all its divine experiences. We do well to remember that the whole message of Christ was that we must go through God to get to the Godhead, which means we must go with our subjective experiences of the divine and live this human dimension to its fullest potential. Thus going with God is our passage to the Godhead or Absolute. Going through God and with God is "the way" to the Godhead that Christ revealed.

Distinguishing Between No-Ego and No-Self

By this time it should be evident that self or consciousness is not an entity or a being; it is not an individual person, a soul or a spirit temporarily dwelling in the body; nor is it divine, eternal or immortal. Self or consciousness is, however, the *experience* of all of the above—entity, being, soul, spirit and so on. Self or consciousness is a specific, unique experience or set of experiences. Take away self, and all its experiences go with it.

So the first thing to understand regarding the nature of self or consciousness is that it is not an entity, being, soul or spirit; rather, it is an experience that we mistake for these things. Between experience and reality or between experience and Truth, there lies a great difference. To discover this difference means traversing the great void between self and the divine—virtually the void between man and the divine. As long as we continue to regard self as an entity, being, soul or spirit, there is no hope of ever understanding what is meant by no-self. This is why interpreting self (and no-self) in terms of any other paradigm, path, or definition than the one presented in these pages, will not only be the cause of much confusion and distortion, but it will be the cause of the true no-self event becoming lost altogether. As it is, this event has already been lost from the literature because there has been no understanding of what self or consciousness really is. Thus some people think self is the divine, the unconscious, the ego, the immortal soul and so on, but none of these is self.

Of all these errors, however, none is more erroneous and misleading than equating *self* with *ego*. As used in modern psychology the terms ego and self are not synonymous or interchangeable; on the contrary, a distinction has been made quite clear in contemporary literature. Where Western philosophy and theology made no distinction between these terms or their meaning, in the Christian contemplative tradition, at least, there has always been a distinction between a lower and higher self—the lower being the ego, the higher being the true self. But now that the specific terms "ego" and "self" are in common usage, it is important to articulate the contemplative journey in the prevailing language. This means we can no longer use the terms ego and self interchangeably or fail to make an experiential distinction between them. By the same token we cannot equate no-self with no-ego or fail to distinguish between these two different events.

As said before, what happens when we fail to make this distinction, or mistake the falling away of the ego for the falling away of self, is that the true no-self event becomes lost. It is lost because no-self has been understood as something it is not—it is not the no-ego event. Instead of two events separated by an entire stage, the traditional path speaks of only a single event, invariably the no-ego experience, but often referred to as "no-self." The no-ego event, however, is a half-way mark immediately PRIOR to the revelation of the unitive state, whereas the no-self event comes AFTER the unitive state has been thoroughly lived in the marketplace, after which it comes to its ultimate ending. Until this error is understood we cannot have a complete account of the human passage; instead, we will continue to believe that realization of the true self or egoless unitive state is as far as man can go this side of the grave—which is not true. But this is how the true end of the journey has become lost—by mistaking no-ego for no-self. We must not confuse these different endings: first the ending of the egoic condition and, later, the ending of the unitive condition.

But this is why, when hearing of the no-self experience or falling away of the unitive state, a great deal of confusion has been generated. Faced with an event we have never heard of before or an experience with which we have no acquaintance, we conclude that no-self must mean no-ego; we think it is a matter of semantics or we believe the author is ignorant of the contemplative path or has made a mistake in interpretation. Since anyone can use the phrase "no-self" we have to be very clear about what is meant by "self" or "consciousness" and continually check on its experiential usage throughout the journey. If self or consciousness is not experiential and not an immediate identity, then it is nothing. If self or consciousness is just another name for the divine, one or the other is dispensable. But this is why, without a clear definition of self in terms of immediate experience, the true meaning of no-self has been mistaken for no-ego and thereby eliminated from the journey. For one reason or another it seems this elimination has been going on for centuries. Our contemplative or mystical literature only hints at a no-self event, whereas the no-ego experience has been well documented in every religious tradition.

It is unfortunate that most of our older religious texts do not make a clear experiential distinction between ego and self. Although the distinction between the egoic and unitive states (lower and higher self) is taken for granted, these texts use the term "self" to define both the egoic and unitive condition. Thus, for example, we hear a great deal about the evils of self, the falling away of self, the realization of self, and the deified self, which does not lend much clarity to the subject of self or consciousness. Then too if we have not had the experiences of which these texts speak, we have no way of discerning their different uses of "self." It follows that if we have not realized the experiential difference between the falling away of the ego-center and the later falling away of the true-self (the divine-center along with the phenomenal self), we do not have the tools for discerning the difference or know what to look for in the literature. From the position of the egoic state we are bound to interpret the no-self experience as the no-ego experience; it cannot be otherwise. Also, to tell someone newly arrived in the unitive state that down the road the divine-center, his whole experience of life and being, will ultimately dissolve, would strike him as unnecessary, unimaginable, erroneous in fact. So even these advanced individuals tend to regard no-self as no-ego. But to dismiss the difference as a "semantic distinction" is unconscionable. It is nothing more than a refusal to examine the experiences and define the terms.

An example of questionable semantic usage might be the following. The Hindu regards the realization of his true self or *Atman* (Brahman in human experience) as his ultimate enlightenment, while the Buddhist regards the realization of no-self or no-*Atman* as his ultimate enlightenment. The question, of course, is what the Hindu and Buddhist mean by "self" or "*Atman.*" If by no-self or no-atman the Buddhist only means "ego" in the sense of a false self, then there is little difference between these two religions; the difference would be only semantic. But if by no-self the Buddhist means no-*Atman* in the Hindu sense of "*Atman*," then the difference between these religions is explosive—and enlightening. As it stands, however, while Hinduism makes a rather clear distinction between the ego (*jiva, ahankara*) and self (*Atman*), Buddhism tends to eliminate the self entirely—be it the ego-self, true-self, divine or absolute self. In some ways the Buddhists throw out the baby (the true-self or *Atman*) with the bath water (its ultimate impermanence). We cannot speak of any cessation or falling away of self or *Atman* unless it has first been realized. Perhaps this is why, with one exception, I did not find the no-self experience articulated in the Buddhist's texts. If from the beginning we assume there is no self or *Atman*, we could not expect to hear of its cessation or falling away. Needless to say I do not hold that self or *Atman*—or ego for that matter—is an illusion; on the contrary, without self, human beings would not exist.

The point is that if we could define the entire self-experience (ego, self, true-self, consciousness and so on) in *experiential* instead of philosophical or theological terms, we could eliminate a great deal of erroneous conjecture, misinterpretation, confusion and bickering. This means paying more attention to the *experiences* behind the terms we use rather than accepting them at face value or as a matter of blind belief. We could then be straightforward with one another and accept our differences without further ecumenical mincing. Although no one is expected to define Absolute Truth, we should be able to define everything short of it because this includes everything we know and experience.

One hope of eventually straightening the path or recognizing two different endings instead of only one may lie with the coming-of-age of Western psychology. Modern psychology has become increasingly aware of the transformation process and hence increasingly aware of the distinction between ego and self. We can no longer brush aside the terms "ego" and "self" as a "semantic difference." On the contrary—and many thanks to Carl Jung in this matter—these terms are becoming increasing differentiated and defined in the light of experience and spiritual development. Because of this we may now be in a position to understand not only the falling away of ego consciousness but ultimately the falling away of the unconscious or "true self" as well. Although we are just now getting used to the notion of transformation or no-ego, and though it seems unfair and

premature to talk about the ultimate dissolution of the true-self and
the divine, we may be more ready for understanding this experience
than ever before. It seems that the history of man's experiences
moves on whether we are ready for it or not; that is, when enough
people arrive at one frontier, another frontier immediately opens
up.

In summary, these few pages have tried to say something about
the difference between ego and self and their ultimate falling away.
We define self as the totality of consciousness, the entire human
dimension of knowing, feeling and experiencing from the conscious
and unconscious to unitive, transcendental or God-consciousness.
The ego we define as the immature self or consciousness prior to
the falling away of its self-center and the revelation of a divine-
center. In the long run, however, it would make no difference how
we defined self or ego when all the experiences on which these
definitions were based are ultimately wiped out. I am not aware of
a single experience we could define as self or consciousness that is
not ultimately dissolved. Though we may arbitrarily wish to name
the divine "consciousness" or "self," these names bring about more
confusion than if we called the divine "air" or "bird." At least these
terms do not confuse the divine with the human experience we
experience and express as self or consciousness. For this reason
when we speak of self we must speak in terms of *experience* and not
in terms of any theory, speculation, philosophy or belief system. If
self is not an experience, it is nothing.

Barring the event itself, the obstacles to a true understanding and
acceptance of the ultimate falling away of all self or consciousness
are formidable. This is a hard reality to face, as hard perhaps as the
ability to grasp the true nature of Christ's death (God's death) if it
were to be truly understood. Christians have never questioned the
nature of Christ's death experience; they think of it as just his
physical death—similar to the physical death of every human being
—and thus their concern does not go beyond its redemptive
purpose. As I see it, however, this totally misses the point, message
and revelation of Christ's death. At the same time I have not found
a consensus in the Buddhists' literature regarding the exact nature
of Buddha's enlightenment. Was it a no-ego or a no-*Atman*-Bra-
hman event? (As a Hindu, Buddha may well have experienced a
divine *Atman* prior to his enlightenment.) By contrast, Buddha's
enlightenment seems easier to accept than Christ's death on the
cross: the former image being one of serenity and peace, the latter
being one of cruel suffering. But what we must not forget is the
picture of Buddha before his enlightenment, the picture of a dying,

starving man, beset by every conceivable temptation, or the picture of Christ after his death, in the glory of resurrection and ascension. We might call the picture of Christ on the cross "before" and the traditional picture of sitting Buddha "after," while not forgetting their reverse pictures—dying Buddha and the resurrected Christ. These two pictures are as interchangeable as their experiences. Where Christ dramatically and physically manifested the no-self experience for all ages to see and ponder, Buddha described the experience, spoke of it to others, and lived out its condition for many years afterward. In both instances, however, the message is the same: self is not eternal, the Absolute lies beyond all we know and experience of the Absolute, self or consciousness. If we believe Christ is God or the one Absolute, the wordless statement of the cross is made all the more dramatic, shocking and powerful.

Conclusion

Unfortunately, consciousness is reluctant to admit that everything it experiences and knows is only as much as its own dimension and capacity permits. Indeed, for the most part consciousness does not even realize its own limitations. Nor will it ever realize its limitations until the human experience has been stretched to its furthest potential, a potential no man knows ahead of time. What this means is that there can be no falling away of self or consciousness until self or consciousness has been lived to the limits of its human capacity, which capacity is obviously its total fulfillment. To expect a kind of mystical demise of something we never really knew, or had never fully experienced or lived, is simply wishful thinking.

The true nature of self is elusive because it is such a continuous, autonomous experience we cannot remember a time we were without it, and try as we like we can never catch it in the act. But the main reason self is so elusive is that it originates at a "point" where the entire system of consciousness borders on no-consciousness, or where self verges on no-self. Whether we think of this as the point where the divine begins or where consciousness emerges from nothingness, or where consciousness merges with the whole body organism, this point is nevertheless responsible for the sense of mystery and unknowableness of the self-experience. Any paradigm of consciousness that does not take this "point" of origin into consideration becomes a closed system. If we assume consciousness or self has no origin, we assume it has no end, and thus as either an eternal phenomenon or one that is unaccountable and purposeless, the entire subject becomes a pointless investigation. The ideal, of course, is to begin our investigation with no prior assumptions, paradigms or belief systems regarding self and to allow the experiencing self to ultimately reveal its own eternal or non-eternal status, reveal its own origin and end. This way we avoid a premature closure which only keeps the subject moving in an endless, pointless, self-perpetuating circle.

But no matter where we begin the investigation of the true nature of self or consciousness, the inherent problem is that we can know only as much of it as we have lived, actually experienced. This fact alone is an inevitable barrier to a full understanding of the completed passage. If we have not lived it all, we can not know it all. Another problem is that consciousness or self cannot possibly imagine or grasp its own eventual ending or non-existence.

The mind is incapable of understanding how this would go; self cannot experience no-self; consciousness cannot experience no-consciousness. Thus because the mind cannot lay hold of any such condition it generally denies such a possibility. As soon as the mind thinks of its own non-existence, when self is suddenly confronted with the imminent possibility of its own extinction, the automatic response is fear, withdrawal and denial. In such an experience (which is quite common) consciousness is confronted with its own annihilation, extinction or non-existence, and at the same time sees nothing beyond. Indeed, consciousness cannot see anything beyond; without itself or without a seer, nothing can be seen.

We must remember that consciousness is not a medium for knowing itself; consciousness is only a medium for knowing what is NOT itself. Consciousness or self does not mediate self-knowledge, but is ITSELF the essence of self-knowledge or self-awareness. This means that at one and the same time consciousness is the totality of subjective experience as well as the medium for experiencing everything that lies outside its own dimension of existence. If we take away self or consciousness, not only is there no self or subject, but there is no medium for experiencing anything else (or other) that exists. This is why, confronted with the possibility of its own extinction, consciousness sees nothing beyond, and why, without consciousness, there could be no experiences of the divine or experience of self AS the divine. The falling away of consciousness opens upon a totally new and unsuspected dimension of existence, one that can never be experienced by consciousness because its dimension is beyond the boundaries and potential of consciousness or the psyche. This is why the falling away of self or consciousness is the only true death experience man will ever know. Short of this, every notion we have of death is not it. (See Appendix II.)

One Way to View the Passage

One possible way of envisioning the human passage is the following. We think of ourselves as originally emerging from the unknown, from darkness, nothingness or non-existence into the light of consciousness. But as consciousness develops we discover the increasing ability to see in the dark, see into the nothingness or mystery within ourselves and eventually realize that this darkness and nothingness is the divine from which we emerged and with which we are one. Thus we discover that our original darkness IS true light. Midway in this passage, divine light (darkness or unknowing) and the light of consciousness are in balance, with neither outshining the other. But as we move beyond this mid-point, divine light begins to outshine the light of consciousness until, in the end, the light of consciousness goes out and only divine light remains. From this vantage point we look back on the passage and see that although consciousness was the veil that dimmed the light, this dimming was necessary in order to make the human dimension possible. But if consciousness makes human existence possible, it is also not separate from the divine, nor does it completely hide it; on the contrary, consciousness or self is man's faculty or medium for experiencing the divine—so long as it remains, that is. Our passage through consciousness is the gradual return to the divine; we leave the divine unknowingly and in darkness, but we return knowingly and in light.

The divine, of course, is not light; we only use this term metaphorically. The essence of the Absolute cannot be known or experienced by the mind or consciousness, for which reason all our names, labels, definitions and descriptions are incapable of grasping it.

APPENDIX I

The Divine Experienced by Consciousness

The terms "self" and "consciousness" are always found in conjunction with man's experience of the divine. This conjunction attests to the fact that consciousness is man's particular faculty for experiencing the divine. Thus the senses and vegetative body are not the medium of the divine's revelation to man; rather, the medium is man's own subjective awareness, his own experience of self or consciousness. For this reason we speak of the divine in terms of a personal or subjective experience—in terms of our self, that is. If there is any problem with this subjective revelation it is man's tendency to conclude that because the divine reveals itself to consciousness or self, the divine IS, therefore, consciousness or self, or at least something akin to it. To avoid this error we must remember that not everything experienced by consciousness—a bird, rock or tree—belongs to consciousness' own dimension of knowing, experiencing or existing; we are *NOT justified in defining the essence of what we experience in terms of our own experience.* If we want to be totally honest, all we immediately know in our experiences is the experience itself, our self in other words. We ARE our own experience. Everything else we experience is "mediated" knowledge or awareness OF: awareness of the divine, of the rock, of everything—which in no way defines the true nature of the divine, the rock, or anything else. By the very nature of the reflexive mechanism of the mind, consciousness' first knowledge or experience is itself; only secondarily is it a knowledge or experience of something other than itself. Thus while the self-experience defines consciousness, it cannot define the true nature of anything else or the true nature of what it experiences.

Consciousness cannot know the "thing in itself" because consciousness cannot be other than itself; it is limited to its own field of knowing and experiencing. The only way consciousness can know something not itself or not of its same dimension is to bring this something or someone into its own field of knowing and experiencing. In doing so consciousness becomes the mediator for everything known apart from itself. Thus in the act of mediating, consciousness imposes its own limitations on the thing known, thereby making it comprehensible in terms of itself—in terms of its own image and likeness so to speak. This means that in order to know anything other than itself, consciousness has no choice but to impose its own limitations on everything NOT itself. So although the direct, immediate object of consciousness is always itself, at the same time, consciousness also mediates knowledge (indirect knowledge) of what is other than itself: things, people, the divine, the universe and so on. We cannot get inside our neighbor's skin; the moment we did so we would cease to be ourself, cease to exist, and at the same time we would suddenly be out of a neighbor. So too, we cannot know the immediate experience of a bird, tree or rock—all we know is our own experience of these things. This means that everything we know that exists, and as much as we know of existence, is only as much as consciousness permits. Consciousness not only defines the perimeters of the human experience, but defines as much of the divine and the universe as this perimeter permits or is capable of knowing and experiencing. Consciousness virtually locks man into the human experience or human dimension of existence.

This is why everything we say about the ultimate nature of the divine or the universe inevitably falls within the perimeters of consciousness. But as the divine and the universe exist beyond consciousness—prior to it and after it is gone—we can give no definition of it in terms of consciousness or its experiences. While consciousness experiences the divine, these experiences are not the divine; rather, the experience IS consciousness, consciousness' own experience *of* the divine. The difference is one of cause and effect. The cause of the experience is the divine, while the effect—the experience itself—is consciousness or self. Earlier we compared our experience of the divine to being stuck by a needle. The experience or what we feel (effect) belongs to us; it does not belong to the needle. We do not know what the needle feels; probably it feels nothing. So too, consciousness feels or experiences the divine, but this feeling or experience is not the divine's feeling or experience. For some people this may be a hard saying, yet its truth is totally verified once self or consciousness falls away. In the meantime the divine is non-experiential compared to consciousness' experiences of the divine, for which reason we do well to seek the divine in no-experience rather than in experience. This is why advanced contemplatives long to experience the divine without any admixture of self. However, the day there is no self in it is the day there will be no self. The whole point is that despite our divine experiences, the divine's essence or true nature is beyond the experiential potential of consciousness.

The ultimate secret, or what man does not know as long as consciousness remains is the presence of the UNCONSCIOUS reflexive mechanism, which is responsible for all self-knowing. Throughout the journey as much as we know of self-knowing is the conscious level, which is but the tip of the iceberg. The mind is not (as some people believe) a "self" prior to its reflexive action. On the contrary, if the mind could not bend on itself there would be no self; the mind only knows a self because of its bending action. The proof of this would be to stop the reflexive action and see if any self remained.   At best all we could bring about in this matter is an impermanent halt to the conscious *reflective* self, after which we would come upon the underlying unconscious *reflexive* self. Thus no effort of self or consciousness can put an end to the autonomous, unconscious reflexive mechanism, because this mechanism is what self IS.

The point is that due to the reflexive mechanism *all consciousness is self-consciousness,* not just on the conscious level, but above all, on the unconscious level. In ordinary experience we usually think that awareness-OF defines only the conscious level of consciousness and that awareness PRIOR to awareness-of defines the unconscious level; but this ultimately proves to be incorrect. *Prior* to awareness-of there is no awareness at all. Because the feeling center is a non-reflexive or non-dual experience, we sometimes think that this feeling-self is, itself, awareness *prior* to awareness-of. While this is true to a point, it does not take into account the whole of consciousness.   Without a knowing-self (reflexive mechanism) there would be no feeling-self or non-dual feeling center; thus if consciousness were not aware of itself there would be no self or consciousness to be aware of. All consciousness is self-consciousness—or better, all consciousness IS self.

Because awareness-of applies basically to the reflexive mechanism or knowing-self, this does not mean that the non-dual feeling self (or center of consciousness) can stand alone, or that we can have a feeling-self without a knowing-self (awareness-of). We cannot have any feeling—energy, will-power, love, the divine—without being aware OF it. The deepest feeling experience is that of simple life and being, an experience so simple that most people take it for granted and do not think of it as a "feeling experience." Although we may regard this non-dual experience as the "true" self or self PRIOR to awareness-of, it still cannot be separated from awareness-of. It is a mistake to think this non-dual experience of life and being can go right on without a reflexive mechanism—this is not how it works. The non-dual experience of life and being is not separate from the reflexive mechanism; on the contrary, this experience (life and being) is the specific *energy* that fuels the reflexive mechanism or makes it work. There can be no permanent cessation of the reflexive mechanism so long as this central energy or life-force remains.

In the unitive experience this central energy (life and being) is known and generally felt to be a run-on with the divine, having been derived from the divine and sustained by the divine. It is very true to say "God IS our existence" because without God we cannot exist. In fact, the unitive experience is this simple singular experience of being and life that we know to be inseparable from the divine. Although this is a non-dual experience, we are also aware OF this experience, aware of our oneness with the divine, and this knowledge is the certitude of the unitive state. We cannot, however, separate the mind's awareness-OF from the experience OF life and being. So, although the feeling-experience of life and being is non-dual or singular, it is totally one with the mind's dual awareness OF this singular experience. This means that the unitive experience is both dual and non-dual: dual because of the reflexive mechanism of the mind and non-dual because of the singular experience of life and being. If the whole of consciousness or self were to fall away—the entire feeling-knowing experience—nothing would remain to be called either dual or non-dual. The divine is beyond both these categories.

Another secret is that because of the unconscious reflexive mechanism, consciousness makes over the divine into its own image and likeness, not in visual images of course, but in ideas and feelings akin to its own experiences of being, self, consciousness and much more. This is why we experience the divine in terms of our own self-experience and tend to believe that the divine is also Being, Self, Consciousness and much more. The divine as it lies beyond all contact with consciousness or the self-experience, however, is not this. I am afraid we have built a lot of theology and philosophy of the divine based on the self-experience, or on the structure and function of our own psyches. But then the divine made the psyche, which means we must be OK despite all our errors and wishful thinking.

APPENDIX II

True Nature of Death and Resurrection

While in the course of our passage we experience a number of endings and new beginnings, experiences we call "death and resurrection," yet the only definitive ending of the passage we recognize is the unmistakable and sudden falling away of self or consciousness. Our particular view of the passage would not be comprehensible in terms of any other ending. Thus if someone mistook the falling away of the ego for the true end of the journey, their view of the journey would be totally different from the one we are presenting. It is important to remember that by "self" or "consciousness" we mean the totality of the psyche including all its levels and experiences. The ego is solely the original self-center of consciousness or self; by no means is it the whole of the psyche, consciousness or self. The falling away of the self-center (no-ego experience) begins the radical change of consciousness which culminates in the unitive state or God-consciousness. It is only after we have completely lived out this egoless unitive condition that we eventually come to the falling away of the "true self" and the totality of consciousness, including God-consciousness. If we do not see how the journey progresses from ego to no-ego and then from the true self to no-self, we cannot have a true grasp of Christ's revelation and the path he revealed to us.

Many Christians regard the experience of the transforming process (Dark Night of the *Spirit* in terms of John of the Cross) as a kind of death of self and self's experience of God. What we did not know prior to the onset of this transformation, however, is that it was the ego or egoic consciousness that experienced God. In other words, until egoic consciousness falls away this consciousness is the only one we know—the only self we know. For this reason when the ego self falls away all its experience of the divine go with it—it cannot be otherwise. When this happens we do indeed feel bereft of the divine and self, but only the self and the divine we knew to this point in the journey. But with the revelation of the divine center and the true self we discover a new self and a new consciousness. Thus the falling away of the ego and its immature level of knowing the divine has forced us to go deeper; from experiencing the divine on our own ground (the ego), we must now experience the divine on its own Ground, a Ground where our being or existence takes its life from the divine.

Initially the interior nothingness, darkness and emptiness that takes the place of the self-center (ego) seems to be nothing but nothing. As it turns out, however, this is the divine, but the divine never before experienced or seen by any ego-self, naturally. Thus, as the divine we have never encountered before, it must reveal itself to us all over again, and this revelation heralds the abiding unitive state. But even before this, unless something tells us this nothingness and emptiness of self IS the divine, we cannot submit our entire psyche to it. But this submission must be done prior to entering the abiding unitive state.

I have noticed that people outside the proper religious context understand neither this interior darkness and emptiness nor the spiritual-psychological requirements of this stage of the journey. The tendency is to be afraid of interior darkness, have wrong views or interpretations of it. Instead of going down into their own emptiness, people try to fill it in with the pleasures of this world. They run from darkness, nothing and emptiness, and often become embroiled in various delusions regarding its true nature. Too few people come to the unitive state because they are outside the proper religious tradition or context for having a true understanding of their experiences. Those who piece together their own path as it suits themselves dodge all the difficult milestones necessary for advancement; thus they go no where. Our well worn traditional religious paths were not meant for egos—which is why their traditional pleasures soon wear off. Either we are in this journey solely for God or ultimate Truth or we are not in it at all. The first to fall by the wayside are those in it for themselves.

Perhaps nothing so articulates the extreme difference between the egoic and unitive levels of consciousness as the notion of death and resurrection. The falling away of the ego-center leaves us feeling our life is no longer in our own hands or that we have no authentic life to call our own; thus the moment the empty center is revealed as the divine, we suddenly see that the divine Ground is our true life and the only life we really have. This discovery of eternal life is a kind of resurrection, for here begins a new life, a new way of living and being in this world. So between the falling away of the ego and discovery of the divine center, there is a sense of death and resurrection, which, for the Christian, is a further revelation of Christ. Here the identity of Christ and the "true self" merge in a remarkable way. Now we know what St. Paul meant: "No longer I, but Christ lives in me."

For all this, however, it can hardly be said that the true nature of Christ's death experience was the death of his human egoic consciousness or immature self—or that his resurrection was the discovery of his true self and an abiding oneness with the divine. From the beginning, or long before his death, Christ experienced an abiding oneness with the divine; indeed, his message was that we too should have this experience or realize this same reality. He spoke to us out of his own experience of oneness, and it was this unitive level of awareness in which he lived his public life prior to his death.   Christ did not speak to us from the level of egoic consciousness; in fact, he may never have known egoic conscious-ness. What his public life in the marketplace revealed was how we too were to live once we had come to the true unitive realization. Thus how one lives out the unitive state is how Christ lived it—in the marketplace. When we come this far (unitive state), however, we have only caught up with Christ when he first appeared in the marketplace. It is at this point that we go forward with him to final death and resurrection.

But if Christ lived in this egoless unitive state of oneness all his life, what was his death and resurrection all about? The Christian notion of "redemption" tells us nothing about the true nature of Christ's death; it only attempts to explain its purpose. But if we, like Christ, can realize our oneness with the divine (the unitive state) and live it out in the marketplace just as he did, we too will come to his same experience of death and resurrection. The way it went for Christ is the way it goes for us. That he is "the way" means that his experiential path is also our experiential path, a path that does not stop at the unitive state or even at the cross.

The true nature of Christ's death was the death of his human ex-perience of oneness with the divine; it was the end of unitive consciousness, God-consciousness—all consciousness, psyche or self. In truth Christ's divine self died; he literally "gave up his self" just as he said—yet who can take this literally? We are always repeating the words "Christ gave up himself," but who knows what this means? We can never know what it means, and *never understand the true nature of Christ's death, until we understand what self is.* When self in the unitive state falls away, we say correctly that "God dies" because God is self's deepest experience and knowing. And beyond this true or divine self, there is no self. So beyond the death of the true or unitive self it turns out that God is beyond all self and its experiences of the divine, beyond union and God-consciousness. God does not die, only the experience of God dies, *which experience of God IS self or consciousness.*

After this Christ descended into "hell" the void of voids that spans the gap between the human (consciousness or self) and the

divine. From this void Christ rose. The resurrection is the disclosure, encounter or revelation of the true nature of the body
(Christ's mystical body) the Trinitarian nature of the Godhead—in
short, the divine beyond all self, consciousness and all its experiences of the divine. While we will not here go further into the
Truth revealed by the resurrection, and the even further Truth
revealed in the ascension, the point is that the resurrected condition
is a dimension of existence beyond psyche, self, consciousness and
all awareness. (See Part III for a further account of this.) The
resurrected condition or dimension of existence is as different from
consciousness as the plant's dimension is different from the
animal's. It is not a different level of consciousness or any psychic
state; rather, it is a different dimension of existence, one that cannot
be described because it cannot be grasped by consciousness or its
intellect.

   If we think Christ's death was the falling away of his ego or self-
center, and that resurrection is the unitive or transcendental state,
then we have tragically fallen short in our understanding of Christ
and what he was all about. As I now see it Christianity has
perpetuated a short-sighted view of Christ and, consequently, a
short-sighted view of the rest of us. Christ's passage was the
revelation of the passage of every human being, and any misreading
of him is a misreading of the whole of humanity. Investigating
Christ's human experiences in terms of consciousness or self opens
up a whole new dimension of his Truth and revelation, and not only
his, but our own and that of the whole of creation.

APPENDIX III
COMPENDIUM OF THE SELF EXPERIENCE

All "self" words are expressions of the experience of consciousness. The deepest experiences that make up consciousness, however, are so subtle and unconscious that we do not recognize them as self or consciousness. For this reason the true nature of consciousness or self cannot be *fully* disclosed as long as we are living it, or are it. Full and final disclosure can only occur when self or consciousness falls away (its experiences cease) and thereby becomes known solely by its absence or what was.

Consciousness or self consists of two different experiences, *knowing and feeling*, as well as two different levels, *conscious and unconscious.* Together these experiential levels are responsible for man's unique dimension of existence; they constitute the essence of man or what he is. Consciousness is the boundary of all human knowing and experiencing, including man's experience of the divine. In fact the most profound experience of self or self-experience is the experience of the divine.

The Knowing Self

Consciousness is a unique function of the human brain, a reflexive function that allows the brain (or mind) to *bend on itself* to thereby know itself. Where the senses look only outward, consciousness looks only inward. This bending action allows the mind to "know itself" ("This is I," "I am myself" and so on) and this knowing or awareness IS self. As an automatic unconscious function, the reflexive mechanism is responsible for the subject-object poles of consciousness. Thus subject and object is one and the same self—the same subject knowing itself as object to itself. We might think of the object-self as a self-image of some sort, which image can be either conscious or unconscious. At the same time, these two levels (conscious and unconscious) correspond to the function of consciousness:

A. *The reflexive level* of consciousness is automatic and, therefore, not under conscious control. This is the *unconscious* where self-awareness goes on whether we are aware of it or not.

B. *The reflective level* of consciousness, however, is under conscious control and, therefore, it is the *conscious* level of consciousness. Thus we can deliberately look within, be aware of ourselves and so on. Developmentally man becomes consciously

self-conscious when he becomes aware of his unconscious awareness. After all, nothing can rise to the conscious level that is not,
first of all, on the unconscious level.

This reflexive mechanism IS the *knowing self*, and all self words
are an expression of this knowing. Also, the reflexive mechanism
is responsible for the development of the intellect and all the
rational function of the mind.   When this mechanism fails to
develop, there is no development of the intellect or rational faculty
—in other words, severe retardation.

The Feeling Self

This is the experience of energy, more especially the energy we
experience as life, life-force, or being. Few people suspect that this
indefinable, pervasive and continuous experience is the deepest
feeling self experience. This same energy is also the experience of
will or will-power, and it is the particular energy that drives the
reflexive mechanism or causes the mind to bend on itself. This
energy is virtually the fuel behind the knowing self. At the same
time, the reflexive mechanism *centers* this energy as the focal point
of its inward seeing. Thus this energy or feeling-self is the *center of
consciousness*. This center is the "point" where the subject-object
poles of the knowing-self converge with the energy that is the
feeling-self. This energy or feeling center is not only responsible for
the experience of physical energy, but also the experience of
physical form. (With regard to physical form, we must remember
that wherever there is a center there is a circumference, and that
due to the center of consciousness man experiences himself as a
discrete or circumscribed entity, form or being.) From this energy
center arises various other experiential energies as well as the entire
affective or emotional system.

Unity of Consciousness

The knowing-self and the feeling-self together give rise to various
subtle unconscious feelings and energies that we do not ordinarily
regard as self or consciousness. Thus consciousness is responsible
for all sense of interiority and spirituality, including the divine
within (immanent) as well as the divine without (beyond or
transcendent to self or consciousness). Consciousness is responsible
for the division of within and without, matter and spirit, body and
soul and all divisions we know of. It is also responsible for the
sense of beauty, a sense of time, physical tiredness, boredom
—the list goes on. The unitary function of consciousness is such
that we cannot have a knowing-self without a feeling-self and vice

versa.   Since the energy center fuels the reflexive mechanism,
without this center there could be no reflexive mechanism.   The
unity of consciousness, then, is its very existence.   That we conceptually divide consciousness into different parts, levels and experiences, does not alter its unitary function and experience.

Consciousness and Senses: Two Separate Systems

While the animals' dimension of existence and knowing is "pure"
sensory perception, man's primary dimension of knowing and
existence is consciousness. What distinguishes man from animal IS
consciousness or self. Functioning together, as they do in man, the
senses are like keys of a typewriter that trigger the reflexive
mechanism. Thus every sensory input bears a subjective stamp. As
long as consciousness or the reflexive mechanism remains, man is
not capable of "pure" sensory perception. While consciousness is
dependent on the senses, the senses are not dependent on consciousness.

Ego Self

Initially the ego-self is the totality of the self-experience; it is consciousness centered on and around itself. This initial self-center is
the ego proper and is experienced as the energy of self-will or
"being for itself."   This self-center, energy or self-will is what
experiences psychological pain and suffering when it does not get
what it wants—the tantrum phenomenon. It is the center of desire,
clinging, fear and much more.   So long as this central energy,
self-will or ego remains, all of consciousness functions according to
this self-center. Should this center fall away, however, consciousness would have to learn to function around an egoless (empty)
center—a divine center. The divine center is an energyless stillpoint. This means that the energy or feeling self that IS consciousness can no longer turn or move toward itself, but is turned
toward the divine even in its first spontaneous movement. The
falling away of the ego-center is the beginning of the true transforming process. Prior to this event we had only been reforming
ourselves, or trying to transform what we knew of ourselves. With
the falling away of the self-center (ego), however, we learn that true
transformation is a divine work, a work to which we can only
submit.

True Self

With the falling away of the self-center or ego, the new center is
two things at once. It is the absence (emptiness or negation) of

ego, and at the same time, it is the positive presence of the divine. The true-self, otherwise known as a unitive self or God-conscious self, is aware of the divine center in the same unconscious act of being aware of itself; thus awareness of the divine and self are given in the *same unconscious reflexive act*. This means that unitive consciousness is our simple, singular experience of existence or "being"—the experience of the deepest true-self being one with divine being. There are not two experiences of being. Unitive consciousness is primarily a "we" or "us" consciousness (referring to self and the divine), and not an "I" and/or "thou" consciousness. This unitive "we" or "us" is indicative of a duality even though the experience of life or being is singular. *God-consciousness, then, is awareness of the singular divine center given in the same unconscious reflexive act as self-awareness.* Because this reflexive act is first of all unconscious and only secondarily conscious, so too unitive awareness is first of all unconscious and only secondarily conscious. Though the unconscious true-self is what experiences the divine, the nature of this true-self is the real mystery of the unitive state or experience. Neither the divine nor the phenomenal self is a mystery; only the middle term (true-self) that experiences the divine on one side, yet gives rise to the phenomenal on the other, remains a true unconscious mystery—which mystery is the unconscious itself. The day this mystery is disclosed is the day the true-self, along with the phenomenal self, falls away. Altogether then, where ego-consciousness was the ordinary self-experience *prior* to transformation, true unitive consciousness is the ordinary self-experience *after* transformation.

Phenomenal Self

Since the egoless or unitive state does not cancel the self-experience, it is important to make a distinction between the deepest unconscious true self (which is one with the divine), and the relatively superficial non-eternal self, which I have called the phenomenal self. As I see it the phenomenal self is the personality, the responsive self or self that other people see; thus it is the self that "appears." In contrast, the true self never appears and is never expressed to the outside. Where the true self seems to be a steady dynamic, immovable center, the phenomenal self arises from the true self, arises to every occasion in response to whatever comes along. In experience, the true self in its oneness with the divine is felt to be a continuous burning inner flame, whereas the phenomenal self is ever changing, moving, coming and going, always called forth by the world and circumstances outside the true self or inner circle. Where the true self is an unknown, the phenomenal self consists of all the experiences we usually think of as self—various energies, feelings, emotions, thinking, and all mental functioning. Although distinct in experience from the true self, the phenomenal self is never separate from the true self; in fact, we might say that the true self is the unconscious phenomenal self, since the phenomenal self takes its energy from, and arises out of, the true self. Without the true self there could be no phenomenal self-experience. We might add that the conscious phenomenal self has no abiding awareness of the divine; its mind, energies and feelings are basically absorbed in the responsibilities of ordinary life. Nevertheless, the phenomenal or conscious self can deliberately reflect (look within) on its own divine center. As soon as it does so, however, the divine center is seen in an objective mode or as object to the conscious reflective mind. The true unitive experience, however, belongs to the unconscious true self, which is the ever-burning central flame, which flame is our experience of life and being wherein we are truly one with the divine. Should this flame ever go out, there would no longer be a true self nor any phenomenal self arising therefrom. The no-self experience is just such an event.

No-Self

The falling away of self or consciousness consists of two different experiences, two because consciousness is composed of two different dimensions of experience—knowing and feeling. First, there is the cessation of the unconscious reflexive mechanism of the mind, which is the knowing-self. On a temporary basis this cessation is similar to ecstasy. Second, there is the falling away of the divine center, which is the living flame and the deepest feeling self. This central unitive flame had been the source and ground of the whole energy experience; it had also been the fuel of the reflexive mechanism of the knowing-self. This second experience, *the sudden dropping away of the unitive center, is the definitive no-self event.* So long as the energy center remains, the reflexive mechanism could just as well start up again, as it does when returning from ecstasy. So the no-self event is first and foremost the *falling away of the divine center, the source and ground of the experience of "life," "being," energy and a great deal more.* Without a ground to stand on there is nothing from which any phenomenal self could possibly arise. Therefore, no-self means: no true-self, no divine-self, no phenomenal self, no knowing-self, no feeling-self, no unitive-self, no center, no interiority, no unconscious, no conscious, no psyche. Without an experiencer there is no experience and no experienced.

Beyond No-Self

What remains beyond self is obviously the body and senses—now, "pure" sensory perception. For the senses to stay awake or function without consciousness is a feat akin to the miraculous. The revelation of the true nature of the body is the resurrection; not only is the body eternal, but its true nature is the Trinitarian Christ—Christ's mystical body. This mystical body, however, is not our usual bodily experience; in fact, it is not an experience at all. Following this is the revelation of the ascension, which is the disclosure of the divine or heavenly state in which Christ's mystical body eternally dwells. In Trinitarian terms this heavenly condition is the Father. If the ascension condition continued for any length of time, the senses would cease to function, followed by the cessation of all bodily function, medical death in other words. The mystical body means the Eternal Form or substance from which all is created, which Form is the divine, eternal Christ. In Christian terms this means: (1) the eternal *Manifest* Form or substance is the divine nature of Christ; (2) the eternal *Unmanifest* (Father) is the glorious state in which the Manifest eternally dwells; (3) the eternal movement or creative *Manifesting* divine is the Holy Spirit. Thus the Trinitarian nature of the Absolute is at one and same time, Manifest, Unmanifest and Manifesting. Beyond consciousness or self, the body alone bears this revelation.

PART II
THREE VIEWS OF CONSCIOUSNESS

PART II
THREE VIEWS OF CONSCIOUSNESS

Hinduism
Carl Jung
Roberts

Introduction

My view of the true nature of consciousness is fundamentally different from the view of consciousness found in both orthodox Hinduism and the psychology of Carl Jung. Because there seems to be some confusion about how my view fits in with these paradigms, I have undertaken the following comparison in order to make these differences clear and unmistakable. It seems that the terms I use ("self," "consciousness," "ego," "unconscious" and so on) have been understood by others according to definitions derived from the Hindu or Jungian view of consciousness. As it happened, however, I did not come upon my understanding of self or consciousness through the Eastern tradition or through any Western psychology or paradigm. By the time I encountered these different perspectives it was too late; it did not change a thing. Thus having taken nothing from these systems there was never any need for conformity or, for that matter, any need for disagreement; one way or the other the idea never arose. Now, however, other people have raised the issue. What has happened is that the terms used to articulate the journey as I know it have been mistakenly redefined according to the Hindu or Jungian version of the journey. But when we define the terms of one journey in terms of a totally different journey, the result can only be invalid and confusing. We cannot lift terms out of their original experiential context and redefine them according to a totally different paradigm and set of experiences.

That everyone has different experiences and perspectives is not a problem; rather, the problem is that when we interpret an experience outside its own paradigm, context, and stated definitions, that experience becomes lost altogether. It becomes lost because we have redefined the terms according to a totally different paradigm or perspective and thereby made it over into an experience it never was in the first place. When we force an experience into an alien paradigm, that experience becomes subsumed, interpreted away, unrecognizable, confused, or made totally indistinguishable. Thus when we impose alien definitions on the original terms of an experience, that experience becomes lost to the journey, and eventually it becomes lost to the literature as well. To keep this from happening it is necessary to draw clear lines and to make sharp, exacting distinctions. The purpose of doing so is not to criticize other paradigms, but to allow a different paradigm or perspective to stand in its own right, to have its own space in order to contribute what it can to our knowledge of man and his journey to the divine.

Distinguishing what is true or false, essential or superficial in our experiences is not a matter to be taken lightly. We cannot simply define our terms and then sit back and expect perfect agreement across the board. Our spiritual-psychological journey does not work this way. We are not uniform robots with the same experiences, same definitions, same perspectives, or same anything. Thus what Jung or a Hindu might experientially define as "ego," "true self," "the unconscious" and so on while it may satisfy their own understanding of such experiences, it would not necessarily satisfy the experiences of other people. To account for this diversity it is important to remember that the human journey is one of gradual change from beginning to end, and that each point *en route* yields to a new and different perspective. Thus the way we see things in the beginning is not the way we see things at the end. This means that everyone writes—and reads—from a different perspective. Another basis of diversity may stem from the fact that the divine is One and, therefore, cannot create two of anything that are absolutely identical. The eternally new and unique: this is the divine. Thus apart from a common divine Ground, diversity is as unlimited as the divine. While man may have no problem with the divine, yet as we know, he has always had a problem with diversity. It behooves us then to be open to new dimensions of experience and to examine our truths every day of our lives.

The problem of making space for anything new or different in the contemplative field is the problem of letting in new experiential definitions for some old terms, terms whose definitions are so taken for granted that they have become sacrosanct, unchangeable and fixed. But as we know, what ultimately determines meaning is not dictionary definitions or someone else's theories and experiences; rather, meaning and definition are derived after experience, or as a result of what has been discovered or learned because of experience. Accepting definitions prior to experience may lead to false expectations and wrong perspectives, which in turn, may lead to false or incomplete paradigms. Authentic self-knowledge is opposed to pat formulas; the search for truth is launched because there is no easy acceptance of what is popularly known or generally accepted. The search for truth must go on until there is nothing left to doubt and no questions left to ask.

In the following pages I use the term "Hinduism" as an umbrella term for various Vedanta and Yoga theories that share the same view regarding the ultimate nature of self or consciousness. Although Hindu philosophy is rich in diversity and has other views of self or consciousness, the most popular or well known is Sankara's view of Brahman, Atman and Consciousness, which is generally considered orthodox Hinduism. Though many books could be cited as reference for this orthodox view, the ones listed in the bibliography are the most pertinent and thorough I have found on our present subject.

Hinduism and Jung's psychology cover a great deal of experiential territory that is not of particular concern here. Our present subject is limited to their particular views regarding the true nature of self or consciousness, and the experiences these terms describe. By putting these views side by side, the purpose is to point out major differences, even profound disagreements. The purpose is not to point out similarities—which are ultimately dispensable anyway—but to put our finger on those differences that make a difference, those which are indispensable. The purpose is not to discredit anyone's views or beliefs, but to leave open the door on alternative or different views and beliefs.

Three Views of Consciousness or Self

HINDUISM'S fundamental belief is that the nature of ultimate reality (Brahman or Absolute) is Consciousness, and that Brahman or Consciousness is the true nature or essence of all that exists. The human experience of Brahman is called *Atman* and is characterized by *satcitananda* or the experience of being-consciousness-bliss.

Although no distinction is admitted between Brahman and Atman, using two terms for one ultimate Reality suggests a distinction.[1] The goal in life is to realize Atman, realize we are Atman, that Atman is our true self or true nature. Since Atman IS Brahman, to realize Atman is no different from realizing our true self as Brahman, or realizing that the essence and ultimate reality of self is Brahman or Consciousness. To distinguish between Consciousness as Brahman-Atman and consciousness as an illusory, false or separate self (*jiva, ahankara*), Hinduism employs the term "Pure Consciousness" for Brahman-Atman, and reserves the term "reflective consciousness" for everything man experiences as an individual self.

It seems that Pure Consciousness or Brahman-Atman is not held to be disconnected from ordinary self-consciousness. Rather, Pure Consciousness is said to be a higher level of one and the same consciousness or just a higher level of self-consciousness. Thus there is no real break in continuity or yawning chasm between divine and human consciousness, the former being a higher level of the latter. At the same time, however, self-consciousness is regarded as an error, an illusion to be dispelled, which would seem to indicate that there is no true connection between self-consciousness and Pure Consciousness. How we get from one consciousness to the other seems to be a particular Hindu problem.

ROBERTS. All consciousness (including the unconscious) IS self. Consciousness or self is unique to man alone; it is not unique to anything else in the cosmos, nor is it the divine or the essence of the divine. Thus consciousness is the basic definition of "man" or what it means to be human. Although the divine is known and

---

[1]As I see it, the distinction between Brahman and Atman is highly significant. It reminds me of the distinction between God and Godhead, where God is man's experience and knowledge of the Godhead—which Godhead, however, lies beyond man's experience and knowledge of It. In other words, as much as man can experience or know of the Godhead IS God; what man cannot know and experience, however, IS the Godhead. Man's experience of the Godhead can go no further than consciousness because consciousness is man's limit of knowing and experiencing. In the same way, I regard Atman as the limit of man's experience of Brahman, which limit IS truly self or consciousness. Thus while I agree that Atman is consciousness' experience of Brahman, I do not agree that this experience (Atman) IS Brahman. (When all is said and done, however, my view of a triune Godhead is not the Hindu view of an unmanifest Brahman.)

revealed to consciousness, the divine, nevertheless, lies beyond all consciousness and even beyond all consciousness' experiences of the divine. Hinduism's experiential account of Pure Consciousness (*satcitananda*) is what I regard as the unconscious' experience of oneness with the Absolute. This experience belongs to the unconscious self; however, it does not belong to the divine. Thus "Pure Consciousness," "God-consciousness" or "unitive consciousness" is man's experience; it is not the divine's experience. While we are on this side of consciousness our experiences of the divine may be characterized as "love", "being", "bliss" and so on, but beyond consciousness and all its divine experiences, nothing remains that could be so characterized. For this reason nothing can be said of IT. Anything known or experienced by consciousness can be articulated, but what is not known or experienced by consciousness cannot be articulated.

CARL JUNG. When asked if he thought anything existed (such as God or an Absolute) beyond consciousness (specifically the unconscious), he said he did not know, but added with certainty that if anything existed beyond consciousness the only way this could be known was through consciousness. Although this response does not exclude the existence of an Absolute beyond consciousness or the psyche, it also does not affirm it. What it does, however, is limit all knowledge and experience of the divine (if it exists) to consciousness, and in this respect Jung's view is closer to Hinduism than to my own. Both Jung and Hinduism limit all possible knowing to consciousness: for Jung it is the limit of man, for the Hindu it is the limit of the divine. Thus belief in anything beyond consciousness would be impossible for both Jung and Hinduism, although for different reasons.

While Hinduism begins and ends every consideration of consciousness from its premise that the Absolute is eternal consciousness, Jung's investigation of consciousness neither begins nor ends with the belief in anything eternal or Absolute. He never claimed that his unconscious self was the Absolute or even suggested it was a soul that continued after death. So in this respect Jung's "self" is quite different from the Hindu Atman. But if Jung's unconscious self is not ultimately eternal, then after death man would have no way of knowing the divine, in which case all man's experiences of the divine would be meaningless—come to naught like a gigantic hoax.

Jung's failure to take a stand on anything eternal colors his entire paradigm of consciousness or the psyche. It leaves his psychology ungrounded and with no foundation in ultimate Reality. For this reason he had no choice but to put his faith in myth with its archetypal or gnostic experiences. Ultimate Reality, however, is beyond myth, symbols and archetypes, and it is unfortunate that few people see the difference. On the other hand, the fact that Jung's paradigm ultimately comes to naught or ends up empty of all Reality is, perhaps, its saving grace. Once religion or Truth has been mythologized, once Brahman, God or Christ is realized as nothing more than an archetype—image, concept or experience of the unconscious self—then we are ready to go beyond all archetypes, beyond the unconscious self to ultimate Truth. This is what Meister Eckhart meant when he said, "I pray God to be rid of God!" and what the Zen Master meant when he said, "If you see Buddha, kill him!" They meant that in the end we have to get rid of all the archetypes—kill them. Yet this cannot be done so long as the unconscious self remains, for to slay every conceivable and experiential archetype is also to slay the unconscious self because it is the maker of the archetypes. (It goes without saying that when there is no unconscious self remaining there is also no conscious self).

HINDUISM begins its discussion of Consciousness at much the same point where Jung leaves off or has no more to say. Hinduism begins with the Absolute and then moves downward or inward to address the mind, intellect and phenomenal experiences. Jung starts with the mind, intellect and experiences, and moves toward the unconscious "numinous self." Jung, however, does not reach the same Absolute "point" at which Hinduism begins its investigation, but then he never claimed to do so. My own point of departure falls between the previous two, which is the "point" where consciousness (and everything else for that matter) emerges from the divine. On one side of this point lies the divine; on the other side lies consciousness. In one direction consciousness develops into our unique human way of knowing and experiencing; in the other direction consciousness moves toward the divine to which it eventually returns. One side is not the other side; consciousness is not divine. But so long as consciousness remains it is also not separate from the divine. On the contrary, consciousness or self takes its life from the divine, and eventually gives it back.

Although these three different views begin from a single point—self or consciousness—this point is regarded quite differently and proceeds in different directions. For Jung the "point" is totally human and basically addresses itself to the content and experiences of consciousness rather than to its ultimate nature, source and destiny. For the Hindu the "point" is totally divine and thus the overwhelming concern is for man to realize this divine point, realize his true self (Atman), or Brahman within himself. My initial "point" is where the human meets the divine and addresses both sides, human and divine, in equal measure.

WHERE JUNG'S VIEW OF SELF and my view of consciousness overlap without wholly coinciding is our view of the unconscious as the deepest level of the psyche. While I hold that "self" is the whole of the psyche or another term for consciousness, Jung reserves the term "self" for the unconscious and uses the term "ego" for the conscious level of consciousness. In my view, however, "self" is the totality of consciousness or psyche that includes both Jung's conscious ego and unconscious self.[2] (As a word, "self" merely expresses the experience which IS consciousness; we can throw out the word, but we cannot throw out the experience.) We agree, however, that the unconscious is the deepest level of experience, but while he calls this deepest level "self," I call it solely the "unconscious self." We often hear the term "true self," but as Jung might use it to define the unconscious and even the numinous, I would not so use it. What I mean by "true self" is consciousness' deepest experience and knowledge of oneness with the divine. Thus "true self" is a middle term, a virtual unknown (not an archetype) that lies between the divine on one side, and the known phenomenal self on the other. The true self is the unknown, mysterious point where the divine touches the unconscious self; it is the point at which consciousness takes its life from the divine. Thus what I mean by "true self" and what Jung means by "self" is quite different. For the Hindu, of course, the "true self" would be Atman, no different from Brahman.

If Hinduism stated only that Atman was the true self or consciousness I could agree, but when it states that self, Atman or consciousness IS the one Absolute, I do not merely disagree, I regard it as incorrect. The difference, however, cannot be reduced to the use of different terms, definitions, interpretations, or even a belief system; rather, the difference is solely rooted in experience.

For the Hindu mystic or contemplative the ultimate experience

---

[2]I make no distinction between the terms "psyche" and "consciousness"; both attempt to account for the self-experience. Thus by "consciousness" I do not mean only the conscious level of self-knowing, but also the unconscious level of self-knowing. In some texts, however, "consciousness" refers solely to the conscious level of self-knowing (Jung's ego, for example), while "psyche" refers more to unconscious self-knowing or to a self that is superior to the ego.

or revelation of truth is that he, his true self or Atman, is Brahman or the one Absolute. The answer to "Who am I?" is "I am Brahman." Now this type of experience is unique to Hinduism; it is unknown in Christianity or any other religion that I know of. Thus experience alone—and not merely different terminologies and definitions, as so many people seem to believe—pinpoints our true differences. While we can argue terms, definitions, interpretations, beliefs and so on, we cannot argue experience; it is impossible. We cannot touch or alter another's experience; all we can do is affirm our own. Thus if through experience the Hindu affirms that his self is the Absolute, I too affirm through experience that, ultimately, there is no self to BE the Absolute. These are two opposite experiences and if we cannot agree to disagree then the only thing left is tolerance—or better, a respect for diversity.

IN THE HINDU AND JUNGIAN VIEW both the Absolute and man are bound by consciousness; if we take away consciousness or self from these systems, then both the divine and man cease to exist. For the Hindu there is nothing outside Consciousness; for Jung, if there is anything, man has no way of knowing it without consciousness. In both views consciousness is central; neither admits to the possible existence of any "knowing" besides consciousness. My comment on this is that the divine was in the know long before man appeared with his "consciousness" and his "self." Also, a view that holds that man alone knows the divine automatically places man at the center of things and makes the rest of the universe inconsequential to the divine. Although man says he believes the divine to be the center of existence, this belief has a curious way of circling back on itself—of being traced back to the believer. This circling on itself attests to the very nature of consciousness, which is totally reflexive. Without a circular reflexive consciousness there can be no center, and without a center there is no divine. Thus self or consciousness is the circle that keeps the divine in, keeps it to itself. As the center of this reflexive arc or circle, however, the divine is still relative to the circumference—relative to our self that is. How to get out of this circle is our human quest and ultimate destiny. The way out, of course, is through the center, and when there is no circumference or self anymore, there is also no center, no interiority—a fact that most people seem to miss or not to understand. What this means is that in the end, the divine is not imminent or "within"; it is only within to consciousness, or due to consciousness. Beyond consciousness the divine is everywhere. What keeps the divine in or "within," is the reflexive mechanism of the mind, otherwise known as "consciousness."

ALTHOUGH HINDUISM BEGINS with a theological statement that the divine IS consciousness or self, it goes on to account for how our human knowing and experiencing falls short of the divine or Pure Consciousness. To account for this shortcoming Hinduism unfortunately employs the term "consciousness" for states less than divine. Thus as a term, "consciousness" is used to refer to both the divine and to man's ordinary states. In order to differentiate these states, the divine is referred to as "Pure Consciousness," while man's unenlightened or ordinary awareness is called "reflective consciousness" or "self-consciousness." This complicates and often confuses the Hindu discussion of consciousness, because there are many levels of consciousness or self, and consequently many levels of experiencing oneness with the divine. Beginners, after all, have authentic experiences of oneness; even children have had such experiences. A rather common mistake in the contemplative journey is to believe we have reached the final or ultimate state of oneness when, in fact, we have not. Perhaps this is why Hinduism has many versions or differing accounts of its own ultimate state. It is easy to confuse self-consciousness with divine-consciousness, and difficult to affirm which level is final or as far as man can go this side of the grave. When we blur distinctions between the divine and our purely human mode of knowing and experiencing (our psychological apparatus, that is), we have no tool for discerning the difference, and it becomes easy to mistake ourselves for the divine or the divine for ourselves. But then, ultimately, Hinduism does not admit to any such distinction. Every distinction that can be made is said to be unreal or an error—an error that includes reflective consciousness (*jiva, ahankara*) or the whole phenomenal self--experience. Instead of seeing the phenomenal self-experience as distinctively human or as the necessary condition for human existence, Hinduism regards it negatively as an error, bad karma, or a mere illusion—all of it to be gotten rid of.

It is impossible to build a helpful or intelligent psychology of reflective consciousness on an error or on what is non-acceptable or non-existent in the first place. The fact that Pure Consciousness is said to be a rare achievement attained after thousands of rebirths attests to the extraordinary tenacity and deep roots of reflexive consciousness. To dismiss these thousands of years old roots as an illusion, error or ignorance is hardly warranted by the rarity of enlightenment. If reflective consciousness is an error, then perhaps man or humanity is an error. I would suggest, however, the problem is not man or humanity, but rather man's beliefs about himself and about the divine.

Christianity's understanding of the distinction between man and the divine takes a more positive view of man's limited condition, a view, however, that does not rob him of oneness with the divine. If we believe that man is the Absolute, then man's powerless human condition is not really explainable, and all attempts to explain it only result in ever more elaborate theories and beliefs. One such belief or theory is rebirth, which holds that man must be continuously reborn until he realizes he is the Absolute. That the Absolute must realize it is Absolute does not present us with a very lofty view of the divine. We can see why this belief is incompatible with the Christian view: if man is *distinct* from the Absolute, then there is no use waiting around (rebirth) for the realization, "I am God" when it cannot happen anyway. Still, the goal of the Eastern realization is based on its belief of no distinction between man and the Absolute, and thus its ultimate goal is to realize we are the Absolute. If such is not our belief, then, of course, such is not our goal.

ANOTHER DIFFERENCE is that while Jung and I agree that consciousness is a physiological structure and function of the brain or neurological system, Hinduism has no such view of consciousness, not even of reflective consciousness—which it perceives as a form of mental ignorance, not as a physiological function of the body or brain. Hinduism regards consciousness as non-material, a soul or spirit; we are told NOT to look for self or consciousness in the body or as any part of the physiological organism. How this agrees with the notion that the divine is "all that exists"—which must somehow include the body—I do not know. If the body were also the divine, then we could not explain the Hindu's insistence that the divine or consciousness is totally separate from the body. The intellectual effort to form a bridge between the non-material and material world, however, is responsible for much of the momentum behind Hinduism's numerous commentaries and commentators. But despite these efforts Hindu psychology remains rooted in the metaphysical, not in the physical. By comparison, no doubt due to Christ, Christianity never lets go of the physical; in some form the body is held to be eternal.

ALTHOUGH JUNG ADMITS TO the physiological roots of consciousness, he dismisses this fact rather abruptly. In an introduction to his psychology he states that the physical structure and function of consciousness is not his particular field of investigation or realm of interest. After these few lines he immediately plunges into the content of consciousness and never comes out again. I find this peremptory dismissal somewhat devastating.

When the body dies, consciousness must die or cease to function, and so much for all the content and divine archetypes; they have ceased to exist. What then? Is there any "then"? Jung said he did not know. The failure to know empties his study of consciousness of any lasting value or purpose. We are no more ahead than if we had studied fruit flies. Without an Absolute or without tapping into something eternal, Jung's psychology literally comes to a dead-end, a dead body in fact. In some respects this is not far from the Hindu notion of man's passage as an illusion; it is all a dream in the mind of Brahman—no bodies need be accounted for.

THIS IS FAR REMOVED from my view of consciousness. The physiological structure and function of consciousness is central to my view because this is the "point" where all energy and matter (structure and function) emerge from the divine, takes life from the divine and are never separated from the divine. This is the "point" where spirit and matter are eternally one, a point, however, that transcends our intellectual definitions of matter as well as our experiences of spirit. The divine is not a function; it is not consciousness, but as long as any function or consciousness remains it cannot be separated from the divine. The cessation of consciousness and the cessation of each successive physiological function—senses, vegetative body—is actually a movement back to the divine; thus each cessation from consciousness backwards, so to speak, is a movement forward to the divine. There is more to the body than function and its complex structure; if we trace the body back far enough we will come to the divine. This means there is no ultimate division between body and spirit—no soul or spirit popping out of the body when it dies. This is not, of course, the Hindu view of how things go; and as for Jung, he never addressed the subject.

Three Views of Ego

FOR THE HINDU, *jiva, ahankara,* or false self includes reflective consciousness, all sense of "I, me, myself," and the whole phenomenal self-experience. While this would not match any Western notion of ego, it is as close as Hinduism comes to making a match. Although the definition of *jiva, ahankara,* etc. would include the Western experience of ego, Hinduism goes further to include what, to the Western mind at least, appears to be the entire self-experience. Hinduism does not share the West's value of the individual ego or sense of personal selfhood; this whole experience would be regarded by the Hindu as the false self. At any rate, once the adept realizes this is not his real self and has discovered the Absolute as his true self or Atman, either no *jiva* or *ahankara* (reflective knower) remains, or else the *jiva* remains as the temporary "play" of the divine. The Absolute (Brahman-Atman) does not play of course; always it remains unmanifest and unmoved. But if the *jiva* or phenomenal self remains as the play of the divine, then the *jiva* and Absolute would be compatible and some form of duality—or union—remains.   If, on the other hand, the *jiva* or *ahankara* ceases or falls away, then only the unmanifest Brahman-Atman remains.

FOR JUNG THE EGO is the entire conscious level of consciousness (or psyche) that includes everything we know about ourselves. Thus the ego is always and everywhere the "known self" or as much as we know about ourselves at any point in time. This known self, however, is the more superficial level of consciousness or the psyche and not its true center. The true center is the unconscious "numinous self," which is an integrating energy and the deepest feeling-self. The ego or conscious "I" is only false so long is it has not yet discovered and submitted itself to the unconscious self and become integrated with it.   But after this submission, transformation or movement from the ego center to the true self center, the ego remains as the conscious level of consciousness.

Jung's notion of a unitive state (mature human state) is the ego's oneness with self, or the conscious level of consciousness being at one and fully integrated with the unconscious level. Offhand this unitive state seems to be nothing more than consciousness' original state of functional unity.   But the paradox is that no one can experience this integral unity of consciousness who has not also realized his oneness with the divine.   Jung stated that few people came to such a state and those who did had done so through a strong religious faith. Obviously what these few people had reached was not Jung's notion of "union" but, rather, the religious experience of oneness with the divine.   This fact should have left Jung scratching his head and revamping his paradigm. That Jung saw no difference, however, and merely imposed his psychological interpretation onto what was essentially a religious or
mystical event, attests either to his own lack of experience and discrimination, or to his determination to force the fit—make over the religious experience to fit his psychological paradigm. No true contemplative who has been through the transforming process would agree that its true nature was the ego integrating unconscious "content," or that the self was a numinous archetype. Nor would they agree that the unitive state is simply the oneness of the conscious and unconscious levels of consciousness; rather, such a wholeness would be regarded as a side product of oneness with the

divine. There is nothing divine about the functional unity or wholeness of consciousness; this unity is simply our self, our own psyche. The real question to ask is whether or not this wholeness or unity can be achieved apart from a religious mystical union with the divine. Jung's paradigm would seem to answer this in the affirmative, though, as he noted, he had never seen it happen.

When Jung heard that in the Hindu system the ego or individual self-experience ultimately falls away, he could not understand it at all. Naturally. The Hindu does not share Jung's view of the ego, and vice versa. Each has a different notion of consciousness and a different view of the ego, false self and so on. Jung never discusses what would happen if, according to his paradigm, the ego fell away. Given his paradigm it would be impossible. His "numinous self" cannot stand alone. Even his two views of "inflation"—ego or self— is not a falling away; rather, inflation is one level of the psyche overpowering the other and rendering it helpless. There is nothing in the Hindu paradigm that could envision such a possibility— though if we look East through Jungian eyes we might see it there.[3]

But Jung was rather astute in picking up a few statements by the Hindu sage Ramakrishna. This great and beloved seer was in the unitive state, yet he affirmed there was still a subtle sense of a personal "I" remaining, but an "I" that was one with the divine and not separate from it. When someone tried to throw this up to him —probably to discredit him—Ramakrishna replied in effect that so long as any "I" remained he would put it to the service of the Lord. Jung did not pick up on this remark to discredit Ramakrishna, but to prove his point that in the unitive state the sense of "I" (Jung's ego) remains. Still, Hinduism has its own distinct notion of *jiva* and *ahankara* and perhaps we do a disservice when we translate it as "ego." What we have to admit is that Jung was confined by his own definitions. Once he determined that the only knower possible was the conscious ego, it then became an absolute imperative for him,

---

[3]Quite possibly Jung got his notion of inflation from the Hindu assertion that their highest state was without the Western ego or reflective conscious-ness—without any I, me, myself, phenomenal self, etc. Jung found this absurd. Evidently the only explanation he could think of was that the unconscious self had absorbed or swallowed the ego leaving the inflated "I am God." Inflation can also work the other way around. When the ego appropriates the unconscious self instead of submitting to it or integrating with it, the ego then becomes a kind of Hitler-type God.

and he could not understand any other perspective. For myself I admit outright that I have no honest understanding of the Hindu *jiva* or *ahankara*. That it is a sense of an individual self separate from the divine is an experience I have never known.

MY VIEW OF THE EGO is different from both of the above. Ego is the specific energy of self-will that resides at the feeling center of consciousness. In experience the ego is the power of self-will that desires, expects, demands and even craves its own good first of all. When this will does not get its own way it can experience interior friction, anxiety, depression, anger, jealousy and so on. The ego is not a harmless mental reflexive "I"; it is not a mistake or an illusion; rather, the ego is a genuine feeling experience and the major cause of human suffering. No matter how unselfish the ego, it always requires some form of satisfaction in return for its unselfishness or altruistic acts. Without this kick-back the ego will not give for long, not even to the divine. When the ego goes in search of its own highest good and satisfaction, however, it goes in pursuit of the divine or Absolute. Now the ego is willing to let go of its worldly attachments and attaches itself, instead, to the divine. In this way the divine (not the world) becomes the object of egoic craving, desires and so on. Obviously there is nothing intrinsically bad or false about the ego; so long as this energy seeks the divine in all things, the ego is on target. It is when the ego is not going in its proper direction that we are being "false" to ourselves.

The breakthrough of the divine into this egoic center of self-will is the onset of the transforming process; this is painful to the ego which does not want to be broken up—or "broken in," as the saying goes. Prior to this breakthrough the ego was in a very good state, enjoying not only the presence of the formless divine, but an almost continuous union with it. That all this suddenly disappears is shattering to the will and its experiential attachment to the divine. Letting go of the world is nothing compared to the enforced letting go of the divine or our enjoyment of the divine. At this point the suffering ego must submit or surrender its entire will-power or energy to the "true divine center" of consciousness, which center initially seems to be no-energy, no-will, no-nothing in fact. In contrast to the ego center, the divine center appears to be no-divine, no-self, nothing but silence, emptiness, a void or hole in the center of our being.

This breakthrough or breaking up of the ego energy will ultimately be the end of it. No longer will we know and experience the divine or this world and ourselves on our own egoic ground; rather, we will know and experience from a divine Ground. The shift is from our own self-centered ground or ego to an empty center or divine Ground. As said before, the empty center is two things at once: the absence of the ego-self, and the presence of the divine. Once consciousness gets to the bottom of its empty center and realizes its abiding oneness or inherent attachment to the divine —a union not brought about by man, but by the divine—it no longer wants for anything because with the divine it has everything. So this is the end of craving, deep desires, searching and so on, and it is the end of all egoic suffering. After this, suffering will be different; all feeling will stop at an interior threshold where consciousness (the feeling-self, that is) meets up with the divine empty center. Feeling then dissolves, as it were, in this empty center and this dissolution gives way to a sense of peace, love and compassion. Without question the ego center has fallen away; it will never be experienced again. All the previous desires and cravings cannot arise because the ego or self-will from which they arose is gone. The center of self or consciousness is now empty of self, and in its place is an empty divine center.

Obviously, my view of the ego is totally different from that of Jung. He could not conceive of any falling away of the ego: not according to his paradigm, the Hindu paradigm, or my own. This is why, when I looked in his works for an account of the trans-forming process—such as I knew it at least—I did not find it there. On the other hand, looking through the Hindu accounts, I could not find it there either. Hinduism does not seem to take into account any gradual or radical transforming process—one that entails real suffering and true grit. Rather, it takes a gigantic leap from statements of the problem (the false self) to statements of a liberated self or Atman. The Eastern religions give the impression that the major problem to be overcome (the false self) is just a matter of intellectual or mental ignorance. If we can just see or understand how it works, then, suddenly, one day we will be free of this false self and land in a state of unending bliss. I realize that no contemplative path wants to advertise the cross or the suffering entailed in the crossing over. On the other hand we must not be naive about this or in any way mislead others. The truth is that getting to the other shore will stretch the human limits to the breaking point, and not once, but again and again. Who can take it? It is not for nothing that the cross is the central Christian symbol.

Although we might say that the result of the falling away of the ego center is a shift from "I" consciousness to "we" or "us" con-sciousness (self and the divine, that is), the real drama, change and struggle of transformation takes place in the feeling-self. The deepest feeling-self IS the experience of life, being, existence; one level up from this is the experience of energy and will-power; another level up is the whole affective system or range of feelings. Almost from birth to death the human struggle centers around the feeling-self, not around a powerless knowing-self. The mind bending on itself, continuously seeing or knowing itself (me, myself and I) is a relative nothing compared to the feeling-self. In the end, the knowing-self will fall away, but for the length of the journey it is the feeling-self that is constantly undergoing change and diminution. Starting at the feeling center of consciousness (as in the center of a circle) divine emptiness increasingly expands outward. The result of this divine expansion is the gradual diminishment of the whole sense of a feeling-self—"feeling selfhood" might be a better way to put it.

As I see it, emphasis on the knowing-self throughout the journey is basically misplaced because the major drama of our spiritual-psychological life revolves around the feeling center; it is there we must look for change; it is there we look for the divine. The one place in Hinduism where I found something akin to what I know as ego made reference to a "knot" in the heart. If the knot were untied, the strings would fall apart and something else (the divine) would be disclosed. The permanent falling away of this knot might be akin to the falling away of the ego-center—such as I knew it, at least. But to call the ego a "knot" would only refer to its negative or suffering aspect, whereas the ego is quite capable of experiencing bliss and ecstasy. The ego has two sides—two strings of attachment, we might say.

Also important to point out is that after transformation the deepest essence of our "true self" is experienced as an unknown, an unknown hidden in the divine. In the unitive state the self is conformed to the divine in that it too becomes an unknown. While existence of the divine and self is experientially affirmed, the essence ("whatness") of the divine and self remains unknown. The reason the deepest self is unknown is twofold. First, compared to the ego-self we previous knew, the NEW self is unknown; it is a new experience and the beginning of a whole new life, a life we have never lived before. Second, the essence of the true self still remains to be known. It is in living out the true self in the marketplace that it eventually becomes known. Just as we learned the true nature of the ego after it had fallen away, so, too, we learn the true nature of the true self when it ultimately falls away. So first we have to live through the ego-self, and then we move on to live through the true unknown self.

UNLIKE THE HINDU, the Christian contemplative never experiences himself AS the divine; rather, he experiences his oneness with the divine.   On a purely theoretical and non-experiential basis, the Christian might just as easily make the intellectual leap and say that the unknown essence of his true self IS the unknown essence of the divine. But the Christian who knows the unitive experience would never make this intellectual leap, simply because it would not be true to his experience; he does not experience himself (or his true self) as the source and Ground of all being. On the contrary, the divine center is the Ground of his own deepest experience of being or life—the same Ground that is the source of all life and being. Thus while we are one with the divine Ground, we are not, ourselves, the Ground. When the Christian affirms that God is his deepest experience of life and being, he recognizes that this is still HIS experience; it is not God's experience. This, however, seems not to be the Hindu experience or interpretation. For the Hindu the divine "in the cave of the heart" is not only his true self (Atman), but his true self IS Brahman, the divine Ground. The difference here is between the Christian unitive experience (self's oneness with God) and the Hindu experience of identity (self IS God). While the Hindu identity seems to be a statement of essence (God IS self, or Brahman IS Atman), Christian union is the affirmation of existence. To paraphrase St. Paul: for me to live is for God (Christ) to live. This is not the same as affirming "I am God." As an experience, self affirms that it exists only because God exists. The experience does not affirm that self's existence IS God's existence. The divine is not my self, or any self.

While this is not the place to discuss the difference between the Christian and Hindu ultimate Truth or revelation, the difference we have pointed out is important to keep in mind. Contemplatives are not interested in theoretical differences and similarities;   their interests focus, instead, on experience, for it is by experience they identify true differences and similarities. Although the uninitiated may think we are splitting hairs over an interpretation of a similar experience, we are actually pointing out a profound difference in Truth between two religious experiential paths. If we hold that the true self or Atman IS Brahman, then there is no way of recognizing or coming to terms with the ultimate falling away of Atman-Brahman.   For the Hindu this could never happen.   For the Christian, however, such an event could be readily understood as the true nature of Christ's death—virtually the death of God. For now, however, we are only focusing on the egoless state of oneness with the divine, which is a midpoint in the overall journey. Comparing individual accounts it would seem that the Hindu identity of self AS God and the Christian union of self WITH God are not the same experiences. Looking East the Christian thinks the Hindu has over-estimated his true self; looking West the Hindu thinks the Christian has not yet realized his true self. Looking at the two, I think they are talking about two different experiences. What we have to face is the fact that not all religious truths and experiences are the same.

Jung made no claim that his true self (unconscious or numinous self) was divine, eternal or Absolute. At the same time his unconscious self was not an unknown; rather, self was identified as a power of integration, an inherited archetype, a model of human wholeness, completeness, union of opposites and so on. Thus for Jung the essence of the unconscious self was an inherited experience interpreted by the conscious ego as its "true self." In other words, the ego or conscious self evidently interpreted an otherwise "unknown" experience AS its true self. That the religious individual would prefer to call this true self the "divine," or some other high ranking conceptual archetype, is alright with Jung. So long as we identify this experience as something meaningful to ourselves it does not matter what we call it. What the unconscious self is then, is whatever we think it is; it is our own archetypal interpretation of ourself and our experiences. If nothing else, the archetype verifies the interpretive nature or function of consciousness, which is the conscious self or ego interpreting its own numinous experiences.[4] But if the unconscious self is an archetype—model, ideal of wholeness, mythical figure or whatever—then so is the divine or Absolute. Unless we believe these interpretive archetypes are eternal, then ultimately there is no eternal self or Absolute. That anything exists beyond these interpretive archetypes, or that there is any truth beyond our ideas of truth, well, we know Jung never came upon

---

[4]Right here we have put our finger on the difference between "experience" and "revelation." Any numinous experience that we can interpret cannot be counted as a true revelation. I will go one further and say that no numinous experience (coming from within the psyche) can ever BE an authentic revelation. Although we can say that any numinous experience is a revelation of sorts, this experience is more a revelation of the psyche than the divine—which lies beyond the psyche. No numinous experience can actually reveal ultimate or eternal Truth.

anything beyond the unconscious; he cannot take us beyond to anything eternal.

It is hard to take any paradigm of human experience seriously when it depends on, or all boils down to, archetypal contents of the mind; for those in search of ultimate truth this could never be satisfying.   This is why Jung's position—self and the divine as nothing more than the mind's interpretation of itself and its experiences—if carried to its conclusion leads to a dark and nihilistic end.   Someday all these archetypes (all content of consciousness) will fall away—and then what?

THE THREE DEFINITIONS of ego presented here each represent a different notion and experience of the psyche. Jung's notion of ego as the entire conscious level of the psyche is not the Hindu notion of *jiva* or *ahankara*, nor are these the ego I know as self-will centered solely in and on itself. For Jung the ego is transformed and never lost; for the Hindu and myself the ego permanently falls away. For Jung the true self is the unconscious level of the psyche; for the Hindu it is the Absolute; for myself it is the point where the unconscious touches with the divine. In each case the ego is something different; it has a different goal or destiny, and it ends in three different experiential states of consciousness. Whatever the points of similarity among these three paradigms there is no evidence to justify that they are the same. All we can really do is compare experiential accounts. Beyond this we have nothing else to go on.

Different Views of the Unconscious

WE COME NOW TO THE UNCONSCIOUS where we find a parting of the ways, a complete split between Western psychology and Hinduism. For the Hindu the unconscious is everything that is NOT consciousness, not the divine, self or subject.   Thus the unconscious is anything that could possibly be an object to consciousness—a table, animal, the body, senses, and even the mind, intellect, and thoughts, self-image or self as object to itself. The unconscious then is the reflective *ahankara* that knows objects to itself.

This splits the Western view of consciousness in half because for the Westerner, the primary object of self is self. If psychology is not studying self as subject then it is studying nothing. The Hindu would say that self can never be an object of study, for any self that could be studied would not be the true self—which is why Hinduism is a religion and not a psychology. Jung's insistence, however, that the psyche and self could be objectively studied is the basis of his claim that his psychology was a scientific and not a metaphysical system or paradigm. What studies or knows the unconscious self—besides a psychiatrist or an outsider—is evidently the conscious ego; thus without the ego's self-knowing, any claim to be "scientific" would have no objective foundation. From the Hindu perspective, however, all we could possibly study scientifically would be the empirical (non-eternal) phenomenal self or conscious ego. The true self or Atman can never be studied; it is not a match for Jung's archetypal unconscious self.

Solely as a psychology, Hinduism basically splits reflexive consciousness in two; it separates ego and self, conscious and unconscious, and even splits the knowing-self from the feeling-self—how this works I will explain later. That it is possible for half of consciousness to be left standing alone is unconscionable in terms of Western psychology. Thus if we ask the Hindu how there could be any knowledge of a subject-self without an object-self he would simply refer to the divine, which is subject-self without an object-self. What we in the West regard as the whole of the psyche (conscious and unconscious) Hinduism regards as "reflective consciousness." True consciousness or Pure consciousness, of course, is Brahman-Atman, and this is basically the beginning and end of Hinduism's view of consciousness. This is the belief system and if we do not share this view of consciousness as the divine self, well, the Hindu would say that is our problem, not his.

Offhand it would seem that East and West are on two different tracks when it comes to discussing consciousness. If Consciousness is Brahman-Atman, then reflexive consciousness studied in the West would be viewed by the East as nothing more than the illusory, phenomenal self-experience exclusive of the revelation of Atman.[5] If I honestly believed this Eastern view were the true status of reflexive consciousness, however, I would not bother to address the subject of Hindu consciousness. It is because I regard the revelation of Atman or the Absolute as being wholly within the domain of reflexive consciousness that I compare my view with that of

---

[5]I agree that Western psychology is totally taken up with the empirical, phenomenal, non-eternal self. Even where it suggests that the unconscious self be given a divine interpretation, Western psychology is wholly concerned with the ego and its comfort.

Hinduism.[6]   While Hinduism is welcome to exclude reflexive consciousness where Atman or self is concerned, I cannot do so. What the Hindu regards as Pure Consciousness, self or Subject, I regard as a state or revelation that is possible only within the field of reflexive consciousness. Take away reflexive consciousness and there is no subject or self remaining—no Atman to BE Brahman.

But the Hindu says this is not the way it goes; rather, take away reflexive consciousness and what remains is Absolute subject or self--Atman or Brahman.   What we have here are two opposite revelations or experiences and, needless to say, they could not both be right at the same time. As I see it, one has first to come upon the oneness of Atman-Brahman (the true self in its oneness with the divine, the unitive state) before Atman-Brahman could possibly dissolve or fall away. We cannot talk about no-Atman-Brahman if Atman-Brahman has not first been realized. And if we do not know the difference between realizing the ego and realizing Atman or the true self, then we can never hope to understand the difference between no-ego and no-self. Jung noted that people often confused the emergence of the ego with the emergence of the self, and so too, I have noticed that people have confused the falling away of the ego with the falling away of self. According to the Hindu and Jungian paradigm, of course, the falling away of the unconscious self or Atman would be inconceivable.

To argue that there can be no subject without an object or that one is only relative to the other would be a waste of time for the Hindu believer. In his view this is an argument from the position of reflective consciousness, whereas Atman is beyond the subject and object of reflective consciousness. While I agree that the true self is beyond reflective consciousness, I do not agree that it is beyond reflexive consciousness. If there is no subject beyond reflective consciousness then whence comes the subject Atman—

---

[6]"Self-*reflection*" refers only to the conscious level of consciousness over which we have some control. "Self-*reflexion*," on the other hand, refers to the unconscious automatic function of consciousness over which we have no control. Consciousness cannot be turned off and on like a machine; we can sit in meditation all our lives with no alteration in its unconscious function. At best, we could only bring a temporary stillness to the "reflective level." "Pure Consciousness" is no doubt beyond "reflective consciousness," but the fact that self remains indicates that it is not beyond the unconscious "reflexive level."   Hinduism seems to ignore or remain ignorant of the wholly autonomous "reflexive" roots of consciousness.

"one's own self"? The reason man cannot have a full understanding of self until it falls away is that he is still IT, still unconsciously living it. So long as we are living it, reflexive consciousness is totally unconscious. It is this unconscious self that experiences the divine, which experience IS Atman. When reflexive consciousness or the unconscious self falls away, this is the end of Atman, the end of Atman-Brahman in fact. For centuries Buddhism has affirmed that beyond reflexive consciousness there is neither object nor subject—no eternal self, subject, Atman or Absolute Self. Because of this Buddhism became a separate religion from Hinduism. If all Buddhism was affirming was no eternal ego, *jiva, ahankara*, or reflective consciousness, it would be no different than Hinduism. But this is not what Buddhism is saying; rather, it is saying there is no ultimate or eternal Atman-Brahman, self or Subject. If after 2500 years Buddhism has not made a dent in the Hindu perspective, it would be pointless for anyone else to give it a try. Thus I leave the objectless self to the centuries of tomes that have addressed this subject—or no-subject.

WESTERN PSYCHOLOGY has a very different view of the unconscious, and for Jung it is virtually opposite that of Hinduism. For Jung self is the unconscious; for the Hindu, self is consciousness. Though I do not see a true correlation between Jung's self and the Hindu Atman, we can probably compare the two because self and Atman is as far as each of them go. But when it comes to the unconscious, their views are not really comparable.

In Jung's paradigm the unconscious is the true subject-self known to the ego or conscious level of consciousness. Thus the unconscious self is an object to the conscious ego; together they form the whole of consciousness or the psyche. The conscious and unconscious levels are but one subjective experience—a knowing-self (I, me) and a feeling-self (will, energy, feelings). Although self can reflect on itself, it is not an object like a chair; on the contrary, without the mind's ability to bend on itself or to be an object to itself there would be no self-awareness, no subject or self—and no psychology. The Western psyche or consciousness then is totally reflexive, even in its unconscious roots. The unconscious is not a negation of self as it is in the Hindu system. (Remember, in Hinduism the unconscious is everything that is NOT the self.)

ACCORDING TO HINDUISM, self or Atman can never be reflected upon; its nature is not reflective; it knows no objects, not even itself as object. Thus self has a way of knowing itself apart from an objective mode, a "knowing" that defies description and cannot be accounted for by reflective consciousness. This knowing is called Pure Consciousness; it is both prior and subsequent to reflective consciousness. Once Pure Consciousness is attained, reflective consciousness is no longer possible. If this is true—that Pure Consciousness is the cessation of reflective consciousness— then it means that the two are basically incompatible and that we cannot have both (Pure and reflective consciousness) at once. In this case Pure Consciousness would not simply be a higher level of one and the same consciousness; rather, Pure Consciousness would be altogether different, something else entirely. Strictly speaking, then, there is no link between Pure Consciousness (the divine) and reflective consciousness (the phenomenal or illusory self). How we get from one to the other and back again is said to be due to ignorance, karma, and its eventual eradication.

Though I agree that in the unitive state the phenomenal self (ego or *ahankara*) is not the primary object of *reflective* consciousness, I hold that the true unconscious self (which is one with the divine) is the primary object of *reflexive* consciousness. Just the fact we are aware of our oneness with the divine attests to the continued awareness of self. In my view Hinduism fails to take the unconscious, unknown self (*reflexive* level of consciousness) into consideration. It is not the conscious ego that is aware of the unconscious self; rather, it is first and foremost *the unconscious self that is aware of itself.* It is this unconscious self that experiences the divine, though neither this self nor its experiences are the divine. For this reason I regard the Hindu's Pure Consciousness or God-consciousness as articulating the experience of the unitive state or deepest level of *reflexive* consciousness.

Still, there is an element in the Hindu view of Pure Consciousness that I can readily understand, only from a very different perspective. Beyond the unconscious (or beyond all self) what remains is what I call Pure Sensory Perception, not Pure Consciousness. PURE sensory perception has no objects. The bird or lion, for example, does not "know" according to man's way-of-knowing. The dimension of PURE sensory perception is totally different from that of consciousness. What the eyes see does not constitute an "object" for the animal. What man calls "object" is always and everywhere an object-to-self, an object-to-consciousness, that is. So I agree with the Hindu regarding a state wherein there are no "objects" and no unconscious. But I have to go further and affirm that in this same state there is also no self or subject—divine or human—none whatever. Once again we are talking about two different experiences: Hinduism affirms there is a state wherein there is a subject (self) without an object; I affirm there is a state wherein there is neither subject (self) nor object. These two states are not the same: what the Hindu calls Pure Consciousness is not what I call Pure Sensory Perception. (See Appendix II)

FOR JUNG THE UNCONSCIOUS is the true self, a mysterious numinous experience or feeling difficult to articulate, but given various archetypal interpretations by the knower or ego. The ego is the basic knower (me, myself and I) while self is the mysterious feeler or the sense of a numinous self. The ego's spontaneous attempt to understand the deeper self gives rise to the archetypes, which are the ideas and images by which we know, identify and understand our deeper self. The archetypes represent how we see ourselves; they are a reflection of our own reality. Thus every archetype is an object to consciousness. In terms of reflexive consciousness in the unitive state, for Jung the ego (knower) is always bending on the subjective self or feeler. There is no feeling without a knower or interpreter; thus even if the feeling itself were divine, there must always be a knower of this feeling.

I would suggest that one key to the difference between the higher states delineated by East and West is that what Hinduism means by Pure Consciousness or Pure Subject could be viewed by the West as the deepest feeling-self standing alone without a knowing-self. The profound, ineffable experience of *Satcitananda* (Being, Consciousness, Bliss) is a feeling type of knowing that Hinduism regards as independent of the mind's reflective way of knowing. If we give it our best thought, we will discover that *while the feeling-self is (or can be) an object to the knowing-self, the knowing-self can never be an object to the feeling-self.* In other words, anything (including our feelings) can be an object to the knowing mind, but nothing can possibly be an object to feeling. The feeling-self cannot know or reflect on a knower; it cannot be an object to itself because this is not its function. Thus the feeling-self just IS; it exists without an object. This is why the Hindu states that the deepest feeling self or Atman is incapable of knowing any object to itself; it just IS— simple existence or being.

Other examples of the feeling self, however, would be the experience of "love," "peace," "sorrow" and so on; these feelings just ARE. But as soon as we give them a label or an interpretation (love of neighbor, or peace of God, for example) we have made these feelings the object of a knowing self. Feelings do not label themselves. While we can reflect on our feelings, our feelings cannot reflect at all—they are not the knower. Knowing, then, is always knowing something, whereas feelings are just there: they know nothing; they simply exist. Knowing and feeling are two non-interchangeable modes of experience.

In the unitive state the deepest subjective feeling is simple being, life, existence, which we know is one with the divine. The question is, can this experience of life and being ever be an object to consciousness? The fact that the knowing mind is aware OF this feeling gives us a positive answer. That we know our experience of *Satcitananda* tells us that a knower remains. The Hindu experience of Pure Consciousness then seems to belong solely to this basic feeling of life or existence, and this feeling is the true self, Subject or Consciousness. Both Jung and I would say, however, that this same feeling is also an object to the knowing mind; the unity of consciousness is such that there can be no feeler without a knower. So the key difference is that, in Western terms, the Hindu ignores or does not take the reflexive knower into account in its higher state of Pure Consciousness. Atman or self is the deepest feeling-self or feeling-being, independent of whether or not we (knower) reflect on this feeling. Thus an abiding awareness of the divine is first of all on the unconscious feeling level, while knowledge of this fact is secondary to its experiential reality.

THOUGH I AGREE WITH JUNG'S UNCONSCIOUS as far as it goes, I would take it further. While the unitive state may include a sense of wholeness or unity between the conscious and unconscious levels of the psyche (Jung's view of union), yet this unity is secondary and totally dependent upon consciousness' realization of oneness with the divine. There can be no stable or balanced unity of consciousness until consciousness has realized its true source or divine Ground. Those who believe otherwise need only meet up with a crisis in life to suddenly throw them off balance and start the old egoic suffering again. Jung, however, does not seem to realize this fact. For him union is basically the functional unity of the knowing-feeling self, the conscious-ego and the unconscious-self. That he never goes deeper or taps into the Ground of consciousness or self is the limit of his paradigm. We will not find in his works a description of union comparable to the Christian unitive state or the Pure Consciousness of Hinduism; Jung does not take us this far.

What is more, the experience of union with the divine is a knowing beyond an archetypal image, idea, experience or perspective. Compared to the thinking, image-making mind, the divine is like "nothing" to the mind; it is void or empty of any archetypal overlay or interpretation that could satisfy the mind in this matter. In fact, the ultimate distinction or discernment between the unconscious self and the divine is the presence or absence of an archetype. A true glimpse of the divine defies an archetypal interpretation, and where we give it one, the interpretation or description is always of the unconscious self; it cannot be an interpretation or description of the divine. When we forget this fact we fall into the grievous error of mistaking the archetype for the divine—that is, mistaking our unconscious self for the divine.

ALTHOUGH JUNG EVIDENTLY THOUGHT he had accounted for the divine in experience—his unconscious self and archetypal experiences—he obviously falls short in this matter. His unconscious self may well be the unknown depth of the psyche, but it is not the divine—and it is to his credit that he never said it was. But this is why the experience of true union (self and the divine) is not to be found in his writings or experiential descriptions. In the unitive state the essence of the true self is unknown, hidden in the divine unknown; archetypes, on the other hand, deal with the known. Jung does not mention, for example, silence, non-movement, no-energy, emptiness, a stillpoint, or the simple experience of being or life, all of which are void of any satisfying human or divine archetypal interpretation. A contemplative is one who must eventually come to terms with "unknowing" or not-knowing. This is his primary way of "seeing," wherein there are no satisfying images, labels, or archetypes.

We have to remember that an archetype is consciousness' interpretation of an experience that it is trying to integrate with its more superficial level of knowing. Thus an archetype is an interpretive knowing of what is essentially unknown. A true experience of the divine, however, is not understandable in archetypal terms—which is why the contemplative is more at home with not-knowing than he is with knowing. But Jung never grasped not-knowing as a way-of-knowing. Instead he was totally taken up with knowing; indeed, this is his gnosticism. But all mythical or gnostic interpretations are so much content of consciousness. They are not consciousness itself, and certainly they are not the divine. In truth, self or consciousness, as well as the divine, can never be a content of consciousness; we cannot pour a glass into itself. The glass cannot be its own content. Whatever is poured into the glass is not the glass. So too, all content of consciousness is not consciousness or self; rather, contents are only notions about self and the divine. So we must not take our gnostic myths seriously; rather, we must continually throw them out as so much weighty baggage. In this matter the true contemplative is very much the agnostic.

DESPITE, OR BECAUSE OF, THIS SHORT-COMING, however, Jung unknowingly points up an important truth, namely, that consciousness often mistakes its experiences OF the divine for the divine. Jung attributes all numinous experiences to our self and not to the divine, or to anything beyond self; thus the experience of self is its own cause. In a subtle way this explains away the divine or makes the divine unnecessary to his paradigm. If self or the unconscious is its own inherited cause and effect, then what need do we have of anything beyond our self? Have we not here mistaken our self for the divine?

Despite this closed circle (we are our own cause and effect) Jung points up a subtle truth of consciousness, which is its tendency to regard its experiences of the divine AS the divine. Consciousness does this when it mistakes the effect (the experience) for the cause (the divine). When our hand touches a flame the experience is totally our own—the experience is not the flame's experience. The flame is the cause; the hand only experiences the effect of this cause. So too, when the divine touches consciousness the experience is our own; the experience itself is not the divine, nor is it the divine's experience.

Though it is generally held that certain touches with the divine can give rise to numinous or even paranormal experiences—visions, voices, energies, interior movements and so on—the danger lies in mistaking these phenomena, effects or experiences, for the divine. We must keep in mind that the cause is not the effect; if we do not understand this we end up deluding ourselves, and perhaps other people as well.

This means that even the experience of emptiness, nothingness, being, life, non-movement, stillness, a center and so on, are strictly our own experiences OF the divine. Although I do not see how the experience of being or life could be called a Jungian archetype or model of reality, we do, in fact, interpret this experience to be either our own life, divine life, or both together. While Jung's description of archetypal experiences does not go deep enough to catch this mistake—mistaking effect for cause—yet this mistake persists on levels unknown even to him. I would go further and say that it may be impossible to catch this mistake until the unconscious self falls away. Once there is no self it can be seen in retrospect that all experiences of the divine had not been the divine; rather, the experiences had been our unconscious self. As it turns out then, none of consciousness' experiences are the divine; instead, they are the unconscious self as it touches upon the divine or is touched by the divine. While discovering this fact is a shock, it is the shock that finally discloses the true nature of consciousness and the unknown self.

THIS MEANS THAT JUNG WAS RIGHT all along: what we believe is the divine in experience is actually the unconscious self. It also means Hinduism is right when it says that the experience of Brahman IS self or Atman. But what neither Jung nor Hinduism addresses is the fact that the unconscious self and Atman ultimately fall away—cease to exist altogether. Thus both the Hindu and Jungian self are not divine and not eternal; rather, the deepest self is that in man which experiences the divine, but is not itself divine. This means that the divine lies beyond all such experiences, beyond all consciousness and beyond anything that could be called consciousness or self. As it turns out then, consciousness' most authentic experience of the divine is NO experience. That we believe our experiences of the divine to be the divine is the final illusion of self to fall away in the no-self experience. I might add that while the Christian contemplative is right in affirming that his self is not the divine, yet he was not really free of this mistake. Although he never experienced himself AS the divine, yet be believed he experienced the divine—I know I did. He was right in affirming the divine as the cause of his experience, but was not right in affirming that the divine WAS the experience. Although philosophically speaking, Buddhism would seem to avoid this mistake—in that it does not believe in an eternal self or a divine in the first place—yet here, too, it is virtually impossible to avoid this mistake. The experience of emptiness or Buddha-nature is still a relative experience or knowledge; it is not absolute or the "unconditioned and unbegotten." It is almost as if by its very nature consciousness has no choice but to make this mistake; in some ways the Hindu is correct in viewing our human passage as a passage through a huge mistake.

Yet this is our life; we have to make the passage and go through all its experiences OF Truth in order to arrive at ultimate Truth. Thus everyone makes the same inherent experiential mistakes regardless of religion or philosophy. What is more, no one knows this mistake until it has fallen away. It could be said that the nature of enlightenment is the falling away of a mistake or error that could not possibly have been seen ahead of time. The nature of this mistake is that even after the mistake is known, this enlightenment cannot be passed on to others ahead of their time. So long as we are living the mistake we cannot see it, for if we could see it then it would not be a mistake. But this is why, so long as we are living self or consciousness, we cannot fully know it. Its true nature can only be fully disclosed when it is gone; all the knowledge and discussion in the world cannot convey such a disclosure.

The Archetypes

QUITE APART from anything Jung had to say about his symbolic mythical archetypes, his real contribution to psychology is pointing out the interpretive nature of consciousness: the knower continually interpreting his feelings and experiences. It is impossible not to do this because feeling and knowing are the two experiential modes that compose the whole experience of consciousness.

Archetypes, then, are interpretations of our various feelings which range from the gross and obvious to the subtle and unobvious. It is easy to understand the self we know but not so easy to understand the self we do not know. We not only experience our unknown, unconscious self, but we are also its interpreters—which means, so long as we think we know our unconscious self, so long do we not know it. This is why when we impose various interpretations on the deeper self we may be subject to deception, thinking we are what we are not. But once we realize that our deepest self is unknown and adjust to living this unknown self, then we stand free of interpretations, free of all archetypes. As long as we invest our unconscious self with archetypes—be they divine or otherwise— we are not truly free; psychological and spiritual freedom is the ability to live with not-knowing. There is no true freedom so long as we demand that everything be known, including ourselves.

But if we cannot stop the interpretive mind, at least we can see it for what it is and no longer be caught up in all its archetypes, its gods and demons. Jung's unlimited number of archetypes are merely the possible cultural masks that can be worn by the unknown self. They are reflections of the known self on the unknown self. Thus archetypes are the interpretations we give ourselves—our self images, in other words. To stand free of all such masks is to stand in the naked unknown and admit our unknowing; until we can do this we will never be ready to go beyond the unconscious self. Although I do not think Jung would share this view of the usefulness of his archetypes—which is the need to unmask every one of them—yet I regard his insight into the interpretive nature of consciousness as his greatest contribution to our understanding of the function of consciousness.

THERE IS A GREAT DEAL to say about the archetypes, and elsewhere I have written at length on this subject. For now, however, I would like only to point out that archetypes continue to arise in the unitive state. In this state the mind continues to bend on itself. If this were not the case there would be no awareness of self and/or the divine.[7] Since all archetypes are self-reflections, we can understand why they appear differently in the unitive state than they do in the egoic state. In the egoic state we regard our self-image or self-reflection as not true to our deepest self; thus we put these superficial images aside and go in search of our true self. The Christian who believes he is made in the image of God will seek God as the mirror of his true self, and eventually he will find his true self in God. In the unitive state, therefore, self-images are far more subtle and less easily recognized as archetypes; this is because they are reflections of the unconscious, unknown, true self and no longer reflections of the known ego-self. I think of this as the difference between archetypes of the "personal unconscious" (egoic archetypes) and those of the "collective unconscious" (true self archetypes), the former being more superficial and easy to recognize.

In the unitive state the mind is now bending on the divine or unitive center, and thus the archetypes reflect how we experience ourselves in this state. The temptation may be to interpret ourselves as someone special—a seer, prophet or healer, mother earth and so on. It could happen that we are tempted to regard ourselves as the divine itself. These subtle notions or experiences are the possible masks or archetypes by which the unconscious understands its self in the unitive state—understands its oneness with the divine.

We have to realize that in this state the unconscious self touches upon the Source of all power, and at times we walk a fine line between identifying our experiences of power as the divine, instead

---

[7]It is difficult to evade the fact that Brahman or Atman is self-reflecting or is aware of itself. The statement "I am Brahman" could not arise without a reflexive, self-knowing consciousness. I do not accept the notion that the divine is self-knowing or "knows itself." In terms of consciousness this fact is unthinkable, yet the truth of the divine is that it IS unthinking and unthinkable. Divine "knowing" has no translation in any terms of consciousness; all that can be said is "not this, not that"—not anything the mind can grasp or conceive of. Because of consciousness man knows himself and knows the divine, and for this reason he believes the divine also knows Itself. Without consciousness or self-knowing, however, the divine can no longer be regarded as conscious or self-knowing.

of our self—which is all it is. It is vital to understand that the true power of the divine is not an experience, and that everything man knows and experiences as power, energy, force and so on is not the divine. The divine has no such experience. This means that when consciousness comes upon the true power of the divine it is the experience of no-power, no-energy, no-force, no-movement. This absence of power is more powerful than all our notions and experiences of power; indeed, this is the powerless Source behind the big bang and everything we call energy and power. From this silent energyless "Nothing" all things come into existence.

So any power and energy we experience belongs to the unconscious self, and all our archetypal interpretations of it are interpretations of our self. If from the position of unitive consciousness Christ and Buddha experienced archetypal temptations to seize this power as their own and proclaim themselves this or that, we can hardly expect to avoid these same experiences or temptations. But if we can understand the subtle archetypal nature of consciousness, we have the ultimate tool for discriminating between the divine and the unconscious self.

Our passage to the divine is a passage through all the archetypes, conscious and unconscious: a passage through the known, and then the unknown self—a passage through all consciousness. When the passage is completed there is the move to the "other shore" where there is no self and no Consciousness. But there can be no passing over until we have seen through every archetypal interpretation that can possibly arise, which means we have to live fearlessly so they can arise and show their faces. Any movement toward avoidance, or any clinging to archetypal notions of ultimate Reality will abort the completed passage. The day we see how these archetypal masks work is the day they can no longer deceive us or move us in any way. At this point the knowing-feeling self has out-worn its usage because it can no longer be moved, a fact that brings us to the river's edge. Self or consciousness does not make the passage to the other shore or cross over. Rather, the crossing is the body and senses acclimating to life without any experience of self or consciousness and all that this implies.

Conclusion

IT GOES WITHOUT SAYING that if there were nothing beyond consciousness there would be no Absolute, nothing perhaps but eternal archetypes—Plato's pagan view in fact. Jung, of course, never claimed his archetypes were eternal, and thus he was no Platonist. But the fact he does not address anything beyond the archetypes brings us to the point at which Jung's vision and experiences fail him. At this point his paradigm closes in on itself and never breaks out of its self imposed circle.

Despite this unfortunate closure, however, I agree with Jung that consciousness or the psyche is man's unique medium of knowing and experiencing, and that it delimits the entire human field of knowledge and experience, including scientific knowledge and religious experience. As consciousness is first and foremost a subjective experience, this experience is the primary object of psychological study and investigation. But where psychology is the study of self as object to itself, the primary concern of science is sensory objects or observable phenomena. Jung's insistence that his psychology was a science confuses two different objects—scientific objects and self as object to itself. Confusing the nature of these two objects and their mode of study is reflected in the limitations of Jung's psychology.

Jung's insistence that his psychology was a science was actually his excuse for not dealing with an Absolute or God and all this implies. By avoiding an Absolute he could avoid coming into conflict with various religions while wandering freely in their sacred domain interpreting everything as he saw fit—all in the name of "science" of course! His excuse was that if he affirmed an Absolute his psychology would become a metaphysical theory, and since he had no credibility as a metaphysician or as a religious individual he sought scientific status for his totally subjective meandering and theories. That anyone can honestly regard Jung's psychology as scientific, or fail to see that his paradigm reflects his own religious unbelief, is evidence that he has been hoodwinked by a very clever intellect. Because Jung could not deal with an Absolute, God or religion, he strove to present us with a paradigm of human experience without an Absolute, without religion, theology or metaphysics, a psychology that does not necessitate any Absolute beyond our self-experiences. This would not have been so bad if he had not stolen everything from religion and its theology and then reinterpreted its truths, beliefs and experiences into a non-religious, non-Absolute paradigm.

Jung stole his notion of self from Hinduism supposedly to translate it into the Western mentality, yet his unconscious self bears no resemblance to Atman-Brahman. That we think it does is his lasting disservice to both East and West. In order to give "meaning" (his own meaning) to a Christianity that otherwise held no meaning for him, Jung stole its experience of transformation (death, resurrection, transfiguration) and presented it to us in

Gnostic archetypal form, a form that has never been representative of authentic Christian mysticism. His stated purpose in all this, to make religion more meaningful, was nothing more than a sly excuse for offering an alternative to religion; as he said, he went in search of meaning because religion held no meaning for him. Our finding meaning where he found none does not indicate his charitable motives. Rather, it demonstrates his conscious or unconscious intent to dismantle traditional religion in order to offer his psychic interpretations instead. For some very personal, deep-seated reason Jung was in competition with religion, not in sympathy with it. His hoodwinking many in the name of giving meaning to our beliefs reveals the almost sinister power he wields over weaker mentalities.

While we are glad Jung found some meaning within the confines of his individual psyche, we have to remember that searching our psyches is no guarantee of coming upon ultimate Truth. In its own right the psyche is quite empty of Truth, which is why it fills in its own truth to compensate for what it does not innately have. All subjective truth is of the psyche's own making, which is why our religious Truths, standing outside ourselves, are a continuous challenge to the psyche. Truth is difficult to come upon because it is difficult to face; it disrupts our psyche and its comfortable notions and experiences of truth, whereas the nature of ultimate Truth is to keep us going—to bother us even. It is a thousand times easier to deny Truth or reinterpret it to suit ourselves than to have to face it. If Ultimate Truth is not larger than ourselves and our limited psyches, then Truth is anything we care to think it is, in which case there is no Absolute, no ultimate or objective Truth.

In conclusion, Jung's psychology is a science only so long as it eschews an Absolute, God and all religion; as soon as an Absolute is adopted, we have a metaphysical and not a "scientific" psychology. From this it is clear that Jung's insistent claim to be scientific depended on no Absolute, and explains why his paradigm lacks any ultimate Truth.

COMING NOW TO HINDUISM. Once it is affirmed that Consciousness IS the divine, no further discussion of Consciousness is really possible. To discuss Consciousness would be to discuss the divine; it would be pure theology. Since Western religions have never held the divine to BE consciousness, their exploration of consciousness is epistemology or psychology, the study of our purely human way of knowing and experiencing. The problem with the Western approach, however, is that it ignores the fact that, along with everything else, consciousness also experiences the divine. In Christianity this study—the divine in experience—has been traditionally known as "Mystical Theology," but it has been studied separately and never integrated with psychology or epistemology. Where psychology attempts to stay clear of these experiences, however, it falls short in its study and becomes as meaningless as Christianity had become for Jung. This is why, to make up for the deficit in Western psychology and to fill in what is missing in Western religion, people in the West are looking to the East, more especially to Hinduism.

What Westerners do not realize, however, is that for the Hindu, Consciousness is first and foremost a central tenant of belief and not really a psychology. Westerners who think they are studying Hindu psychology are actually studying Hindu theology. Its psychology arises from its central belief that the Absolute IS consciousness, and thus its psychology all leads back to the same point. Few people have come far enough in their investigations to realize the essential difference between Western psychology and Eastern theology; in fact, Westerners probably know more about Eastern theology than they do their own. For this reason they do not understand that when they adopt Eastern psychology with its various practices and techniques they are actually adopting a whole theology, a religion, a particular mentality and perspective, along with all its explanations and interpretations. Those who have gone far enough to realize or see this, at least have a conscious choice; those who fail to see the difference have no choice at all.

The often heard notion that Hinduism encompasses or subsumes all other belief systems is true only if every belief system holds with Hinduism that the Absolute IS consciousness or self (Atman). If a belief system does not hold this same view, it cannot be compatible with Hinduism. While every religion shares certain views and experiences in common, when it comes down to the fine line we have to admit our differences. If there were no profound differences, we could not account for different religions.

A major problem in Hinduism is how to account for lesser states of consciousness if consciousness is essentially divine. If man, like the divine, is consciousness, how could we NOT be enlightened? The attempt to solve this problem is the core of all Hindu philosophy and speculation. For some people the notion of rebirth seems to resolve this dilemma, and yet enlightenment is then needed to resolve rebirth. So the circle keeps going round and round.

The Hindu problem, however, is not our Western problem. When consciousness is not regarded as divine or Absolute, then the Hindu problem does not arise. The West, however, has is own set of problems. Western theology has never really addressed the subject of consciousness or self, but it should do so if it wishes to have a fuller understanding of Christ's humanity, his experiences, his ultimate Truth and revelation. To say that Christ's self or consciousness was eternal gives an entirely different picture and meaning to Christ than if we say his self or consciousness was not eternal. As it stands, the unexamined notion seems to be that his self or consciousness was, in fact, eternal. I think the West will come upon its own set of problems when it faces the impermanence of Christ's self or consciousness, but, at the same time, this will reveal an entirely new dimension of Christ's revelation—of this I am certain. If, on the other hand, Christianity maintains that Christ's self or consciousness is permanent and eternal (and our own as well), then Christianity is no different from Hinduism, and Christ is but another incarnate being who periodically comes to enlighten the world.

FINALLY, the purpose of this writing has been to call attention to the fact that basic, profound differences exist between psychologies just as they exist between philosophies and theologies. It is because there is no single view or definition of consciousness, self, ego, and the unconscious that we have different psychologies and epistemologies, even different religions. While it is easy to bridge superficial differences, profound differences do not give way because they were not meant to give way. Our minds and experiences were never meant to be identical. If they were, the divine would have created robots instead. So diversity is essential; it serves a great purpose, even though this is sometimes hard to appreciate. The desire to do away with all differences, the longing for sameness and unity of minds may be symptomatic only of the inability to tolerate differences, or the inability to appreciate the diversity of divine creation. As I see it, diversity arises from the oneness and uniqueness of the divine reflected in creation, wherein there is nothing identical because each reflects the One. While we can love all paths, we cannot live them all or live more than one at a time. To completely live one will demand everything we have to give—and more.

We cannot move around from one paradigm to another and expect the same outcome, or naively believe they are all the same. Each psychology or view of consciousness builds on a different basis, represents a different point of view and is derived from a different set of experiences. We cannot take words like "self" or "consciousness" and expect them to be defined (or even experienced) identically wherever we go. For this reason I cannot address those who believe or have experienced that the divine is consciousness or self. I can address only those who believe or have experienced that the divine is beyond consciousness or self.

There is no easy crossing-over into a new perspective, religion or psychological paradigm. If we think we can take all our baggage with us—our usual mind-set—we may be in for a shock when we learn we have to drop our familiar baggage because it won't fit in. In some ways Jung warned us about this when he spoke of Westerners trying to put on Eastern mentalities in the belief that they could have the best of both worlds without giving up a thing. Yet I like to think that Westerners have the ability to absorb the best of all cultures (and mind-sets) without compromising their own. This does not mean hopping around or trying to straddle different paths at the same time, or piecing together our own religion; rather, it means staying with one path and absorbing the best of all others. If we can do this we service our own path and all the people on it; if not, we end up serving no one. It seems everyone is keen on stealing from religion, but the question is, who is giving anything back to it? How have we enriched our paths for those who come after? Those who steal and run off to put together their own "thing" will soon be left behind and forgotten, while the great rivers of our traditional religions will move right on whether we are with them or not.

APPENDIX I
ESSENCE OF THE DIVINE

To say that the divine IS consciousness is actually a statement of its "essence" or "what" it is. In my view consciousness is not the essence or "whatness" of the divine; rather, consciousness is the essence or "whatness" of man. Christian theology holds that the essence of the divine is totally unknown; it cannot be grasped by the mind or consciousness; thus it cannot be defined or even named. On this point Christianity is silent. St. Thomas stated that in the case of the divine its essence and existence are the same or identical. What this means is that the essence of the divine IS its existence. "What" the divine IS, then, is "That" it Is—a good koan, I think.

APPENDIX II
PERSONAL DISCOVERY OF BUDDHISM

With regard to recognizing an experiential account I would like to offer the following incident. Shortly after the no-self event I began looking in the Eastern literature for this particular experience. It did not take long to learn that in Hinduism the ultimate experience is the realization that Atman-Brahman is "one's own self." I could not identify with this experience or realization; in fact, it struck me as quite the opposite of what I was looking for. In Hindu terms, Atman is not only man's experience of Brahman—often described as *Satcitananda*—but ultimately Brahman itself. In the no-self event, however, both the experience of the divine and self fall away in one unitive piece, taking with it the Center (divine stillpoint or fire of love) along with the entire experience of life and being. This is not only the falling away of the divine in the "cave of the heart," but also the falling away of the cave itself. I found no account of any such experience in the Hindu literature.

Then I went to the Buddhists' literature and came upon their doctrine of no eternal self and the cessation of self. Instantly this struck me as true, yet I could find no experiential account of the event that would have allowed for a comparison. Indications of it given by Zen masters and others were in the form of changed perspectives rather than the cessation of psychological experiences. Also the perspectives that were given were more indicative of the no-ego experience rather than the much later no-self event. These two different events and their ensuing perspectives are often mistaken for one another because of certain features and descriptions in common. These two different events and the Truth discovered following these experiences often sound alike; for this reason they can easily be confused in the literature, though never in actual experience. I am convinced that due to this confusion the no-self event has been lost to the literature. Today we hear of only *one* event (no-ego), whereas there are *two* events—separated by many years. Someday I hope to put these two events side by side in order to make the difference forever unmistakable.

At any rate, I gave up looking; Buddhism has less in the way of personal accounts than Hinduism, which has almost none. I was used to my Christian literature with its wealth of personal, contemplative accounts. But three or fours years later I picked up a book on the life of Buddha and came upon a few lines—supposedly said by Buddha—regarding his experience. Comparing self to a house, Buddha said that suddenly the "ridgepole" collapsed or was "split" and the rafters had fallen down—the house of self was no more.[8] The key word was "ridgepole," the sturdy, seemingly eternal divine Center—God in Christian terms, Atman in Hindu terms, and perhaps emptiness or Buddha-nature in Buddhist's terms.

The tone of the lines was "Ah ha, finally I caught you (self); finally I have discovered your true nature!" But where Buddha's tone was of one who had caught a thief in the act, my reaction was one of having been cheated all my life. For over thirty years there was total certitude that the sturdy immovable Center was God, but with its sudden falling away (and extinguishing of the "flame of love") it was discovered to have been only the unknown, unconscious self, which self also had been the entire experience of "life" and "being"! The deception is shocking. What had truly fallen away, of course, was not God; rather, it was the *experience* and *experiencer* that fell away and took the *experienced* (God) with it. If there is no experiencer there can be no experience and experienced. Consciousness or self is the medium of experiencing God, and without this medium there is no Consciousness, self or God. Thus God is something else entirely, and far beyond consciousness or self's experience of God.

The deception aspect of the no-self experience is important because Truth becomes known only when deception falls away; thus the revelation of Truth must, at the same time, always be the revelation of a deception. This is why the sudden falling away of self is equally the disclosure of a great Truth—namely that the divine lies beyond all our experiences of the divine, and that these experiences had only been the unconscious self which we had mistaken for the divine. So the disclosure of the deceptive self is the hallmark of the no-self experience. What falls away is the

---

[8]House-builder! I behold thee now,
   Again a house thou shalt not build;
   The ridge-pole is split
   All thy rafters are broken now,
   My mind, its elements dissolved,
   The end of cravings has attained.

I have found about a dozen translations of these eight lines in various books; unfortunately, I do not have the specific reference for this particular translation, which was jotted down about five or six years ago.

"experience" and the "experiencer" which takes the "experienced" (Absolute) with it—the whole unity of consciousness falls away in one fell swoop.

For the Christian this "death of God" is a particular revelation, that of the true nature of Christ's death, an event that is not, however, the end of the revelation. What is interesting is the almost identical Buddhist account of the "splitting of the ridgepole" and the Biblical account of the "renting of the veil of the temple" at the time of Christ's death. The Buddhists' is a personal experiential account while the Christians' is an externally manifest event, though the meaning is the same. What separates the Holy of Holies (the Absolute) from the rest of the world—man and the universe—is the veil of self or Consciousness. The veil is not some egoic rag; rather, the veil is sacred, mysterious and impenetrable, seen and acknowledged as the gateway to the ultimate Truth of God. Tearing down the veil is almost blasphemous because now there is no distinction or separation between the Absolute and man or between the Absolute and the whole universe. This is an incomprehensible and unthinkable Truth, yet this is the great Truth revealed at Christ's death and Buddha's enlightenment. Self or Consciousness is the veil, as well as the seemingly indestructible central ridgepole of the psyche.

The ridgepole is not the ego-center of the psyche that buckles with the winds of fate; rather, the ridgepole is the stable balanced divine center, a stillpoint that does not bend with the fluctuating circumstances of this world. We only come upon this abiding divine center or ridgepole after the ego-center has fallen away. This fact is brought out in the lines of the verse already quoted:

> House-builder! I behold thee now,
> Again a house thou shalt not build;

The word, "again" implies that the center and its house had fallen away before, but had been rebuilt around a new center—this time the ridgepole. So too, when the ego-center falls away we feel we have gone to pieces; yet afterwards we discover a divine center and a new unity is established around this new (seemingly) absolute center—the ridgepole. But further on, once the divine center or ridgepole collapses, there is nothing left with which to rebuild a house; there is no self—no center and no circumference—remaining. Quite possibly, Buddhists may have attributed the rebuilding of the house to the notion of rebirth, but if we take away this belief (which Christians are free of anyway) we can see that man comes upon an abiding stable center, refuge or stillpoint only AFTER the ego-center falls away. There is no balanced, stable or enduring unity of psyche so long as the ego is its center. Only a divinely-fixed stillpoint or ridgepole meets this requirement. Buddhists, of course, have their own interpretation of these lines. I can only say that coming upon them was a moment of enlightenment, one I compare to an arrow shot at the beginning of time suddenly hitting a bull's-eye. This is the only experiential account I found in Buddhist literature that could be identified as the true no-self experience. Everything else beats around the bush.

A few days later I came upon the Five *Skandhas*. On reading the short translation of these five terms I immediately recognized the entire self experience. This was another remarkable find because without the no-self experience no one can possibly account for the entire self experience; as said before, as long as we are living it, we cannot have the whole story on self. Thus whoever nailed down the Five *Skandhas* knew this event, knew the permanent cessation of the *Skandhas*.[9] Together the Five *Skandhas* constitute the true nature of self; their experience is the entire self-experience including the experience of the divine. This might be called a piece of esoteric knowledge in that the Five *Skandhas* can be disclosed AS self only when the whole experience permanently ceases. We spend our lives being unconscious of the complete self-experience; while we can identify its conscious experience, we cannot identify its unconscious roots because we ARE it. Thus, for example, who would think self to be man's entire experience of "life" and "existence"—which, in the unitive state, is also our deepest experi-

---

[9]FIVE *SKANDHAS*:

Rupa = experience of bodily form and other physical experiences connected with consciousness.

Vedana = emotions, and numerous subtle feelings we never think of as "self."

Samma = perceptions. The senses and consciousness functioning in conjunction—so long as consciousness remains, that is. All knowledge, ideas and concepts arise from this conjunction. PURE sensory perception, however, is void of consciousness.

Sankara = experience of energy, life-force, will-power. This is the fuel that runs the reflexive mechanism of the mind.

Vijnana = consciousness or awareness, including the unconscious. Also the reflexive mechanism of the mind or brain, the knower and discriminator, image-maker and so on.

ence of the divine? That self IS our deepest experience of the Absolute is something we never counted on. Then, too, who can imagine what remains or how things would go without this experience, without any self or *Skandhas*? Most people think they would be dead. At any rate coming upon the ridgepole and the Five *Skandhas* told me all I ever needed to know about Buddhism; everything else is beside the point. Without question, Buddhism has hold of a profound and difficult Truth.

From both my reading and discussion with others, however, it seems the Buddhists do not believe "no-self" means the falling away or permanent cessation of the Five *Skandhas*. Rather, the general belief is that the *Skandhas* are only transformed or perfected, that only their defilements are eventually overcome, or that they are only discovered to be "empty" or void of any permanent or eternal self. I regard this view, however, as only articulating what I call the "no-ego experience" or discovery. Once we come upon the empty center of self we know that at bottom the *Skandhas* (our self-experience or experience of our own being) are empty of self-being. This is similar, if not the same, as the Christian encounter with the central void and nothingness in the Dark Night of the Spirit. Here the center of self is void of self (seemingly the divine), then one day this same emptiness, darkness or nothingness is revealed as the Source or Ground of Being—the Source and Ground of self. Although the Ground is not the self, yet self could not exist without the Ground. This unitive state of affairs might be likened to a doughnut (or *doughnaught*). The hole in the doughnut is not the bread, just as the divine empty center is not the self; yet we cannot speak of a doughnut unless we have both the hole and the bread. So too we cannot speak of a unitive or non-dual state unless we have both the divine and self. The unitive state does not do away with the phenomenal self-experience or the Five *Skandhas*. In both Christianity and Buddhism this egoless unitive state is held to be a purified transformed state, a state purified of ego defilements. In this state the skandhas do not cease to function or to be experienced; rather, they are seen as the impermanent, phenomenal, conditional self-experience and by no means eternal.

It is only AFTER we come to this state of oneness that there comes a turning point and we enter the marketplace. The marketplace is the free exercise of the phenomenal self, a life of egoless giving and living. It is when there is nothing left to give that the phenomenal self comes to an end or ceases to function. It ceases because once it has been fully lived, none of life's challenges can move or effect the phenomenal self anymore. Sooner or later repetition is without challenge, and when there are no challenges left, the conditional self has outworn its use, its function and purpose. The unexpected surprise of the cessation of the phenomenal self, however, is that its very Source, Ground or Empty center falls away; it is this latter event that is the true no-self experience. This is the collapse of the divine ridgepole, the falling away of the empty center. It is the definitive end of the entire self-experience the cessation of the Five *Skandhas*. As I see it, then, in Buddhist's terms, *the true articulation of the no-self event would be "NO-Five Skandhas."* Because the *Skandhas* were the medium of experiencing the Absolute or empty center (the *Skandhas* being relative to emptiness, as a vessel is relative to its content), the Buddhists affirm that without this medium there is no Absolute to speak of. The "unconditioned and unbegotten" is beyond all consciousness, self or *Skandhas*, and thus nothing can be said of it—its dimension is mute.

So the no-ego experience is the disclosure that at bottom the Five *Skandhas* are empty of self, and that this emptiness IS the unconditioned and unbegotten. The much later no-self experience, however, is the falling away (or permanent cessation) of the Five *Skandhas*, along with their empty center. Now there is no dough-nut—no bread and no empty center. At this point man must span the Great Void between the human and the divine, a void that is totally different from the *Skandhas'* empty center; without the *Skandhas* there can be no empty center. Self or the Skandhas may be likened to a container or a circumference that can be either empty or full, but take away the container or circumference and there is nothing left to be empty or full. Now there is only a Great Void. When all form is absolute void (and not merely empty) then Form IS the Absolute. In experience there is a great difference between "emptiness" and absolute void.

As I see it, Buddha was a Hindu who had realized Atman: the true self and its oneness with Brahman. But he realized this state was not perfect, for suffering was still possible—albeit not egoic suffering. From this position Buddha glimpsed or experienced a further perfect state and determined to attain it. The ultimate falling away of Atman (or Atman-Brahman) is the true no-self event, an event that could not have taken place if there had been no Atman in the first place. When Buddha affirmed no eternal self he was speaking AFTER the event (his enlightenment) or AFTER Atman (self) had fallen away. Obviously then it is a mistake to believe there is no self to begin with; no-Atman or no-self makes no sense unless it negates an experience that actually exists. So although Buddha went a step further than the Hindu realization of

Atman, no one can take this step or be in line for this event who has not first realized Atman. For there to be no-self or no-Atman, first there must be self or Atman. This is the way the path goes. Because Atman ultimately falls away it is obviously not the Absolute or Brahman. That we think it is, however, is the deception we spoke of earlier, a deception that IS self. The term "deception," however, does not mean that self is a lie; it means that it is only a relative truth and not Absolute Truth,

In conclusion, that Buddha (or whoever) accounted for the entire self-experience in the short formula of the Five *Skandhas* (put it in a nut-shell so to speak) is actually an amazing feat. Whole libraries are filled with discussions of self and the self-experience, but without ever nailing it down or making it clear. As the concise, exact formula of self the Five *Skandhas* is a true revelation, virtually the revelation of the essence of man. This, I think, is Buddhism's great contribution to man's knowledge and understanding of himself, his present condition, and the goal that lies before him— the destiny he is to attain. In all our religions we are presented with a great Truth or Truths that we eventually take for granted as a kind of foregone conclusion. Thus we hear and read about Truth and go on our way, without, however, actually realizing the enormity of its revelation. Perhaps the ultimate paradox is that our great religious Truths can only be revealed when everything we know and experience as these Truths has fallen away. Truth, after all, is "that" which can never fall away.

BIBLIOGRAPHY: PART II

These are the books on Hinduism I found most pertinent to the subject of this chapter. I have said nothing regarding Hinduism that cannot be found in these works.

Beidler, William, *The Vision of Self in Early Vedanta*.   Delhi: Motilal Banarsidass, 1975.

Seksena, S. K., *Nature of Consciousness in Hindu Philosophy*. Delhi: Motilal Banarsidass, second edition, 1971.

Sinha, Jadunath, *Indian Psychology* (two volumes). Calcutta: Sinha Publishing House, second edition, 1958. (According to the author in the 1933 first edition, his is the first attempt "to give a comprehensive account of the psychology of the Hindus." It includes views of all the renowned Hindu scholars and commentators through the ages.)

PART III
THE CHRISTIAN PASSAGE

CHAPTER ONE
AN OVERVIEW

INTRODUCTION

Consciousness or self underlies everyone's journey regardless of their religion or particular path. While an understanding of consciousness and its developmental milestones is the goal of psychology, religion carries this study further because it recognizes that consciousness is also the medium of the divine's revelation to man. Unlike psychology the goal or end of religion is not limited to self-knowledge, but goes beyond to divine-knowledge or knowledge of the divine. Thus religion includes self-knowledge or psychology, while psychology does not of necessity include religion or knowledge of the divine. Without religion, then, the study of psychology or consciousness can never be complete, and any psychological paradigm that fails to take religious revelation into account can never give us a complete picture of man. Religion not only adds dimension to consciousness or self, but reveals its path and ultimate destiny.

I define religion as the divine's revelation to man, the revelation of ultimate Truth. The major religions of the world are each known by their particular revelation, particular because each religion has its own revelation regarding the nature of Truth. What is not called into question by these different religions is that ultimate Truth or the divine exists; what differs among them is their revelation regarding the nature of this Truth or the nature of its existence. Thus the diversity in our religions is due to their different revelations regarding the nature of final Truth, while they are one in affirming its existence.

Also unique to each religion is that along with its revelation a particular path is unveiled, one uniquely conducive to the realization of its own revelation. It seems that the overwhelming appearance or revelation of the Absolute instantly sets up a contrast between Its existence and ourselves and our ordinary mundane existence; thus we begin looking around for a path or some means by which to bridge this gap. The path we find will depend on the gap to be bridged, the gap being the difference or contrast between ourselves and the Absolute—God or Truth. Thus, for example, if the revelation were the disclosure of the divine in nature or as nature, the path would be mapped accordingly, with the goal of becoming one with nature. If, on the other hand, the revelation were the disclosure of the divine within ourselves, this would have a different path with the goal being the discovery of the divine as one with our deepest self. Again, if it were the revelation of the utter transcendence of the divine beyond both man and nature along with the laws for "right living," the path and goal would be living according to laws revealed by the divine. Once again, if the revelation were that Christ incarnated the ultimate nature of the divine and ourselves, this too would have its own unique path with the goal of realizing Christ's Truth or the Truth he is. The whole point is that these paths are not alike because their revelation and ultimate goals are not alike. In each case the Truth to be realized is not merely the existence of Truth or the divine, or merely an "experience" of it; rather, the goal unique to each revelation is the final or fullest possible realization of its own revealed Truth. Thus even if every human being in the world experienced the divine and believed in some form of ultimate Truth, this would not make all religions the same; what makes the difference is the particular revelation that defines the goal or end to be realized.

While we can take for granted that beyond the grave final Truth is the same for all, yet as this Truth pertains to human existence, to our path and our present lives, religion is diverse. Beyond the grave, of course, there is no religion or revelation, no path and no goal; in the end (or heaven) all will be known. In the meantime, the fact that each religious path points to a specific revelation of the divine or Truth—its ultimate nature and not merely its existence—means that even if we realized the divine according to one religion's revelation, this need not include another's revelation, much less all possible revelations. Thus, for example, to realize the true self as divine is not a Buddhist's goal; to realize there is no eternal self is not a Hindu goal; to realize that the divine transcends man and nature is not the Christian goal; and to realize that the Trinity or Trinitarian Christ is the ultimate Truth of the divine is not the Judaic goal. So it goes with our different religious revelations. It seems that the challenge a specific revelation presents is the very means by which we keep going—that is, each revelation tells us we must not settle for anything other or less than the fullness of our particular, unique, religious revelation.[1]

For the Christian the ultimate revelation of Truth is Christ; thus Christ is the goal to be fully realized. While this revelation does not exclude the divine in nature, it also does not end here. Also, while Christ's revelation includes realizing oneness with the divine, it does not end here either. Nor does it end with the realization of the divine as transcendent to man and nature, or the divine as One Absolute, or the enlightening revelation that form is absolute void, and Absolute Void IS Form. While the ultimate revelation of Christ includes these revelations, in themselves these revelations do not include Christ. They do not do so because these revelations were around before Christ; thus Christ is not necessary to their revelation or their realization. We do not need Christ, for example, in order to realize oneness with nature and the divine, or to realize the divine within or transcendent to ourselves; all this can be realized without Christ. However, Christ adds something more to these revelations. To find out what this "more" is, or how Christ is a further revelation of the true nature of the divine, is the ultimate Christian goal. While a further revelation can include all that went before, what went before cannot include a further revelation or what came after. This means, for the Christian at least, that until the revelation and mystery of Christ has been exploded to reveal and include all Truth, the Christian cannot rest in any lesser Truth

---

[1]Someone asked, "Does this mean there is no realization outside a religious tradition? Do the traditions cover all potential revelations?" My answer to the first question is that I am not aware of a single realization of ultimate Truth (God or Absolute) that falls outside the revelation of our major religious traditions. People like to think they are outside a tradition when, in fact, they have been influenced and surrounded by it all their lives. Failure to acknowledge their indebtedness may be due to sheer ignorance or an un-divine pride and prejudice. In answer to the second question, we will never know if there is anything left to be revealed until it has been revealed; since we cannot miss what we do not know, we cannot even ponder a potential—something more to be revealed. One rule of thumb might be to ask if our revelations leave any questions unanswered. The problem with this, however, is that the relative, rational mind cannot deal with absolute Truth because this Truth belongs to a different dimension than the questioning mind. Thus even in the face of final Truth the rational mind will go on questioning forever. Beyond the rational mind, however, there are no questions because no questions can possibly arise.

no matter how wonderful this lesser (or less than complete) Truth may be.

Of all religions Christianity is the most difficult and challenging; it stretches the human limit beyond itself because the nature of its Truth neither stops with ourselves, nor can it be attained by ourselves. In the truest sense Christianity is not a do-it-yourself religion: whatever we can do ourselves goes no further than ourselves. This is why the Christian path and goal cannot be realized without the divine's special help, a help we call "grace"— grace being defined as the divine's special life in man over and beyond his purely natural life. Though grace is not developmental in itself, in man it is more developmental and transforming than the process of ordinary physiological and psychological development. It is difficult enough to grow up physically and psychologically, but far more difficult to grow up spiritually or in accordance with the path of grace or divine life.

A modern error is to mistake psychological maturity for spiritual maturity, whereas the two can never be synonymous. The requirement of grace is beyond anything ordinarily required of the psyche; it is almost as if grace were a separate faculty in itself. This path of grace, however, is very difficult. More often than not it does not go along with our notions of how things are supposed to go; in fact, it usually goes contrary to our paradigms and expectations. Sometimes it feels as if we are going against the tide, against the grain of ourselves, so much so that I would even define grace as the divine going against our self, never with or for our self. (From a divine perspective, of course, it is all in our favor.) The divine does not follow our development; rather, we follow the divine's development in us. But this is why the Christian path of grace is so exceedingly difficult: in truth, God's ways are not man's ways. Although not everyone perseveres on this path, it is nevertheless open to every human being. There is no such thing as the divine favoring one human being over another or giving more grace to one and less to another. The divine chooses everyone, but not everyone chooses the divine: thus the choice is on man's side, not on the divine's side. If there is any difference between the haves and have-nots it is not due to any divine favoritism, but to those who seek with their whole being and those who do not. Those in desperate situations know well what grace is; those in comfortable situations may never know what it is.

The path to the final Truth of Christ is an ongoing challenge from beginning to end. The way is transforming and never static; as we go further and deeper Christ is increasingly revealed, never the same, and in the end, not what we thought at the beginning. The journey is all a preparation for bearing the fullness of Truth; if we were to see this Truth at the beginning, we would die before we got started.

Since the Christian path is the only one I know experientially, the pages that follow represent what I learned on this path, especially as it pertains to the ultimate revelation of Christ. The latter half of this account gives the sequence of the path's major milestones as I experienced them. While my account and what I have to say may not be typical of someone else's Christian journey, it nevertheless testifies to the variety of experiences within a single path, a variety due to different psyches, mentalities, and, above all, the divine's unique design for each of us. No single account or its findings can speak for everyone in a tradition; all it can do is speak for the possibilities within a tradition. It seems that even within a single tradition, variety is the spice of divine life. Though I would like these pages to be a source of encouragement for others, it is important that we do not settle for anyone else's journey or account; we have to have our own. The great Revealer will take care of this; It alone knows us and maps our way, a way that will be unique and like no other.

CHRIST'S REVELATION

Since God had already revealed himself to the Jews, we cannot say that Christ was first of all a revelation of God to man. What Christ added to the Judaic revelation was the ultimate nature of God, that is, the Trinitarian nature of the one God. Perhaps nothing so testifies to the profound mystery of this Trinitarian nature than that many non-Christians have been convinced over the centuries that Christians believe in three Gods. Obviously this revelation is not available to the intellect, and neither is it ordinarily available to the contemplative or mystical psyche. Mystics and seers in various religious traditions have come and gone without any account of the Trinitarian nature of the one Absolute. This further affirms that the Trinity is a unique one-of-a-kind revelation, a great Truth that cannot be known apart from God's specific intervention. It also means that the Trinity is not discovered in the ordinary course of our spiritual journey, not even for the Christian; rather, the Trinitarian nature of God is the final ultimate revelation that may or may not be known by a Christian this side of the grave. However this may be, the central aspect of this revelation is that it comes through Christ, which means that only Christ can give way to this revelation, not Yahweh, Allah, Brahman, the Tao—or even the

Father or Holy Spirit. The Trinity is virtually tied to Christ; it is Christ's ultimate revelation, the revelation of Christ's divine nature or mystical body. Without Christ this revelation could not be forthcoming or known at all—for which reason it is unknown in other religious traditions.

Yet for most Christians the full and open disclosure of the Trinitarian nature of God is the culmination of their journey. From the outset, however, it is basically a matter of faith, and as a matter of faith, the mystery of God's Trinitarian nature is responsible for Christianity's mystical flavor. Neither the existence of God nor the life of the historical Jesus is a mystery, but what can never be taken for granted is the enormous mystery of God's true nature, a nature that can never be revealed without Christ since it is equally Christ's true nature. But if this is the ultimate Christian revelation, there is another side to Christ's revelation that is of immediate concern to man. This revelation is not the true nature of God, but the true nature of man—that is, the true nature of self or consciousness. Thus Christ not only reveals God to man, but man to man—reveals our self to us, that is. In doing so Christ revealed humanity's oneness with God as well as its ultimate destiny in the Godhead or Trinity. We begin, however, with our individual self, and to understand our individual journey we look to Christ's human journey.

It is a hard saying, but if we are truly to follow Christ, the first thing we must realize is our oneness with God. At this unitive point we begin to understand Christ, to understand in what way we are other Christs and, therefore, what it really means to be fully human. The realization of oneness with God does not mean that we are the historical Jesus or the incarnate Christ—of whom there is only one—rather, it means that at this point we see Christ as "that" mystery of our being which is truly one with God, one with the Father. Though we may equate this mystery with the unknown "true self," it basically goes beyond this. This specific revelation of Christ is not the revelation of God within (God as immanent), nor the realization of our oneness with God; rather, this revelation is over and beyond the unitive realization of oneness with God.

Although it is one thing to draw the intellectual conclusion that because we are one with God we are, therefore, "other Christs," it is quite another to see how this mystery works. This specific revelation of Christ is not an intellectual conclusion or a leap of faith. While those in other traditions tend to think that Christ is any human being who has realized oneness with the divine, this is not Christ's specific revelation. Christ is the middle term that bridges the gap between man and the divine and brings them together—is responsible for our oneness with the divine in the first place. This is quite different from any notion that man is God (or can become God), different even from the belief or experience that God is immanent or within all that exists. The mystery of man's oneness with God is neither the mystery of man nor God; rather, the true mystery of this oneness is the middle term or bridge between the two, which mystery IS Christ. The revelation of this mystery is not part of the unitive revelation but is over and beyond it. Though we tend to equate Christ with the unknown "true self," Christ is actually the link between our true self and the Father. To see how this works is the gradual unfolding of Christ's divine nature.

In my childhood and youth I often thought that the historical Christ, because of his physical form and personality, was more an obstacle to understanding the formless mystery of God than he was a help. Eventually, however, I came to see that without the historical Christ we would have missed the furthest reaches of both God and man, which is the oneness of Form and Formless—Christ and the Father in the absolute sense. Because of this purely Trinitarian oneness (Form and Formless) Christ's revelation neither begins nor ends with our realization of a formless divine. There are a number of levels of understanding the oneness of form and formless, and we begin with the human form of the historical Christ by understanding his divinity as his formless divine nature. In this way the historical Christ immediately clues us in to the oneness of Form and Formless.

As a youngster, however, I was put off by God with form or the belief that God could assume a particular form; what kept me from total rejection of Christ was the Eucharist—the incarnate Christ without form (as I then saw it). The point is that the divine Christ taking on human form is the beginning level of a great Truth or revelation—namely, the oneness of Form and Formless. Since, like Christ, we too have form, the historical Christ illuminates or verifies our own human experiences of oneness with a formless divine. Our identification with Christ in this matter, however, is but the first step of his revelation. Beyond realizing we (and Christ) are one with God, there is much further to go. What we must come to first of all, however, is Jesus' own human experience of oneness with God; only after this can we begin to penetrate the true mystery of Christ's Trinitarian nature—and consequently our own ultimate destiny.

TWO DIFFERENT TYPES OF ONENESS

There are two ways in which Christ is "one" with God. In his eternal divinity this oneness IS the Trinitarian nature of the Absolute, and in this respect we cannot say Christ is merely one with God; rather, in the Trinity Christ IS God—is the Trinitarian Absolute. In his humanity or incarnation, however, there is another type of oneness, a purely human oneness with God, and this type we ourselves can experience. This abiding certitude or seeing (not merely a passing experience) is what we call the unitive state. At this point in our journey or when fully established in the unitive state, we realize in what way we are "other Christs." We are not claiming Christ's Trinitarian oneness, but rather his human experience of oneness with God. And when we experience this oneness it is much the same oneness that the historical human Christ experienced. In this purely human experience it can be said we are equal with Christ.

This first type of oneness is of a particular nature, and its experience is difficult to adequately articulate. This oneness is a true union of two that could never be articulated as "I am God" or that God is my "other." True union is neither the experience of identity (I am God) nor merely an experience of relationship (I-Thou); rather, true union falls between these two. This experience is our deepest experience of "life" and "being." We cannot say we are "related" to our experience of life and being, nor can we claim that our experience IS God's experience of life and being; after all, life is more than our experience of it. But if we ourselves are not divine life or the Source and Ground of all life, we nevertheless know that our life and being is not separate from God's life and being. We are one with It, but not IT.[2]

This same unitive experience is also a profound mystery that ultimately gives way to a dimension beyond union, a oneness that is the ultimate revelation of Christ's Trinitarian nature. This second type of oneness is neither identity, union, nor relationship; it is beyond them all. It is not "we," however, who know or experience this Trinitarian oneness; only Christ IS this oneness. The fullness of Christ's divine condition (heaven or the divine state in which Christ dwells) is incompatible with continued earthly existence; it is

---

[2]A good image or analogy for understanding the unitive experience is to think of a single doughnut. Consciousness or self is the dough, and God is the empty center. If we take away either the dough or the empty center, there would be no doughnut—no experience of union or oneness.

beyond all our notions of "experience." While this glorious condition is man's ultimate destiny—and Christ's original state before his incarnation—the fullness of this eternal condition is not compatible with the human condition. If it were, there would be no need for death.

So it is important to understand and distinguish the difference between our human oneness with God (also the historical Christ's experience) and the much further and very different Trinitarian oneness of Christ's Godhead. One will lead to the other, but one is not the other. What we experience in the unitive state is not the Trinitarian oneness; rather, it is consciousness' or self's experience of oneness with the divine—a purely human experience. The Trinity or Godhead, however, lies beyond self or consciousness and all its experiences of the divine. The divine nature neither is, nor has, consciousness; thus our human experience of oneness with the divine (consciousness' experience, that is) is not the Godhead's experience or condition of existence.

Sometimes we overlook this fact and base our whole understanding of God or the Trinity on our unitive experience and its knowledge of God. We forget that Christ's divine nature, his Godhead or Trinitarian Reality, lies beyond his human experiences of the divine, beyond his unitive experience of oneness with the Father. This means that the historical Christ's purely human experience of oneness or union was not eternal; it was not heaven or the ultimate divine condition of Trinitarian oneness. To return to this original condition (heaven) Christ had to die and, in dying, go beyond the human unitive experience of oneness with the Father. Surrendering this human oneness for the infinitely greater oneness of the Godhead is the true nature of Christ's death; we know it was not easy. Although the historical Jesus was as real as ourselves, his eternal divine reality is beyond his historical humanity, beyond even the incarnation and ascension. What remains beyond these events —which are not merely historical events but revelations of Truth— is not the historical Christ, but the Trinitarian Christ. The only way in which Christ's humanity or incarnation is still with us is the Eucharist; this is the mystical Christ and quite different from the historical Christ. The bodily form of the historical Christ that people saw in passing was non-eternal, but in the Eucharist we have Christ's true eternal body—Eternal Form or mystical body.

LIMITATIONS OF THE HISTORICAL CHRIST

When we focus our attention solely on the historical Christ we cannot help but miss his ultimate truth. That Christianity tends to do so is a great flaw: it stresses only his humanity without giving equal stress to Christ prior to his incarnation or after his ascension. Although the Trinitarian Christ existed before the incarnation, our usual view or understanding of the Trinity envisions only the historical Christ instead of his eternal Godhead. My impression is that Christianity too often takes for granted or only gives lip service to Christ's absolute eternal Godhead. As a result of the inability to deal with this, Christ's ultimate truth and mystical dimensions have been thrust into the background, or have gone underground to receive little articulation on the surface of the Church. In this age especially, Christ is envisioned as little more than a glorified social worker, and love of God has been replaced by love of neighbor. Little wonder that the Eastern religions, which have infiltrated the Western mentality or perspective more than we realize, have a powerful attraction for Christians looking for the mystical dimensions so lacking in the Church.

The problem with this exodus to the Eastern religions, however, is that these religions, by the nature of their revelations, are inherently incapable of coming upon the ultimate truth of Christ. Those who go East will not find there his Trinitarian Truth; what they will find is only his human truth, and sometimes not even this. Furthermore, Hinduism, for example, stops at an experience of God that is not even that of the historical Christ. According to the Hindu belief system Christ is someone who realized he was God— the goal of the Hindu realization. But this was not Christ's experience, not as a human being and certainly not as the Absolute —we cannot imagine any Absolute that has to "realize" itself as the Absolute. Even if we come to Christ's human experience of oneness with God, this still falls short of Christ's Trinitarian oneness and the true nature of the Godhead. Thus we have to push on beyond this purely human union in order to come upon the divine or Trinitarian nature of Christ—which we are called to do.

So there is a further step in Christianity that is unknown in the East. Christ is more than an historical human figure who realized his oneness with God; Christ IS God apart from any human realization or experience of oneness. Also, unless the historical Christ had an ego (a non-divine self-center capable of sin) to transcend or to be transformed, we cannot even say he "realized" oneness with the Father. Born without sin means born without an ego; thus Christ never had to realize oneness with the Father because he was born to this union—in it or with it. This means that once we have realized our own oneness with the divine we have only caught up with the human (egoless) state in which Christ was born. After this we go forward with Christ to death and resurrection in order to go beyond the purely human limits of union or oneness.

Another limitation with regard to the historical Christ is the tendency to equate the incarnation solely with the appearance of the historical man Jesus. The incarnate historical Christ appeared 2,000 years ago, yet the incarnate Eucharistic Christ is with us today—still in the here and now. The historical Christ is different from the Eucharistic Christ. In the former we have the human body that appears; in the latter we have Christ's mystical body that does not appear. Yet both are equally the incarnate Christ. This tells us that there is more to the incarnation than the historical Christ and that as long as we tie the incarnation solely to the historical Christ we miss the furthest reaches of his revelation. The Eucharistic Christ reveals a dimension of Christ and the Trinity that the historical figure could never do; it is to reveal this further dimension that Christ remained with us. The Eucharist is all part of Christ's revelation of ultimate Truth; where the historical Jesus is the Christ that WAS, the Eucharist is the Christ that IS. Thus the Eucharistic Christ goes beyond the historical Jesus—it is a further revelation of Christ's incarnation and Trinitarian nature. By itself and with nothing further, the historical Jesus reduces the Christian belief to an unbelievable myth.

We can see that there are many levels of understanding Christ and how our journey moves to ever deeper levels of his mystery and revelation. It is a tragedy to settle for a one or two dimensional view of Christ; this not only limits Christ and our understanding of him, but it limits our own self-understanding. Christ enlightens the true nature of our self, and thus wherever we stop in our understanding of Christ, we stop in an understanding of our self. The historical or biblical Christ is only our beginning level of understanding. How or in what way his life, death, resurrection and ascension revealed the ultimate truth of God and ourselves is the further dimension to be revealed. The one dimensional answers we find at the historical or purely biblical level cannot be final or definitive; they may even be naive.

We go deeper when we strive to follow Christ by living his first commandment—love God above all things, above all people, above nature and, above all, love God above ourselves. Unfortunately many people settle for the second commandment—love your neighbor as yourself—which in and of itself goes round in circles and has no need of God at all. Self-love is incapable of true love of neighbor; it may even be bad for him. Furthermore, self-love can never reach Christ's ultimate challenge of loving our enemies or those who do bad things to us. We cannot begin to understand the second commandment until we have come to the unitive state and thereby mastered the first commandment. The unitive state gives us the ability to see God in others with the same eye by which we see God in ourselves; thus what we love in others is the same God we love in ourselves. This love bypasses the whole phenomenal self or the person that appears, be he good, bad or indifferent. So before we can truly follow the second commandment, we must first have mastered the first commandment which means that true love of neighbor is impossible until we first love God above our neighbor and our self.

If we could really do this—love God above all things, people and self—we would come rather quickly to a deeper dimension of Christ, which is our identification with him in the unitive state of oneness with God. In this state we identify with Christ on a profound subjective level wherein Christ is no longer confined to an objective historical personality or human form, but is now realized as equally the manifestation of our own life and historical reality. This does not mean Christ's historical humanity is left behind, but it does mean that having seen the limitations and impermanence of our own historical personality and social circumstances, we now see these same limitations in Christ's historical manifestation. It goes without saying, of course, that we can no more leave Christ's humanity behind than we can leave our own behind. But at the level of union with God, the emphasis is not on the past historical or biblical Christ but on the living manifestation of Christ in the here and now.

What is revealed in the unitive state is that we are one with God only because we are one with Christ, and "that" in us which is one with God, "that" is Christ. Now this is a profound mystery and one we are called to penetrate. At this point we are asked to see that our love of God is actually Christ's love of God, that our virtue is his virtue, that our reality is his reality. But if this is true, what need is there for "me" anymore? Up to this point we had thought it was our self (me, myself or I) that was one with God, but here we learn we are not one with God; rather, Christ and Christ alone is truly one with God. So where does this leave us—"self," that is? Some people seem to think that the answer to this question is the realization that "Christ IS me" or "I AM Christ." But this answer is not satisfying because it still leaves "me." So long as there is a "me" to BE Christ, then "I" obviously remain. If I were really Christ, however, there would be no "me" to BE Christ.

St. Paul's articulation of the unitive state was very accurate. He said, "For me to live is Christ," and "Now, no longer I, but Christ lives in me." Not only does the "me" remain, but without it there would be no Christ to be me or be in me. In the unitive state, then, self obviously remains. When we have come a long way into this state, however, or lived it for many years, we eventually realize that the imperfection of this state or the fact it is less than heaven is BECAUSE self remains. Now the question arises, "Is it possible to go beyond the unitive self that is one with God?" Of ourselves, of course, there is no way of going beyond because self is incapable of its own extinction; the falling away of self is a divine doing and not a self-doing. But the first step for eventually going beyond all self is to see or realize that "that" in us which is one with God is NOT me (I or any aspect of self); rather, "that" is Christ. Christ, then, is THAT unknown mystery in or about us (all human beings) which is one with God. When we truly see this we press on to find out what that mystery is—what Christ in us really is. Before we can come upon this query, however, we must first have come upon the "true self" and its oneness with God. In and of itself the unitive state need not be a revelation of Christ's true nature or a revelation of Christ at all. Many people outside the Christian tradition have come to the unitive state of oneness with the divine without any revelation of Christ. Thus to conclude that the divine we realize IS Christ, would simply be a blind leap of faith like putting two and two together. This is why I say that Christ is a specific revelation over and above (or beyond) the unitive state. Strictly speaking, for the Christian, Christ is not the realization of the true self; rather, Christ is beyond even this—beyond even our oneness with the divine. To understand this better we might focus for a minute on the Christian experience of oneness with the divine.

EXPERIENCE OF ONENESS AND BEYOND

Once we come to an abiding consciousness that the deepest center of our existence runs into the divine (like an umbilical cord, so to speak), we realize that this awareness is much like the historical Christ's abiding consciousness of oneness with the Father, and for this reason we call this state "Christ-consciousness." This does not mean we are aware of Christ. Rather, like Christ, we are aware of our oneness with the divine—the Ground of our being and all being—the Father, in other words. This is not the experience "I am Christ," but only the recognition of an identity with Christ through oneness with the Father. Because of this similarity we can see in what way we are "other Christs," see that because we are one with

God we are also one with Christ. At this point we see God in everyone and everything, and thus we see that because they too are one with God, they too are Christ. But this ability to see God in all things and to understand how all things are one in God still falls short of the specific mystery of Christ. Though we see God as the center, creator and unifying force of all that exists, this in no way answers the question of "what," within all that exists, the divine is one with; nor does it tell us the true nature of this union or oneness. Though we may know this missing link to be Christ, how this could possibly work is such an enormous mystery we usually go no further with it. The sole purpose of the unitive state, however, is eventually to penetrate the furthest mystery of Christ and the moment we have done so will be the same moment the unitive state comes to an end—falls away.

As we can see, then, it is a great mistake to regard the contemplative unitive state as the end or goal of our journey or as the final understanding of Christ and the Trinity. The ultimate mystery of Christ cannot be grasped at this unitive level of insight, revelation or experience. As said before, the revelation of Christ is not a necessity for coming to the unitive state. To go beyond this unitive state, however, Christ is not only a necessity, but without Christ, there is no going beyond. It is from the unitive position, however, that we begin to tap into a more profound dimension of Christ's divine or Trinitarian nature. If we ask the way ahead or what goal lies beyond this state, the answer is difficult because until we have gone beyond or seen what lies ahead, we have no way of understanding in advance. When first emerging from the transforming cocoon, the completeness of the unitive experience is such that nothing seems wanting to us; having God, we have all. Nothing can add to this completeness, and nothing can take it away. So what further goal could possibly lie ahead unless it be heaven itself? Looking ahead we see no path; there is no goal but that of immediate service to God whatever the circumstances. From here on we seem to be on our own, yet we know that whatever we do, we do with God, and wherever we go, we go with God. The only thing I know that moves us ahead and leads to a further revelation of Christ and the Trinity (true nature of the Godhead) is the Eucharist.

THE EUCHARISTIC CHRIST

As already noted, the incarnation has a dimension beyond that of the historical Christ who appeared in human form and consciousness. In the Eucharist we have a more perfect coming together of the divine and human; Christ's historical presence could touch very few people, while in the Eucharist Christ can touch us all. Here we are confronted with Christ's physical body in a way not seen by the senses or known by the intellect, and this fact alone should clue us into the mystery and true nature of his human body. Although we call the Eucharist Christ's "mystical body," we should not forget that Christ's body is also physical. There is no great mystery in a non-material spirit that does not appear to the senses, but there is enormous mystery in a material, physical body that does NOT appear to the senses. The fact that the Eucharist is Christ's physical incarnate body or form is the clue to his ultimate divine nature. To see how this works explodes the whole revelation of God and man, reveals their true nature and the true nature of all that exists.

People have various notions about the Eucharist and Christ's mystical body, notions that are really too erroneous to repeat here. It is important to emphasize that the Eucharist does not stop with Christ's humanity; it is equally his divinity inseparable from the Trinity or true nature of the Godhead. Thus the Eucharist is not only the body of the incarnate human Christ but equally Christ's mystical body or divine nature prior to his incarnation and humanity. To go one further, the Eucharist is not only the mystery and reality of Christ's eternal body but the ultimate mystery of our body as well. This means that our body is more than its present historical physical experience—what we see, know and experience of it. Just as Christ's physical body in the Eucharist cannot be physically seen, known or experienced, so, too, the true nature of our own eternal physical body cannot be seen, known or experienced. So the Eucharist is telling us that the body is of a different nature than what we ordinarily see and know; it tells us our true body is what we do NOT see and know. But whatever this body is, or whatever its eternal form, we know it is not separate from the physical body we see and know—anymore than Christ's incarnate body is separate from his eternal mystical body. Ultimately then, the physical body we know is not separate from the physical body we do NOT know. This is a tremendous truth to ponder; it means that there is no separation between our eternal body (that we do not know) and our physical body (that we know) and that in death there is no non-physical spirit leaving the physical body. In a word, there is no such thing as the separation of body and spirit, or separation of a physical and non-physical body. To think otherwise is not what the Eucharist reveals to us. Christ's physical body is not separate from his eternal divine or mystical body, and anything Christ reveals to us is our Truth, not merely his Truth.

The Eucharist, then, goes beyond the visible form of Christ's physical body as it walked this earth, and beyond our own body as it, too, makes this same passage. Neither at his death nor his ascension did Christ "leave" his body, and so, too, neither at our death or dissolution into God do we "leave" the body. Nothing so reveals this truth as the ascension experience when Christ's body seemingly evaporated into a cloud—disappeared from sight. Yet his body remains ("I go in order to come."); it has gone nowhere, and being nowhere in particular it is everywhere. Since we cannot point to everywhere, the Eucharistic Christ is the microcosm of everywhere and no different from "everywhere." We do not know where Christ is NOT, but we do know where Christ IS—the Eucharist.

We might compare this mystery to the fact that the Eucharist as One and indivisible is nevertheless multiplied the world over. It belongs to no one, is never exhausted, and is always with us leading us from the One (microcosm) to everyone, to everywhere. In truth the body of Christ is the true body of all that exists, all that is manifest of the Father. This does not mean Christ is "matter" as it is defined scientifically, but "matter" as it cannot be defined or seen with the senses and known with the mind or intellect. It means Christ is the Eternal Form of the Formless Father and the backbone of all we know to exist. So the further revelation of the Eucharist is that it is not only the physical incarnate Christ, not only the mystical Christ, not only the cosmic Christ, but Christ of the Trinity AS the Eternal Form of the Godhead. Christ is not multiple forms but, like the Eucharist, is One Absolute Form.

THE UNITIVE MYSTERY OF CHRIST

With the help and revelation of the Eucharist we come closer to answering our previous question—"What is 'that' in us that is one with God?" This inquiry, remember, stems from a particular experience or realization that Christ is "that" in us which is one with God. It is not ourselves or any aspect of our known self that is one with God; rather, it is truly Christ alone that is one with God. This fact explains the burning love we experience, a love we know is beyond us completely, a flame that seems to have a life of its own quite apart from ourselves. Realizing that this love and oneness is beyond self's capacity and that this flame is Christ's love for God (the Father), the question arises as to the true nature of Christ in ourselves that is responsible for this phenomenon.

To understand this particular situation and why the question arises, we have to remember that Christ was never identified as our divine Center or Ground of Being: this was never the revelation.

Instead, Christ was initially revealed as the "unknown" about ourselves that was one with the divine Center, an unknown that we may have taken for our unknown true self. But now we have come a long way; we see that Christ is the connecting link between God on the far side of the Center and ourselves on the near side. We see that Christ is the connecting link between the human and the divine, and this link is the true mystery of the whole unitive state of affairs. We did not see this earlier, and some people may never see it. Inquiring into the true nature of Christ, the unknown link or middle term between self and the divine, is a major turning point of the journey, one that occurs toward its ending—unbeknown to us, however, except in retrospect. This is when we realize that we ourselves never were one with God, that the love we experience is not now and never was our own, and that from beginning to end the whole unitive experience was beyond ourselves. At this point, the mystery of Christ emerges as never before, with the impending impression that the burning flame (love between Christ and the Father) is about to completely consume or burn up the remaining self-experience leaving no self at all. In the face of such a burning love this is not a frightening prospect. On the contrary, we would not wish matters to be otherwise. But then there is nothing we could do anyway since the flame is totally beyond us; it is not us. It is overwhelming love, then, that finally consumes all self. As long as any sense of self or any self-experience remains, God cannot be all.

We could not expect this particular situation to have arisen if we had ever identified the divine center as our self (true self) or even as Christ. As soon as we identify our self as the divine center or God, we ARE God; in this case there is no union but identity. "I am God," "I am Christ" or whatever the identity, obviously retains the "I" or self. Also, if we identified the divine center as Christ, God is wholly "other," an I-Thou relationship that is not true union. In both cases we have closed the door upon any further possibility, event or revelation; at this point the journey would be over, finished. But neither identity nor relationship expresses the truth of the unitive experience, and so long as we do not make this mistake, the journey moves on to an entirely different ending—the ending of all self. So long as any self remains—identity or relationship—the journey is not complete, nor can our understanding of the divine be complete. Christ IS the mystery of the unitive state and experience. He is the unknown link or middle term, as it were, between ourselves and the divine, the "point" at which we leave off and the divine begins—this is Christ.

So the day we see that the union we experience is beyond ourselves is the day we realize that we (self) are not and never have been truly one with God—never. That we ever thought we were is now seen as a great mistake. We remember, too, that Christ said as much—that no one (no individual self) sees the Father or is one with the Father—only Christ sees the Father, only Christ is one with the Father. This means that the reality or truth of our experience of oneness is not what it seems and that the reality or truth of union or oneness lies beyond the experience itself. In other words, we think an experience indicates such and such, whereas its reality is altogether different from what we think the experience indicates. In this case, what we thought was our own self's oneness with God turns out to be a mistake. It takes a tremendous preparation, however, to see this mistake because the reality and truth beneath our experience leaves out any and all self.

For the Christian, neither the existence nor the experience of God is a mystery; rather, Christ is the ultimate mystery because Christ alone can reveal the Trinitarian nature of God, without which there could be no incarnation. Thus to crack the mystery of Christ is to crack the mystery of the Trinity, Christ's divine nature, his incarnate nature, on down to our own nature and the nature of all that exists. So the quest is to uncover the mystery of "that" in us which is one with God, "that," of course, being Christ. Although we may know and believe Christ is God, in experience a distinction remains between the utterly transcendent (Father) and the burning flame or love that IS the incarnate Christ's own love for God or the Father. Christ's love for the Father, of course, we think of as the Holy Spirit. While we might call the Holy Spirit the "link" between the Trinitarian Christ and the Father—the link between Form and Formless, Manifest and Unmanifest—yet the incarnate Christ stands on man's side of the Holy Spirit as the love that consumes all self. This is the way it worked in the incarnate Christ, and this is the way it works in us. The divine flame is not ourselves, but the incarnate Christ's consuming love for the transcendent Father, a fire in which self will be totally consumed. If we have never come upon this distinction (an incarnate and nonincarnate love), we may never be able to understand how or why the eventual no-self event comes about.

So what we know or experience in the unitive state is this: God is the center of our life and being, IS our deepest experience of life and being, and a burning love. This is no small center of self; the flame spreads outward to include all we are but our own awareness of it. Can this love ever reach a point where it could exceed all self-awareness, overrun and obliterate this awareness once and for all? But if we lost all self-awareness would we also lose awareness of the divine? The question cannot be answered ahead of time. What lies beyond all awareness no one knows—obviously there would be no one or no self to know. The day we approach such a possibility is the day we become aware of the fine line between this burning love and a permanent loss of self-awareness, permanent loss of all experience of self.

THE FINE LINE BETWEEN TWO DIMENSIONS

By "fine line" I mean the unexpected confrontation with the immediate experiential possibility of all awareness permanently falling away. It is the fine line between self and no-self. At this point we do not see how life could continue in such an event; after all, if "we" (self) are not aware of God and our surroundings, then what is? It is not a matter of personal self-awareness falling away, of which there is little left anyway, but of all awareness falling away. The impression is that this could only mean death. Self, which IS consciousness or awareness, is obviously incapable of imagining its non-existence or imagining how life would go on without itself. The overriding mystery, however, is how, without awareness, there could be any awareness of the divine—or heaven. In death we may not miss the world, but we do not want to miss the divine. The "fine line," then, is the awareness of an unusual kind of death, one that is not physical and not even spiritual. Instead, it is the death of awareness itself, awareness not merely of self but, equally, awareness of God.

The fine line between self and no-self is also the fine line between a purely human union or oneness with the divine (experienced by self or consciousness) and a Trinitarian Oneness, which is beyond the human experience or beyond any self or self-awareness, and thus beyond consciousness' experience of oneness with God. In terms of Christ's reality this is the fine line between his human experience of oneness with the Father (similar to our own) and his divine oneness with Father and Holy Spirit in the Godhead or Trinity. The difference here is not merely one of experience, but of two different dimensions of existence.

To pass over the line takes not only the falling away of all self-awareness, which is the first step, but the extinguishing of the unitive flame or center of being along with all to which it gave rise —it gave rise to our self or consciousness. This is like having the divine Ground pulled out from under the whole self experience and taking the self with it. Such an event could not have been anticipated in a million years; it is unthinkable and unimaginable. Self, of course, can never put an end to itself anymore than it created itself in the first place. Only the divine that brought self or consciousness into being can bring about its non-being or consummation. It should be remembered, however, that self or consciousness is not a being or an entity—as so many people mistakenly believe. In fact, one of the errors discovered beyond self is that self or consciousness was responsible for the whole experience of "being" or the feeling of being a discrete entity, individual, soul or immaterial spirit; consciousness or self was this experience. But the Reality or Truth beyond this experience is another matter entirely.

Obviously the falling away of the phenomenal or superficial self-experience is not the central issue of the no-self event. At this point of the journey (the "fine line") the self-experience has all but disappeared anyway. The central issue is the falling away of the divine center, the burning flame of love and oneness that had already been seen as beyond all self. This flame, as we said, was the love and oneness of Christ and the Father, but now this oneness has gone—gone and taken the whole self-experience with It. On the cross Christ affirmed that the Father had left him, after which he too died. The Father, of course, could not "leave" the divine Christ, so what really happened? Christ's purely human experience (self or consciousness) of God fell away, and with self or consciousness goes its entire experience of the divine. Christ's human experience of oneness with the Father dissolved because this was self's experience of God, and not God as He lies beyond all human experience. Though we say of this event that "God died," this refers only to the EXPERIENCE of God (which IS self), certainly not to God beyond all experience. The closest we can come to God dying is the incarnation event, which is a God-Awful event beyond the imagination, endurance or capability of any human being. I regard Christ's incarnation as the true saving act, not his death on the cross—which was a divine release from the human condition.

Without self, of course, there is no one—me, myself or I—to BE God. Thus even at the resurrection Christ made no claim to BE God. As we will be discussing later, all claims to BE someone or something have nothing to do with God; all such claims belong solely to self or consciousness. What is realized beyond self is the All and Everywhere of God, meaning that the divine is no-thing and no-one (discrete entity) and, therefore, cannot be pointed to or brought into focus. Consciousness provided a pinhole or center, like a microscope or telescope, through which it could glimpse the infinite and bring it into focus. Without this apparatus, however,

God as Everywhere cannot be focused upon, not even in experience. The human mind, of course, can never understand how this works. Due to their totally limited nature, neither the mind nor consciousness can apprehend the infinite or the All and Everywhere that IS God.

THE DIVINE BEYOND THE UNITIVE VIEW

It is important to point out the difference between God as All and Everywhere as this is seen and understood from the perspective of the unitive state, and as it is later seen and known beyond this state or beyond all self or consciousness. While the statement that God is "All" or "Everywhere" is a great Truth regardless of our perspective, how we see and understand it (the All and Everywhere of God) changes as our journey progresses. The basic unitive view sees God IN all things and all things IN God which is the realization that the divine as immanent (within us) is, at the same time, transcendent (without or beyond us). In other words, God is not only IN us, but we are also IN God. Because we see God as the Center of all that exists, we know that everything that exists is one and united by reason of this divine Center. Because all that is created or exists arises from this Center, we see how the many are one in the divine. Thus once we see the divine in all that exists it becomes impossible to look anywhere or to see anything wherein the divine is not present. For this reason we say the divine is All or Everywhere because It is IN all that exists. After all, we cannot look anyplace where nothing exists. From this unitive perspective we see everything in its pristine miracle as God's manifestation, virtually a revelation of itself. Thus everywhere we look we see the sacredness and oneness of the manifest, and we are uplifted to the divine in the marvel of its manifestation or creation. Beyond union, however, this whole perspective falls away. The All and Everywhere of the divine means something else entirely—although it is but a further extension of the unitive dimension of seeing and knowing.

First of all, beyond union there is no divine Center, no center anywhere. Few people realize that without the experience of a center there is also no experience of interiority or within-ness. Without a center nothing can arise within ourselves: no feelings, no energies, no divine presence—nothing. This means we can no longer experience or see the divine within ourselves and, consequently, within anything else that exists. And when there is no divine within (immanent), there is also no divine without (beyond or transcendent). Thus beyond union the divine is not the center of anything; it is not immanent or IN anything and also not

BEYOND or transcendent to anything. What was responsible for this way of seeing or knowing was self or consciousness. In fact, consciousness or self was not only responsible for this whole experience and way of knowing, but consciousness or self IS this particular experience and way of knowing. In other words, the deepest unknown mystery of consciousness IS its whole unitive knowledge or seeing of the divine. It falls away because its seeing and knowing is purely relative and thus incapable of coming upon the full Truth of the divine. Self or consciousness knows some Truth but is incapable of knowing all of it—final Truth, that is.

So beyond self or consciousness there is nothing for the divine to BE IN, and nothing for it to transcend. Self or consciousness had been the vessel experiencing the divine as without and/or within. Without a vessel or container, however, there is nothing the divine can pour itself into, nothing for it to be either within or without, and nothing to which it can reveal itself. Without a vessel there is no "one." And without a one there is no multiplicity of ones. Thus the "All" of the divine is not the sum of ones or the sum of any multiplicity—such as drops of water in the sea. It is a mistake to think that the All of God consists of many entities or beings. The divine is not an accumulation of all that exists. To say God is "All" means God is all that eternally exists or all that has permanent existence. The point is that as long as we know any multiplicity or oneness we are still seeing the divine from the perspective of the unitive dimension or vision. Beyond this, however, there is no one (entity or being) or many (entities and beings) to BE one and united. There is a subtle but important difference here between the divine as "Being" and the divine as "Existence."

So beyond self or consciousness the new dimension is seeing in what way the divine is all Existence; what is responsible for this particular seeing or knowing is the revelation that Christ's divine nature is the eternal Manifest of the Godhead. This means that there was no time when the divine was not Manifest, or that from all eternity the divine exits in some Eternal Form—or unknown substance. Usually we think of the manifest as something brought forth in time or as something created. But this is not what is meant by the Eternal Manifest or Christ. The Eternal Manifest means that Christ's eternal divine nature always was and always will be. It is from this Eternal Manifest that all is created, and because of this the created and Uncreated (Eternal Manifest) are one. In other words we were not created from nothing, but from the Eternal Manifest. What is eternal about the created, however, is not what we see with the senses or know with our minds (multiplicity, in other words), nor is it anything passing, impermanent or temporary. Rather, what is eternal about the created is "that" from which it was created—the Eternal Manifest Christ. As we know, the divine Christ existed from all eternity, before the incarnation and the historical Jesus. Prior to the incarnation, however, we did not know about the Trinitarian nature of the Godhead; thus we knew nothing of the Eternal Manifest. We did not know how or in what way the divine was connected with creation. Christ was to reveal all this, reveal not only his (and our own) human oneness with God but the divine Trinitarian oneness of Form and Formless, Manifest and Unmanifest. Thus the revelation of Christ's divine nature as the Eternal Manifest reveals the ultimate nature of the Godhead—Trinity or Absolute.

Solely from the perspective of consciousness this is like saying that Christ is matter or that matter is eternal. Although I would prefer this error to many other errors going around, we have to be very specific about what the Eternal Manifest is NOT. Science does not really know what matter is or know its true nature, and nothing the mind is capable of studying or defining is the Eternal Manifest. This is because the divine is a dimension of existence beyond the grasp of consciousness, self, the mind, intellect and senses— intuition and insight as well. Whatever these know of the divine is purely on their own terms or own ground so to speak. But the divine solely on Its own Ground is beyond all possible ways of knowing and experiencing. Sometimes we forget that the divine was around long before man appeared with his various faculties or ways of knowing—before anything appeared, for that matter. It is the divine PRIOR to all we know that exists, that is the Eternal Manifest. This is why, in order to come upon the Eternal Manifest, all we know to exist must first be removed, must cease to exist. It is only on the other side of this Great Void (beyond all we know that exists) that the Eternal Manifest can be revealed—revealed as all that remains when everything we know has ceased to exist. This Great Void is the journey from death to resurrection. When nothing exists but the void, THEN we see that the void of all form IS Eternal Form or the Eternal Manifest. From this position we say that God IS ALL that exists because here we realize God is not only Formless, but God is Form as well. Thus all that is created does not arise from nothingness or a sheer void but from the Eternal Manifest divine. This means that the forms we see are truly one with the Eternal Form we do not see.

We have to be careful, however, not to confuse the created with the Uncreated, the begotten with the Unbegotten, temporary forms with Eternal Form, or the Eternal Manifest with the manifest we see, know and experience. In terms of the Trinity this means the Father is the Formless or Unmanifest (the divine or heavenly state in which the Manifest dwells); Christ is Eternal Form or the Manifest divine; and the Holy Spirit is the Eternal Creative Movement of the two. Once we see this spectacular Truth we see how or in what way God is All and Everywhere.

Another difference between the unitive perspective of the divine and the perspective that lies beyond union relates to the experience of oneness. It may happen that in our whole lives we never felt separate from God; from the beginning we may have intuited this mystery or experienced the divine within ourselves. In this case we did not go in pursuit of the divine in order to become one with It but to know the divine more perfectly and, above all, to attach our will to Its will in order to lead a good and holy life. For this reason the bottoming out of the original self-center (the ego) and the ensuing process of acclimation (or transformation) may even have come as a surprise. After this, however, our knowledge and experience of oneness with the divine is very different. As said before, in the unitive state the divine is experienced as our deepest life source or the deepest experience of our own self existence. This experience of simple existence, being or life, is singular and one— we do not, for example, experience two existences. But at the same time we know that while we cannot exist without the divine, the divine, however, can exist without us. But what would the divine be like without us?

When this experience of oneness or union eventually falls away, there is no longer any experience of oneness or union. Beyond self or consciousness the terms "one," "oneness" and "union" no longer apply; they have no meaning anymore because there is no truth to back them up. Here we see that the divine is beyond the one and the many, and that God is not just non-multiple; God is also non-One. Though it is true to say there is only One God, to say "God is One" imposes a subtle limitation on the divine in that it implies the multiple—as does the notion of God as "non-dual." The mind has no other way of understanding "one" except as relative to many; a relative one, however, can never be divine. But this is why the divine beyond union or oneness cannot be articulated in any such terms. Here the divine is known as All with no reference to ONE and no apprehension or experience of ONE. The problem with the term "All," as mentioned before, is that it is often mistaken as the sum of ones, which is an error as it refers to the divine. To keep it straight we might remember that All is relative to None or Nothing, and that these relative terms (all or nothing) are so close to absolute Truth that we can let them stand without detriment to the divine.

One reason for pointing out different perspectives regarding ultimate Truth is that we cannot adopt easy cliches to articulate the divine. What do we mean when we say, "God is All and Everywhere," "God is One," "God is transcendent and/or immanent," and so on? Everything we say about the divine is from some particular perspective or level of our journey; thus everything we say about the divine is not so much a revelation of the divine as it is a revelation of where we are in our journey. In other words, what we give away with our descriptions of the divine is not the divine but ourselves, so to speak. When, however, we borrow handy phrases without verifying our particular perspective, specifically what we mean by them, our terms for the divine become misleading cliches. We have a tendency to throw out terms we have never defined or terms for which we give no experiential referent. Thus we constantly pass around terms such as ego, consciousness, love, light, oneness, Everywhere, All and a thousand others, without substantiating them by any experiential referent or perspective. Use of similar terms or phrases, however, is obviously no guarantee of similar or equivalent perspectives.

The nature of our journey is a continual change in perspective. Truth does not change; it is we who change. And nothing so reveals this personal change as our perspective on the divine. Because of this change we have different philosophies and theologies—different people seeing Truth from different perspectives. All disagreements, of course, arise from different perspectives. We have to be cautious, then, when encountering other people's perspectives and, above all, when stating our own. The criterion is to look for and apply experiential referents for all terms used. This would avoid a great deal of confusion and dispute, and it would verify the changes in perspective that take place as we go forward with the journey. If there were no change there would also be no journey.

We do well, then, to note the different perspectives from which the divine or final Truth is articulated. Use of such small terms as "within," "center," "union" "emptiness" and many others may tell us a great deal; in fact, it may tell us all we need to know. The above terms, for example, always indicate the divine known to consciousness or self, which means self still remains. So the fact we use similar terminology does not indicate similar perspectives, or even similar Truth.

EXPERIENCE VS REALITY

Beyond self or consciousness one of the most shocking truths is that, by its very nature, self or consciousness not only precludes the fullness of Truth, but even forbids it. To come upon the fullness of Truth is not within the human dimension; whatever we know, even by way of our most mystical experiences, is still through a glass darkly. Self or consciousness precludes or hides final Truth in order to make the human dimension possible, or for man to exist. As discussed elsewhere the fullness of Truth or the ultimate divine condition (heaven) is incompatible with human existence; if this were not so, there would be no need for death. An authentic unmediated glimpse of ultimate Truth and man would go out like a light. It is good then, that man does not see too much. The question for us, however, is how consciousness or self actually precludes ultimate Truth. What is there about consciousness that more or less keeps man in his place and does not allow him access to final Truth?

The answer is so simple that it may just appear meaningless. In simple terms, consciousness or self IS experience, and on this experience we base everything we know. Experience, however, is not the same as ultimate Reality; none of the experiences of which self or consciousness is capable is ultimate Reality. Thus while consciousness (which IS experience) is responsible for our human reality, this is not ultimate Reality. Let us give some examples.

Man has the experience (and knowledge) of "being," "life," "soul," "individuality" and a thousand other experiences. On these experiences he bases his life. But these experiences, while authentic in themselves, do not give us the ultimate Truth of things—the Truth beyond our experiences. When self or consciousness falls away, all these experiences fall away because they were not final Truth. As it turns out, the Truth of man—and everything that exists—is beyond all man's experiences and way of knowing. So the first notion to dispel is that the falling away of consciousness or self is the annihilation or extinction of some entity, being, soul, spirit. Rather, it is the falling away of the EXPERIENCE of being, soul, life, spirit. Consciousness or self, which IS experience, falls away because it is not ultimate Reality, not eternal, and not capable of coming upon final Truth. Consciousness, then, is not only responsible for our human experiences, but consciousness IS the human experience.

So the shocking truth of self or consciousness is its deception, but a deception unknown to us as long as it remains. Where we had believed ourselves and the divine to be a "being" or an immaterial spirit, we discover this was all based on experience which turns out NOT to be the ultimate Truth of things. So, too, experiences of the divine as love, power, life and much more, turn out to have been only our experiential selves, whereas the divine is beyond all such experiences. Not only is the divine beyond all our experiences of the divine, but our own ultimate nature is beyond any and all experiences of ourselves. It is important then not to mistake our experiences of Truth and Reality for Truth and Reality as they lie beyond all possible experiences. The difference between experience and Reality is so great that it cannot even be expressed.

Some people believe that the true nature of self or consciousness is beyond its own experience anyway, and thus even if the experience fell away, self or consciousness would remain. But by what criterion, knowledge or experience, could we make this claim? If there were no experience of self how could we know it still exists? Many people believe that once self falls away, either the divine appears in its place or some higher self or consciousness is revealed. While this might be true of the no-ego event—where the self-center gives way to a divine Center and the "true self" is discovered—this is not the case when the true self and divine Center later fall away. As long as any self appears, be it divine or otherwise, we have not yet gone beyond all self. Those who believe that beyond the unitive state a divine self is revealed can never have a true understanding of Christ's death, the death of a divine self—or as divine as any self can be. Beyond self, the body and senses must bear the burden of revelation and Truth. When acclimation to this new dimension has reached a certain point, the true nature of the body is revealed, and this revelation IS the resurrection.

Here it has been asked: If self is the experience of life, energy, being and so on, where does it go when it falls away? Strictly speaking, when an experience ceases it does not "go" anywhere—when we stop laughing or our heart stops beating, for example, where does it go? In this sense, the question makes no sense. But the question is valid because the falling away of self is not just the cessation of a passing experience (or many experiences); rather, it is the falling away of the whole energy or power responsible for experience. The power responsible for our experiencing the whole range of consciousness or self, however, is not so easily dismissed. After all, the falling away of this power leaves the body energyless or lifeless—though not in the way we usually think of this. Our usual notion of a body without energy or life is a dead body. While the falling away of self or consciousness is the only true death experience man will ever have, its falling away reveals a great truth: namely, that eternal life is beyond all our experiences of life. Thus no human "life" experience is eternal; purely by contrast, eternal life is the experience of no life.

This means that the divine is not any power, energy or life that we (self or consciousness) can experience; rather, God is the life and power we DO NOT experience. Though it is true to say that God is the power or life behind our experience of energy or life, yet God is not energy; in fact, we do not know "what" God is or its true essence. So the energy we experience is just ourselves; it IS self or consciousness, while God-beyond-experience is no energy. God, then, is the non-experiential Ground from which our experience takes its life, the same Ground that fashioned and continues to sustain our experience of life and being. If this experience should disappear into the non-experiential Ground, it would disappear, cease, become non-experiential. The answer, then, to what becomes of self or consciousness is that the whole experience disappears into the non-experiential divine. The experience that was, is no more.

From one perspective, the snuffing-out of the particular energy that IS self or consciousness may seem to be a divine un-doing, that is, an un-doing of its original doing or creation. But if we understood the true nature of the human passage we would see that this un-doing is actually a divine creative act. In other words, by a single non-perceptible act the divine brings us (self or consciousness) into being, and by another such act we move into eternal life or the divine. This is no backward movement; what we may think of as an un-doing, is actually a further doing. By one act we come from God; by another act we return to God. It is as simple as that. Between the coming and going, however, is our human passage, virtually the whole of human existence. The divine, of course, is unchanging while we are always in a process of change, and this movement is our homeward journey.

The true nature of death is, therefore, a positive forward movement into eternal life. Without it there is no resurrection or realization that the true nature of the body is Christ's eternal mystical body and his divine nature in the Godhead. In general, man is unwilling to face the side of creation that he deems negative: illness, suffering, old age, any form of dissolution or cessation, and ultimately death. He sees this as a backward movement instead of a continuation of one irreversible forward movement. Due to this ignorance, man idolizes and clings to youth and maturity and has an enormous fear of its decline or undoing. Even in our theories of psychological and spiritual development we go no further than the so-called "mature" years or stage of life. Once we get there we see nothing further to be achieved; we may even cling to this stage. One way or the other the second half of the human journey goes unnoticed, or if noticed, is judged to be regrettable. Beyond maturity, however, there begins the true homeward movement. If we think of the journey as a circle tour, we can see that at the point of greatest maturity man is the most distanced from the divine, but once beyond this midpoint the movement is toward the divine and no longer away from It. Thus our initial development and maturity is not nearly as positive or in touch with the divine as is our eventual undoing.

In the creation of man, an imperceptible divine act is required for the structure and function we know as consciousness. When the fullest potential of this function has been exhausted there begins its undoing—virtually the undoing of consciousness with all its experiences. And ultimately, not only the function and structure of consciousness will come to an end, but that of the senses and vegetative body as well. While we might say that these were temporary functions of One Eternal Form or Christ, we must remember that the divine is not a structure or function of anything. The divine clay from which we were made is not changed or affected by any temporary structure of function. By the time this function comes to an end, however, we have already seen beyond it, seen "that" in us which is truly one with the divine, which IS Christ. Beyond self we understand why Christ "gave up his self," understand this was necessary not only to reveal his divine nature, but for his return to the Father or the divine condition from which he came. Prior to this event, however, how can we possibly understand the death of Christ's self? Who can even believe it? Until we ourselves can face the death of our unitive experience of oneness with the divine, we can never understand the true nature of Christ's death or come upon the great Truth that lies beyond it.

We must not stop, then, with our experiences or ever allow them to become the gauge of ultimate Truth. In the long run, in order for us to come upon final Truth, every experience we know of or are capable of must eventually fall away. In the meantime, until this happens, we really have no choice but to go with our experiences; after all, we did not make or choose self or consciousness. We cannot turn our experiences off or on. Despite the disparity and the hidden deceptions that lie between our experiences and final Truth, the fact remains that self or consciousness is our human passage; about this there is no mistake. Without consciousness man would not exist because he *is* consciousness. Thus consciousness with all its experiences was fashioned to lead man to Truth; its passage moves in one sure direction to the divine, its true end. Though man, as we know him, is not eternal, man as we do not know him is indeed eternal. As I see it, man is eternal in the same way Christ's mystical or Eucharistic body is eternal. For those who truly know this great Reality, nothing more need be said. Man's ultimate destiny is magnificent indeed.

KNOWING WITHOUT A KNOWER

Once self or consciousness falls away, apart from pure sensory knowing, there is no way to account for the non-sensory knowing that is specific to the no-self condition. Where charity, unconditional love and compassion had characterized the egoless or unitive state, knowing is what characterizes the no-self condition. Apart from this particular knowing, nothing else really characterizes the no-self condition; all it is about is knowing. This particular knowing, however, is not omniscience, nor is it a scientific or rational knowing. It is also not "knowing by not-knowing"—which best characterized the unitive condition. The knowing characteristic of the no-self or resurrected condition is different yet. I call it the "cloud of knowing" in order to differentiate it from the "cloud of unknowing." Where the latter unknowing revealed a psychological dimension beyond the rational or intellectual mind (a kind of third-eye), the "cloud of knowing" has no connection with the mind or psyche, nor could it be called a "way of knowing." Here, what is known is not connected with the mind, the brain or any physical structure; it is totally non-experiential. Where "unknowing" had been first a negation and then a transcendence of intellectual knowing, the present "cloud of knowing" negates unknowing and is quite absolute without any unknowing about it. (Both unknowing and this new "knowing" may be called a "cloud," however, because both are beyond the usual rational, intellectual or scientific mind and its way of knowing.)

The knowing I am referring to has a very specific knowledge. Its sole domain is God's revelation to man and how man knows and experiences the divine; it is knowledge of the journey from one end to the other, a complete overview of it. This knowing is not, however, concerned with God prior to man's existence or as God exists beyond man; it does not define God's essence or "what" God is; it cannot utter a word of description regarding man's final or heavenly state; nor can it convey the particular dimension of existence (no-self or resurrected state) that lies beyond self or consciousness. Regarding all this, nothing can be said. This particular knowing, then, deals solely with man, his true nature or essence (self or consciousness), and the divine's revelation of ultimate Truth. Whatever pertains to this domain is known; whatever does not pertain to it has no relevance to the journey or the divine's revelation.

The reason for bringing this up is to affirm that beyond self or consciousness there is a particular knowing that is neither omniscience nor unknowing, nor a knowing that has any need of a knower. The proverbial question people ask regarding the no-self condition is "Who knows?" The question, of course, requires an answer in terms of self (a knower) or in terms of the same dimension in which it was asked. To respond, "There is no 'who'," could never satisfy a knower and its way of knowing. Obviously the mind cannot grasp the fact that beyond self or consciousness there is no "who" or knower—as said before, self cannot imagine no-self. But this is why, beyond self, such a question (who?) cannot possibly arise; instead, what immediately arises is the question of the true nature of "that" which remains when there is no self or knower.

As already pointed out, although the "cloud of knowing" is without a knower, it is not omniscience. While omniscience is also knowing without a knower, unlike the "cloud of knowing," omniscience is not concerned with the divine's revelation to man. Omniscience was around prior to man and man's need for revelation. Since omniscience IS the divine, this knowing is not of man's intellectual dimension. The divine does not see creation as man sees and understands it; thus omniscience answers no human questions because it asks none. I bring this up because some people have odd ideas about omniscience, putting it on the level of a Mensa mentality or some kind of ESP experience, or equating it with "mystical knowledge," perhaps. Invariably man thinks of omniscience in terms of his own mentality, his own experiences and way of knowing. He thinks God can answer his questions in a manner satisfying to his own limited mind. But God's answer to man would never satisfy the mind because God does not see things as man sees them in the first place. But what, then, does it mean to "know all"? We say the divine knows all because the divine IS ALL. Thus, to account for omniscience, the divine need know only one thing—that it is ALL. The fact that we know the divine is All is not the same as omniscience. For man, this knowledge is just one piece of knowledge among many; for the divine, however, there is nothing else to know. Man is not only incapable of omniscience, he is also incapable of grasping any form of knowing without a knower. The reason for this inability is that the mind which tries to grasp such a condition IS the knower or self.

But more important than the question of whether or not a human being could come to such a condition (knowing without a knower) is the question of whether or not the divine knows in terms of a knower or self. Does the divine know "itself"—that is, does it have the same reflexive way of knowing by which man knows himself? If we asked "Who are you?" would the divine respond "I am God"? While anyone can say "I am God"—and perhaps believe it—the statement could hardly be a criterion of Truth. "I am God" is not even a true identity statement. The only thing that can identify itself IS self; apart from this, self gives identity to whatever is not itself. Thus true identity statements might be: "I am myself," "I am who I am," or "I am that I am," but never "I am God." As soon as I am no longer myself but something else—say, a rose, an angel or God—there is no true identity. If there were no self or consciousness, of course there could be no identity statements. The point is that any statement identifying self as the divine or God is not a true identity statement, since it is true neither of God nor of man. Beyond self, then, if we ask "Who knows?" not even the divine could answer. Without self or a knower there is no answer because the question cannot rightly be asked.

But the statement "I am God" is also invalid for another reason. Apart from implying self or consciousness, it implies that God knows God or something other than himself. Strictly speaking, however, God does not know himself as God; only man knows God. By and large "God" is the term we give to an otherwise nameless divine or Godhead, and while this term works for purposes of communication, it would hardly be the way the divine knows or identifies itself. As was said elsewhere, the Godhead known to consciousness is "God," and thus God is everything consciousness knows of the Godhead. If there were no consciousness, there would also be no God.

The real question, however, is whether the divine knows itself at all or if the divine is, or has, self or consciousness. Naturally we think God knows himself because we know ourselves; we cannot imagine how God could not know himself when we know ourselves and we know God. But the divine's knowing is not our knowing, and to think it is has been a great human problem—Job's problem, to name one. But because we know "ourselves" does not justify the conclusion that God knows "himself" or "itself." This is pure projection, an imposition of human knowing on the divine. Not only is "myself" indicative of reflexive consciousness, but so are "I," "me" and all other self expressions. Divine knowing is not reflexive, however, and without the reflexive there can be no consciousness or self, no I or I am. The question of whether or not the divine is or has self or consciousness is not a matter of semantics as some people would have it; rather, it is a question of the true nature of the divine.

Because of consciousness man both knows himself and knows God, and because man knows God only in so much as he knows himself, the greater the degree of self-knowledge the greater the degree of divine knowledge—or rather, knowledge of the divine. If man had no self or consciousness he would neither know himself nor God. Self then mediates man's knowing and experiences of God, and thus the God he knows and experiences is always in terms of self or consciousness. Because the same consciousness knows both self and God, man often experiences God as part and parcel of his own subjective being, or knows God in much the same way as he knows his own true self. Thus what consciousness knows of the divine is according to its own self-nature, its own self knowledge and subjective experience. But the God known and experienced by consciousness or self is not the ultimate reality of God, which Reality or Godhead lies beyond the limits of self and its self-knowing. Although our path to ultimate Reality lies through consciousness, once on the other side there is no self-knowing, identity ("I am me") and so on; this is not the nature of divine knowing.

If the knower and experiencer came to an end, so too would its knowing and experiencing, its known and its experienced. But if God had been known and experienced, how, without the medium of self or consciousness, is God to be known now? In terms of consciousness or self, God is not known or experienced. No description is possible of the knowing that lies beyond self or consciousness; no idea of it can even be formulated. To say that, in the end, the divine is not known and does not even know itself is obviously dissatisfying to the human mind. The mind, however, can never be satisfied with divine knowing because divine knowing is beyond the mind and its way of knowing. But if divine knowing is such that the divine does not know itself as God, we could hardly expect any human being to know himself as God. What would not be the Truth of the divine could not be the Truth of a human being. This brings us to ask if the incarnate Christ knew he was God.

DID CHRIST KNOW HE WAS GOD?

As we have said, anyone who knows or experiences himself as God is not God; being beyond all self, God does not know himself as God nor know he is God. Thus neither in his humanity nor divinity did Christ know he was God. That we claim Christ knew he was God attests only to our ignorance regarding self or consciousness and our limited understanding of Christ, human and divine. The general thinking is that if we know Christ is God then certainly he must have known he was God. Often Christ's sayings such as "He who sees me sees the Father," or "Before Abraham, I was," are given as proof that Christ knew he was God, but these sayings easily lend themselves to other interpretations. Much stronger statements are Christ's continuously addressing God as "Father," praying to Him, affirming he was sent by him, even saying "If I give witness to myself I am a liar." Christ gives witness to the Father, not to himself or to his self. Even if Christ had said he was God this would not make it so, any more than it would be true if someone else made this claim.

To say that Christ never knew he was God is very upsetting to the Christian mentality. Yet the fact Christ never said he was God or knew any such thing IS his Truth. If people only knew the truth of divine knowing and the truth of consciousness or our purely human way of knowing, they would understand that any claim to BE God is NOT God. In this sense it could be said that Christ was God because he never said he was.

We think Christ knew he was God because we know he is God, but this reasoning is due to our limited way of knowing. It is not God's knowing. The rule of thumb is this: where any self is involved (me, I, or I am and so on) be it in the form of any knowing or experience, then the divine or ultimate Truth is instantly ruled out. The divine is beyond all self, and thus identifying God as self or a self, or as any level of self-experience or self-knowing would not be true of God, and if it is not true of God, much less is it true of man. So either way, as a matter of human knowing or divine knowing, Christ did not know himself as God. It would be as absurd to say that "God knows himself" as it would be to say that a lump of sugar knows itself. Only man (consciousness) knows a lump of sugar, and only man knows God.

If in looking at ourselves we also see God, we see God in the same human way that Christ saw God; he knew himself as one with God, but not himself as God. Thus how we see God in ourselves is the same way Christ saw God in himself; this seeing is solely our *human* seeing of God; it is not God's seeing. We think God sees himself because we see ourselves, yet every time we make such a leap in judgment we make God into our own image and not the other way around. Something else to consider: if we (I or you) were God, we could not explain why we did not know this from the beginning, or why some people claim that man's goal is to "realize" himself as God. It makes no sense to think that God must realize he is God. Because God in his Godhead never realizes himself as God, he could never create anything that could possibly realize itself as God. In fact God cannot create himself (his equal); anything created has to be of less stature. Our goal is to realize our human oneness with God; beyond this we cannot go. Beyond this even God cannot go because from the beginning there has never been anything for God to "realize."

This is saying only that the way we see God in ourselves and know our oneness with him is the same way Christ experienced this in his humanity. Purely in his divinity, however, Christ never had to realize he was God because this is not even up for realization. It is man who realizes Christ is God, whereas Christ in his humanity and in his divinity never realized this or knew it at all.

As to how we know Christ is God when Christ did not know this himself, my answer is that we do not know Christ is God anymore than he did. Though he IS God, we cannot know this from any position or level of self or consciousness or purely with our intellect and human way of knowing. In fact, it is always an embarrassment to hear people trying to prove Christ's divinity; we can no more prove Christ's divinity than we can prove the existence of God. Even when we realize our most mystical oneness with God, we still do not know that Christ is God. It is at this point of union, however, that we enter into his human experience of oneness with God and begin to have insight into the Trinity. It is at this point we begin our true identity with Christ as a human being.

So the only answer to how we know Christ is God is that we know this by FAITH alone. This faith is a very specific grace in that it never gives up on Christ; it does not depend on the intellect or on any experience, it does not stop with any experience of Christ even when we know and experience our oneness with God. This grace, which is God's mysterious life and as close to divine knowing as man can get, pushes on and never rests satisfied until Christ is understood beyond all possible understanding and all possible experiences. Grace demands that we do not rest until we know or see first hand the truth of the incarnation, death, resurrection, ascension—the fullness of Christ's truth. Faith is not content with seeing "through a glass darkly" or intuitively, conceptually or symbolically, but seeing beyond which there is nothing left to see and no one (self) to see. This is true Christian faith. For the Christian contemplative especially, there is no rest in this matter; rest only means there is no further to go to the mystery of Christ. The nature of grace has a way of pushing and stretching the human limits, pushing them until there is no mystery remaining—pushing them right over the fine line, in fact.

So to realize we are one with God is relatively easy, but to realize how and in what way Christ's divine nature is the eternal Godhead is another matter altogether. After the Christian has realized Christ's same human oneness with God, he still has much further to go. It is from the point of union or oneness that he now has to go forward to Christ's same death, resurrection and ascension. But who can understand death and resurrection coming after a life of union and oneness with God? Who can understand the true nature of this death and what the resurrection reveals of Christ's divine nature? Because of this mystery I regard Christianity as the most difficult and mystical of all religions; Christ is the most unbelievable and unknown Truth there is—and the most difficult of all Truths. Christ is the key to the ultimate nature of God, ourselves, and all that exists. It seems that a greater truth takes a greater realization; we can always find rest in lesser truths, but if there is anything more to be known or realized, we have to push on.

In conclusion: Since human nature is not God, it never knows itself as God; since divine nature IS God, divine knowing has no need to know it is God. Divine knowing is beyond self-knowledge or any other purely human way of knowing.

THE ULTIMATE MYSTERY OF CHRIST

As said earlier, the true mystery of the unitive state is neither God nor the true self; rather, the mystery is the true nature of "that" in us which is one with God. While this mystery had been revealed as Christ, we neither experienced Christ as our true self nor as the divine Center. In other words, Christ is beyond anything we know and experience of God and beyond anything we know and experience of our true self. In a word, Christ is the mystery beyond the unitive state, beyond even our oneness with the divine.[3]

---

[3]It seems that from the beginning many people equate the divine center as Christ. I could never do this, however, because such was not the revelation. Instead, the revelation was that Christ was "that" which united the divine and self. That other people do not see things this way suggests they

The final resolution of this mystery is the revelation of the resurrection—that is, the true nature of the body beyond all self or consciousness. In this revelation Christ's divine Reality is the Eternal Form from which all matter is formed and into which it ultimately disappears. An analogy of divine Form might be clay; whatever we shape with this clay or however this shape is made to function, no aspects of its form or function is divine. Nor is the eternal substance of the clay in any way changed because of the various forms made from it. Christ then is Eternal Form from which our own physical body is fashioned; the revelation of this, Christ's Mystical Body, IS the resurrection. This mystical body, however, is not the body we usually know and experience; by contrast, Christ's mystical body is non-experiential and without any bodily experience.

Staying with the analogy of clay, in terms of the Trinity, Christ is the Eternal Form or substance of which the Father is the "Formless Unmanifest" or the divine state or dimension in which Eternal Form exists. In itself a heavenly state cannot be manifest, and thus it can never be form or the manifest. Just so, the Father or ultimate state of the Godhead is formless and unmanifest. The Holy Spirit is the "Eternal Movement" or the manifesting of Eternal Form, and this Movement is the divine's eternal creativity. Because of this the universe was fashioned and continuously moves and changes—man included. Because of this everything we know comes and goes, while what we do not know never changes; the Trinity remains the same and untouched from all eternity. As we can see, without Christ there would be no universe and no one to see or question its mystery; if the divine were not Manifest we could not even speak of an "Unmanifest."

Although we know that every analogy falls short of the divine and can never represent its true nature, I have found that some people forget this fact and treat analogies as if they were statements of ultimate Truth. Using a piece of clay to illustrate how the Trinity works is just what some people are waiting for in order to condemn anyone who would do so. What is behind this condemnation, however, is the fear that there just may BE no eternal self or consciousness. There seems to be a certain fear that without self, God will somehow turn out to be an impersonal, indifferent "cosmic

---

probably will not understand what I am saying here about Christ as the link between man (self) and the divine.

soup," as one theologian put it, or a blind, unintelligent energy, on down to no theistic God at all.

In the history of our religions, however, no one has reported the divine to be an indifferent, impersonal hunk of clay or cosmic soup. Such notions belong only to scoffers. But with regard to the Trinity or the ultimate nature of the divine we might remember St. Augustine's discovery that God is closer to us than we are to ourselves. Now nothing, of course, could be more personal or closer to us than we are to ourselves, yet he says God is even closer than this, more personal than personal. In other words, God is beyond self, yet closer than self. But how does this work? Beyond or underlying all personal self and even its experience of oneness with the divine is Christ's Mystical Body. From this Eternal Form we were unknowingly fashioned and to this Mystical Body we knowingly return. The body we know, however, along with its structures, functions and experiences, including self, is not divine or eternal. But what could be closer to us than the body, the ultimate nature of which is Christ's Mystical Body? Those with experience could never call this Mystical Body "impersonal." Indeed, it is beyond anything we usually know as personal or impersonal. While there are no words to express its Reality, we can at least affirm what It is not; thus we can say that any notion of the divine as impersonal is a complete error.

It is important to distinguish between God as "relatively" personal and God as "absolutely" personal. Usually God is only regarded as personal relative to man, relative to ourselves or to creation. But the Trinity tells us that beyond man and creation God is personal in himself. Thus to be "personal," the Trinity has no need of creation or of man, no need of self or consciousness. Thus without the Trinity there can be no valid claim that God is intrinsically or absolutely personal. If God is only personal relative to ourselves, then the Trinity has no meaning; it would be irrelevant. Beyond all self, however, God is personal simply because God is Trinity. If this were not so, the beyond self God might well turn out to be an impersonal hunk of clay or cosmic soup. The revelation of the Trinity, however, dissolves all such fears and nonsense. If Christ had not surrendered his entire unitive self to God, there would have been no revelation of the Trinity. Though a subsequent matter of faith to his followers, the truth of the Trinity as a personal God can only be verified beyond all self.

Christ's link with consciousness, then, is the unknown substance of our physical body that underlies the function and energy of consciousness along with all its experiences. Christ, however, is none of these experiences; nor is Christ the empty divine Center or the Unmanifest's heavenly state. If it were not for Christ there would be no consciousness or self because man as we know him would not exist. As the Eternal Manifest, Christ is a greater mystery than the Unmanifest, which is why to explode the mystery of Christ is to reveal the mystery of God, Its Trinitarian nature, the mystery of man, ourselves, and the whole universe.

THE ETERNAL BODY OF CHRIST

As wonderful as it sounds to say that man is an image of God, the paradox is that deep in himself man has never felt very good about himself as an image of God. One reason is that God has no image and, thus, man also has no clear image of himself. But if man could just have an image of God, then he could also have an image of himself and thus know himself and his own true nature. Although, ideally, man fashions himself after his image of God, yet where this image is not clear or where it is false, man fashions God after his own self-image. Thus if our self-image is unclear or false we can hardly expect to have a true image of God.

So man's continuous longing for a true image or knowledge of God is equally a longing for his own true image and self-knowledge. For this reason man has never been satisfied with his own man-made images of God or the mythical characters he concocts in his own brain. Man longs for a true, living image of God, a human being in his own likeness that gives him the certitude that God really understands the human condition. Because self or consciousness is the essence of person or personal, it follows that man longs for a personal, close, subjective God, one that can help him fulfill his personal life (self or consciousness) in the best way possible. This longing is so innate in the deepest nature of consciousness that the instant God created consciousness the incarnate Christ was in the making. There is no greater assurance of God's caring or closeness to humanity than that God should take on consciousness or self and walk among us as a fellow human being. This is no far-off esoteric God or one seen every so often by a few privileged seers and prophets. This is God rubbing elbows with everyday people in the marketplace. What greater proof of God's caring for man could we possibly think of?

This is why consciousness and Christ go together; the incarnate Christ is not only the fulfillment of our image-making consciousness or personal self, but equally the revelation of man's true nature and connecting link to God. The historical Christ was virtually God making the human passage through consciousness; anyone less than

God cannot validate or enlighten the path; no one else can be the "last word," as it were, regarding our human passage and its milestones. God is the only one capable of revealing the furthest reaches and ultimate end of the passage; anyone less than God is incapable of doing so. Although all men ultimately come to the same end, none of these has ever revealed the passage in its completeness, or physically demonstrated it, or remained with us as a living presence—the Eucharist. Because of this living presence (Eucharist), the unfolding depths of Christ's revelation is as much with us today as it was in his historical incarnation, death, resurrection and ascension. In one sense Christ is the unfolding of our own lives; we are the truth of Christ because in the very movement of our passage, Christ is revealed again and again; his passage is lived over and over in each human being—if only we had eyes to see how this worked.

So the point of Christ's incarnation pivots on consciousness or self, its journey, milestones and turning points, even its ultimate end or ending. It can be said that our whole journey is Christ's human consciousness taking over (transforming) our own. This transformation takes place on a level of existence we do not know because Christ exists on a level we do not know. For most of the journey what we know and experience of Christ is akin to our deepest unknown self, yet Christ exists for us even beyond this personal, experiential self-dimension—closer than close, that is.

The critical point of this journey occurs the moment (known only in retrospect) when an equivalent match is made between our consciousness and Christ's consciousness at the time of his death. This is the point or moment when we have reached the threshold or limits of consciousness; it is the "fine line" between consciousness and no-consciousness, self and no-self. This is the point at which consciousness, its whole potential for self-knowledge and divine-knowledge, has been spent or fulfilled, and, like a balloon that can expand no more, consciousness or self gives way, dissolves forever. But "who" really dies here? For some people the answer is difficult to understand. The answer is that only Christ dies—and only Christ rises. "That" which spans the great void between man and the divine is not man; it is not self or consciousness. Rather, Christ alone can span this void because only Christ, having come down, knows the way back; only Christ is man's guarantee of the Father's (Unmanifest) heavenly estate. The only way man can get to this eternal estate is by Christ dissolving our consciousness or self in his own divine nature. There is no other way. Consciousness was fashioned for this world, this earthly existence; it was not made to bear the final Vision which is incompatible with earthly existence. Those who believe they can openly see God and have this world too are very much mistaken.

In a certain way the dissolution of consciousness is Christ's death all over again, and the resurrection is the revelation of Christ's Eternal Manifest Form—his Mystical Body, the truth of our body and "that" mystery in us which is one with God. The physical body is not self or consciousness; consciousness was but one function of the body. But take away all physical structure and function— virtually the body we know and experience—and there is Christ's Mystical Body in its divine Form. Consciousness gets in the way of this great Truth. In fact, consciousness generally regards the body as a temporary shell that houses an inner, immaterial spirit, a spirit that pops out when the body dies. But this whole scenario is consciousness' view of things based on its own limited experiences and way of knowing; ultimately there is no truth to it. The resurrection reveals that there is no distinction, as we had thought, between matter and spirit, body and soul, and so on. Obviously what consciousness had regarded as matter and spirit turn out to be of a different nature altogether. Thus we must not mix our present notions of matter and spirit with their Reality or Truth. As said before, beyond self or consciousness there lies a dimension that cannot be articulated. All that can be pointed out are those notions and experiences of consciousness that ultimately turn out to be incorrect, limited or misleading.

In the end, then, the true nature of Christ's Mystical Body is the ultimate Reality of our body. And just as the Mystical Body dwells in a divine or heavenly estate—the Unmanifest Father—so too, Christ brings all that is manifest to this same estate, brings all to the Father. While we hear a good deal about experiences of love and bliss in our spiritual journey, we hear little about the revelation of the Trinitarian nature of the Absolute. Obviously this revelation belongs to Christ. The path he revealed does not stop with blissful experiences or even our human oneness with God, but moves on to reveal the Trinitarian nature of the divine, because this is his divine nature. To eventually see how this works is what our Christian passage is all about. While the resurrection is the revelation of Christ's Mystical Body or Eternal Form, the ascension is the further revelation of the Unmanifest Father or the heavenly state in which the Mystical Body eternally dwells. But before we can come to this —and every man will—we first have to die with Christ.

CHAPTER TWO
STEPS IN MY CHRISTIAN PASSAGE

Introduction

What follows is a brief account of the major milestones of my Christian journey. With few exceptions these milestones were recognized only in retrospect or when there had been sufficient distance to recognize a particular experience or event as a major turning point. Without this distance or perspective we never know where we are at any given moment, which is why the present moment, and not any particular experience of the past, is of the essence. Without distance we cannot always tell, in the immediacy of experience, which events are most important to the overall journey. After all, not every outstanding experience is a milestone, and not every milestone is an outstanding experience. A milestone could be so simple that it warrants no immediate emphasis and may only be recognized when it is long past. What I mean by a milestone is an irreversible change in awareness—awareness of ourselves and awareness of God; it is a grace that comes out of the blue and cannot be attributed to anything we have done. Some people seem to think we can account for every experience and change in terms of external circumstances, other people in our lives, something we have done, or perhaps a particular practice. But this reveals a disbelief in anything beyond our mundane lives, ourselves and our own doing. Grace is not dependent upon extraneous factors or even "who" we are. It does not follow us around or wait upon our good time; rather, it is we who follow grace as it lights the way—this much, we can do. To be a witness to grace and to testify to its reality is not really to be a witness to ourselves, our mundane lives, or anything we have done. This is hard for some people to understand or believe, yet this is the truth of it.

I
God as Immanent

My journey got started at the age of five with an overwhelming experience. From within there was a sudden infusion of tremendous power. If a balloon could feel, this infusion might be its experience when someone blows air into it. For a moment I thought, "I'm gonna bust!" There was a moment of fear that this power might totally overwhelm me and I would cease to exist. What this meant, I had no idea. When it became apparent that I would not bust, the power turned into a joy beyond description. Although it gradually subsided, the power never completely left. On many occasions it would suddenly reveal itself until, finally, I realized I could always find it within. I knew this power was not myself; it belonged to a dimension unknown in my ordinary experiences. Also, it gave no impression of being a person or an entity; it was completely formless. Initially I did not think of it as God—of whom I had heard a great deal—but sometimes this idea did, in fact, cross my mind. Thus, for example, one day in school this power suddenly leaped when sister told us that God was present in all things. Putting two and two together I decided this power was God and ran home to tell my father. My father, however, told me no one could experience God as he was in himself, and though I did not really understand what he said, I believed him. The experiences, however, went right on. Although this power was somewhat aloof and not too personal, I came to regard it as a rather awesome, friendly teacher. How this worked—by its movements, a little more or less air in the balloon—I cannot go into detail here. The initial experience, however, was a major milestone because it marked the beginning of the quest for the true nature of this power; if it was not myself, what was it?

The first thing I did was to go around and ask everybody I knew if they also experienced this particular power within themselves. Nobody seemed to understand, so I decided that adults had forgotten, and that kids were still in line for it. Many times I returned to my father with various questions, and though I received a lot of answers that were meaningful later in life, he dodged any affirmation of man's ability to truly experience God as He was in Himself. But his insistence in this matter turned out to be a great benefit. Eventually I learned to maintain a distance on my experiences, and when they were not overwhelming I even adopted a skeptical attitude toward them. It seemed the best policy was to forget them and go on my way. Sometimes, however, this only increased the experiences—the power's way of saying "Pay attention!" In these early years, between five and nine, this was no small power.

I was always hesitant about trusting this power because I felt that if it so wanted, it could take over my life and obliterate me completely. I knew it was completely independent of me, had a life of its own, and did its own thing quite apart from me; I had no say or control over it. Sometimes I had the impression of being "used" —for what end I could not guess—and that who I was did not count at all. Based on this I had an intuition at six or so that ultimately proved to be true. Somehow I knew that this power had a plan for my life, a certain work to do in me with a specific purpose or end in mind. I knew that whatever I wanted in life or whichever way I wanted to go would be of no concern to this power. In a word, I was not going to have a life of my own. This intuition could hardly be flattering to a self that did not matter. Though I spent a good deal of time in life making sure this intuition was nothing but a figment of my imagination, it was all to no avail.

At the age of nine I came down with a bone disease. My parents and others became so upset over this that they managed to create a dark cloud that seemed to hang over my head. I will not go into detail, but the cause of the real trouble was a terrible mistake on the part of a doctor. I knew he was wrong, but no one believed me. This overhanging cloud of some unknowable, impending disaster gradually got thicker, darker and lower down; I had the impression that the interior power was somehow holding it aloft so it would not descend or touch me. One day, however, when praying God to help me in this matter, I suddenly realized I might as well be praying to the ceiling; God, if he even heard me, was not about to help. I then turned inward to my friend of four years and for the first time put all my hope and trust at its disposal. As I looked at my friend—comparable to a light center in myself—I saw its light slowly fade before my eyes, and at the moment of its total disappearance, a large black hole suddenly appeared in its stead. At that moment the black cloud over my head descended, inside and outside, and I collapsed.

If it had not been for a miracle three days later, I doubt that my mind would ever have moved again. My interior friend did not appear again for eighteen months, and it was just as well. I verged on feelings of hate for this power because it had let me down in my hour of need. Yet because there was nothing "within" anymore or no interior power to hate or to be angry with, these feelings not only dissipated, they gave way to a feeling of emptiness and a genuine loneliness and longing to see this mysterious power again. I would always look upon this abandonment at age nine as the most tragic event and trial of my life; even in retrospect I believe the event was improper for my developmental age and that God overstepped himself and pushed the human limits too far. The result, however, left me with the decided intuition that God's work in this human form was actually a piece of research, or that God was testing to see just how far he could stretch the human limits— possibly with the idea of refashioning them. But this is why it took a miracle (which I will not go into) to revive my psychic life; otherwise it would have been over before it had barely begun.

As for the bone disease, my father took me to the Shrine of Our Lady of Guadalupe in Mexico to be cured. With this he seemed satisfied and assured; thus once more peace returned to the home front. I switched my whole allegiance from God and the interior power to Mary, and this was a happy switch. After God abandoned me I never again prayed to him for a single thing—it would have been a waste since it was obvious he was going to do his own disastrous thing anyway. But Mary, she works the miracles, and always in our favor. I had ceased to consider the possibility that the former power was God; I figured that God could not be anything that comes and goes, much less leave a black hole in his wake; at the same time, however, I seemed unable to make contact with God anywhere else that I tried. At the Shrine, however, there was Mary, and a promise. While my parents prayed for my bones—which I knew would get well anyway—I asked only to see God, and this Mary promised.

II
God as Immanent and Transcendent
Christ as the Vessel

Though I waited every day expectantly, it was almost a year before this promise was fulfilled in a glorious experience in the woods, high in the Sierra mountains on an Easter Monday. For sheer spectacular magnificence this sighting probably outdid all the experiences of my life. I might compare it to a sustained flash of lighting that blinded the beauty of nature around me, as well as the one who saw it. For weeks afterwards the world was void and empty; life was solely in the remembrance of this sighting, which gradually faded away as the world slowly became more livable again.

The unusual aftermath of this event, however, was the quiet reappearance of the former interior power, which, after eighteen months of absence, I had never expected to see again. I found its reappearance upsetting because now I had an interior object for my anger, blame and distrust. Then, too, since I had now seen God in the woods, I knew this interior power was not God, and thus I was not about to put any faith in it. Instead I determined to stick with the great vision and Mary, and ignore its presence. In the woods there had been instantaneous recognition of God; nothing would ever call this in question. It was a different case, however, with the interior power. To label this power "God" would have been only an intellectual judgment, a judgment that did not stick because it was constantly subject to doubt; I could put no faith or trust in anything I could doubt. So the interior power remained a mystery, which means I had no certitude of its true nature. But if this power was not myself and not God, what else could it be? Since there was nothing else within, it had to be one or the other. The quest for the truth of my experiences went on.

In the meantime, my father had finally conceded that the saints had in fact experienced God. "But," he added, "the only purpose of these experiences was to increase their faith." From this I concluded that the saints were people obviously low on faith and that "experiences" were a sign of weakness. Because of this I developed a certain skepticism and genuine dislike of spiritual "experiences." I was convinced that God could be nothing that came and went, but only "that" which remained beyond all and any type of experience; this, at least, was the God I searched for. Though destined to have certain experiences, I eventually decided that only people who were skeptical of experiences could really afford to have them. Without a certain distance or a non-experiential divine (or a naked faith, perhaps) to stand on, experiences can be an entrapment that carry us off to a totally false end. If the truth be known, the only permanent eternal and unbroken "high" man will ever experience is not in this world, for such a condition is what heaven is. In this final heavenly estate the world is neither seen nor heard, for heaven is that which man has never seen nor heard.

Despite this knowledge, however, I eventually found that ignoring the inner power was not easy. My impression was that it wished to regain my trust, break down my resistance and skepticism; it even tried to impress upon me that it was God. Naturally, I did not want to believe this; I was sure that as soon as I believed it, it would disappear just as it had done before. Still, this was no little power; it could knock me down and leave no doubt that it was God—for a while at least. The struggle to ignore this power went on for four years, a struggle that in the meantime was compounded by other factors as well.[4]

One factor was the struggle between two different levels of myself. One level was the external self so obvious to others, while the other was the deeper "real" self that was incapable of being known or seen by others, and whose major concern was the quest for Truth, God, and an understanding of my experiences. Not for a minute did I regard the interior power as my real self. As said before, it did its own thing, came and went as it pleased; there was no second guessing it. To get on with my life I had to ignore it as best I could. There was a certain reluctance to go with the real self, however, because it took little interest in social life or the things of this world; instead, it was totally at home in solitude, nature, music and books. Thus I felt that the moment I gave it free reign or precedence in my life, I might as well go off and live in a cave. Which level to go with?—that was the question.

The second factor I had to struggle with was of a religious nature. At one point I realized that I did not see how I could honestly believe that Christ was God. My experiences of God had nothing to do with Christ; in fact, the idea that the historical Christ was the Absolute All and Everywhere struck me as unbelievable. How could this possibly work? The problem was not with his life or that he was specially sent to reveal God to man; rather, I could not see how the Almighty could be contained in a single human being and how the world could go on at the same time. The sole Christ I could hold out for which inhibited total rejection was the Eucharist. If it had not been for the Eucharist, I do not see how I could have remained a Christian. In this form Christ was not a problem; in focusing on the mystical or Eucharistic Christ, I did not have to deal with the images or the human form and personality of the man who lived two thousand years ago. I figured that if he was not God,

---

[4]Part of my struggle was the difference between God in experience and God as a more conceptual truth. These are two different dimensions: experience and knowing. Thus a gap exists between the two that has to be resolved (or integrated). In the end it was God alone who eventually resolved this dilemma; of myself I could not do it.

then his historical humanity was dispensable anyway.[5] Thus I realized my problem with Christ was not the mystical Christ, Christ of the Godhead or Trinity, but with the historical Christ who came and went. I had already learned the hard way that anything that came and went was not God.

Something else about Christ bothered me: the notion that he died a terrible death for my sins. This struck me as absolutely preposterous, unbelievable. To begin with I never felt I was a sinner, nor did I see the good people around me as sinners. That the only reason for the incarnation was sin was a notion I instinctively rejected. But then the question arose, "Well, if he did not die for our sins, what was his particular death all about?" Elsewhere I have recounted the story of my going into Church one day and putting this question to Christ. Though it could be said I received no answer, in the moments of silently waiting for one, I did indeed come upon something. It struck me forcibly that the real tragedy of Christ's death was that nobody understood it. Without any feelings of tragedy, for a moment I was overwhelmed by the presence of a tragic mystery here, and this sense of a profound mystery would never leave me. At the same time, however, I was certain that sin was neither the true nature or purpose of Christ's

---

[5]I might add that as a youngster I was thoroughly acquainted with the Gospels. That I found them fairly uninspiring and not pertinent to my quest may have been due to an overkill or too much early familiarity. At twelve I undertook to read the Old Testament from front to back, a project that turned into a test of endurance because I found it utterly shocking and distasteful; one thing I knew—this God I never knew. In Christianity the anthropomorphic images of God are acknowledged images of Christ's humanity; they are not images of his divinity such as I found in the Old Testament. Due to my early experiences I basically got hold of God before I was exposed to various religious concepts, images, theology and so on. While I learned from God not to get wrapped up in my personal experiences —God being beyond them all—I also never bogged down in the opposite— the rational, conceptual, historical view of God. Both extremes can go off the deep end and eventually miss God completely. Nevertheless I am obliged to the Gospels for bearing witness to the facts of Christ's life, or to the revelation of God inherent in his human manifestation—his death, resurrection, ascension, and eucharistic presence.

death and that its truth remained to be known.[6] From that time on, every time I looked at the cross (which was almost daily in my life) there was ever renewed this sense of a profound unknown mystery and the need to find out its true nature and purpose.

At the time of this incident, I was eleven. For the next four years I struggled with the question of whether or not I was really a Christian and whether or not I could ever be one. It would take a small volume to recount my discussions with my father on this matter. Let me just say that, to this day, I have never come upon anyone who had a better knowledge of his faith than my father. The history of the Church, the ancient Fathers, theology—especially St. Thomas—and all things Catholic were the love of his life. His library also contained the lives and writings of the great Saints and mystics. And, to go one further, as attorney for several religious orders, it was said at the chancery office that he had a better knowledge of canon law than the canonists themselves. So education in my faith could not have been better; in fact, if I had had to rely upon the religious instruction I received in twelve years of attending Catholic schools, I do not see how I could have stuck it out.

But it was something he said one day, almost in exasperation, that finally put me over the line. I insisted that in baptism I had never received the gift of faith. I could not find it in myself; thus there was no use our kidding ourselves about it. I was an intrepid arguer, and to a point my father welcomed this; an unexamined faith, he would say, was not worth its salt. But one day I put a strategic question him. After adding up those things I could honestly believe and those things I could not honestly believe, I discovered that I believed more than I disbelieved. While this was good news to me, I knew that the notion of a "seamless garment" meant that either you believe it all or you cannot be counted as a believer. So I asked my father, "If I believe most of what the Church says (or believes) but cannot believe a few things it says, does this mean I am not a Christian?" Without hesitation my father replied adamantly, pounding his fist on the table, "The Church does not say you have to understand the mysteries of faith. All it asks of

---

[6]In some ways its tragedy is that in the failure to understand it, we have blamed Christ's death on our sins. While this view of atonement and redemption might make sense to some people, and even be comforting to them, I would always regard this view as a tragedy in itself. Christ "saves" us by transforming us into himself; there is no other way to get to heaven.

you is that you practice the faith. If you do not practice you will never understand; if there is any hope of understanding it will only come through practice. So PRACTICE, PRACTICE, PRACTICE!" After this he went back to eating his dinner, and no more was said. This unexpected answer filled me with joy. What he said I could indeed believe and understand. Now I no longer had to worry about being a Christian; instead, my goal was eventually to become one. Faith, then, was a process—it was not a pre-fixed either/or proposition. And so I set out in earnest to practice my religion with the hope in mind that someday I could truly say, "I am a Christian."

Between the ages of eleven and fifteen, then, the struggle was three-fold: it was a continual effort to put no trust in the interior power; it was the growing pull between the superficial self and the real self; and it was the more intellectual problem with Christ and the search for an honest faith in him. I count this as the only period in my life when I experienced a true interior dichotomy; yet it was this pull in different directions that gave rise to the recognition of a need for unity within myself, a pressing need to get it all together.

At fifteen there came an important breakthrough which was an intuitive glimpse of the path ahead or the way I had to go. Here I understood that, although God as he was in himself was beyond all human experience, in order to get to God as he was in himself I had first to go through God as he was in myself. This meant that I had to go with my experiences and stop all the resistance, all the struggles and battles, doubts and searching. These were only a resistance to taking the human experiential journey to God. In order to take this journey, I was to believe that the interior power was God, I was to go with my deeper self, and I was to have a naked faith in Christ because his was the way to God as he was in himself—and beyond ourselves. Thus I saw that going along with my experiences and trusting God for them was the way to get to God beyond all experiences. While this knowledge of the path ahead was quite definitive and unquestionable, it was also disappointing and humbling. This insight might be compared to standing on a mountain waiting for the ascension, when suddenly God appeared and told me to go back down the mountain, walk the full distance round the earth and then ascend the other side. This was not entirely good news. I foresaw that going with my experiences would bring on a pile of troubles, and it did. Then, too, there would be the extra burden of carrying with me (on this trek) the knowledge that God was beyond all my experiences. How could anybody give themselves up to their experiences if they knew God was beyond them all? Seeing the way to go and what to do is one thing, but actually being able to do it is another. One thing, however, had become obvious: there were no divine short cuts or quick ways to God. I had to take the whole human journey and live the human experience to the fullest extent of its potential.

A major milestone occurred a few months later that gave me the confirmation I needed to get started. First, I saw that the God within or "immanent" (the power or presence I experienced) and the God without or "transcendent" (beyond myself as God in the woods) were identical. They were just two different manifestations of God and, therefore, two different experiences. This told me that the God I experienced within myself was the same God that transcended myself, the difference being that God within was experienced by self (and, therefore, subjective), whereas God "without" transcended self and was ultimately non-experiential to self (God overshadowing self, that is). It was the same God only experienced either by self as "within" or as ultimately transcending all self and its interior experiences of God. Another way to put it: while all things are in God, God is also in all things—much like the air inside a balloon is the same air as that outside the balloon. At first I was overjoyed with this piece of information, but a few days later it dawned on me that somehow I had been left out of the Godhead: God within and without, but what about me—me, myself and I? I could see how I was totally unnecessary and inconsequential to God; I was devoid of any eternal life of my own. I was just a passing, non-eternal piece of creation, a temporary vessel (like a balloon for example) and nothing more. The sense of having no real life of my own and of having no real connection to God was terrible, so terrible I was convinced that this "seeing" or understanding was incomplete. For the first time in my life I sincerely prayed for help.

The answer was the second part of this milestone and another, far more brilliant "seeing." This was the Trinity wherein Christ was midway between the Transcendent Father (without) and the Immanent Holy Spirit (within). The understanding was that Christ (the vessel) stood for every human being and that his human mission or goal was to bring us to his same position in the Trinity or Godhead. Without Christ there was no oneness between the created (the vessel) and the uncreated (immanent-transcendent divine); in fact, without Christ there would not be the created. Without Christ or the middle Ground between Immanent and Transcendent, the Godhead does not work. Christ, then, is the Vessel uniting the divine within and without, immanent and transcendent. But in order to come to his same position we had first to follow Christ and become as humanly perfect as he was perfect, which meant giving our whole life to this journey to the Godhead. This breakthrough or "seeing" was the only time I ever had a sense of Christ "saving" me—saving me and every perishable form that existed. I might add that every major breakthrough or revelation of God was always all-inclusive, meaning that it never had reference solely to "me." It seems that the nature of revelation, or at least any truth I ever came upon, is never really "personal," both because it is beyond us and our wildest expectations and because its truth is obviously the same for all. For this reason I never felt the journey was a "private" affair; rather, it was the direction and truth of everyone's journey. This milestone was so powerful that whatever else was going on in my life, it instantly fell away. At this point the journey began in earnest; the path ahead was looking up.

The first insight into Christ that resolved the problem of why I had always experienced God within, rather than Christ, was the realization that this was also the way it went for the historical Christ; this was also his experience. Christ did not experience himself within; rather, Christ experienced God within—the Father, as he called him. If Christ had experienced only himself within, he would have said he was one with himself, or solely referred to himself as the "Father." But if Christ is the Father, then one of the terms—"Christ" or "Father"—becomes dispensable, in which case the Trinity is dispensable. In human experience, however, just as in the Trinity, there is a distinction: the manifest and unmanifest are one, but they are not one another. In this matter, consciousness (our human mode of experiencing God) does not belie the Trinity or truth of the Godhead; indeed, consciousness "reflects" this truth even through it cannot lay hold of it. As we know, Christ spoke of his oneness with the Father, prayed to the Father and gave witness to having been sent by the Father; obviously Christ's human historical experience of God was like our own. He experienced the divine within just as we do. With this insight I could begin to identify with Christ's interior experiences, the goal of which was to come to his same abiding experience of oneness with God—or Father.

Thus I saw that to follow Christ meant to have his same interior experiences and to follow the inner, not the outer, movement of his life. This is the only way we can ever come upon his same perspective or behave in the virtuous way he prescribed. We cannot put Christ on like a coat, for even if we copied his behaviors, followed his words or did everything he said, this would still not be true following. Christ's first commandment to love God above all things is the sole key to his interior life and his experience of God. As beginners we aim for love by the practice of virtue through self-discipline, but later the practice of virtue arises automatically out of love and is not a matter of self-discipline or curbing the ego-self. So I realized the priority of coming to Christ's own intense love of the Father; everything else, including love of neighbor, was seen as secondary.

Somehow realizing this priority is, I think, the essence of a contemplative and how he differs from a non-contemplative. The latter strives to do two things at once: to be of service to God and to this world at the same time. This is why he travels more slowly toward union with God. Though he sees no dichotomy between God and involvement in human affairs, his whole struggle is centered on bringing them together. The contemplative, on the other hand, is sooner able to get things together because he is acutely aware of this dichotomy from the outset. Thus he follows the first commandment until it leads automatically and *per force* into the second. This way he travels much faster than does the non-contemplative.

III
Transformation Process
or
Dark Night of the Spirit

The third milestone was almost predictable. After being on the path for about two years the inevitable happened; the divine within (God immanent or the ever present power) suddenly disappeared and left a black hole again. Over my mind there descended a cloud like a shroud that inhibited its usual functioning. I recognized this situation from my experience eight years previously (I was now seventeen.), only this time the maturity and insight were not wanting. I did not collapse, but was determined to hold still and not flinch come hell or high water. The task is to get to the bottom of this dark hole, to see it is God and to surrender our whole being to It. This predicament is very difficult; it is the Dark Night of the Spirit and the onset of a radical change of consciousness—transformation, as some people call it. The divine, of course, did not fall away or disappear as the experience leads us to believe; rather, it was only the self-center (ego) that fell away.

Up to this point in the journey we unknowingly experience the divine through the self-center or on our own ground, so to speak. But now the divine shatters the self-center in order that we may experience him as our deepest abiding experience of "life" and "being." At first the empty center seems to be empty of both self and the divine, but in the definitive revelation, which is a "seeing" or disclosure of the abiding divine Center, there will also be the discovery of the "true self" or the unknown self which is one with the divine. This final unitive revelation, which came almost two years after the falling away of the self-center, marked the end of the transforming (or acclimating) process and the beginning of a new life. I might add that my goal was never to attain the unitive state or any state, for that matter; I simply did not think in these terms. The desired goal was a continuous awareness of God that no activity or thought could alter or disrupt. Perfect love of God was the goal, and selflessness was a goal. Perhaps this is why the unitive revelation came as a quiet surprise, but then, this is probably the way it goes for everyone. From this position it was possible to look back and see the path up to this point or milestone, but looking ahead I saw no path. This abiding union with the divine left nothing to be desired, nothing wanting. I could not see how it was possible to go deeper than the Deepest Divine Center this side of the grave. What remained to do now was to go forward to the full exercise of the unitive state in the ordinary affairs of life.

IV
The Marketplace

In the unitive state the ordinary self-experience (impermanent, phenomenal self) was no longer a problem or deterrent to continuous awareness of God; it was also no deterrent to full involvement in the purely external affairs of life. In a word, I no longer experienced any dis-unity in myself and, therefore, no authentic concern with the phenomenal self. Prior to the unitive state, I was trying to transform this superficial, phenomenal self, but this self is not the level of the psyche that is divinely transformed or even primarily affected by transformation. Rather, it is the deeper unknown self (or "real" self as I called it) that undergoes transformation, and experiences an abiding oneness with the divine. In the unitive revelation this fact came as a surprise; where I had thought the phenomenal self would be transformed (the self we ordinarily know, that is), it turns out that this impermanent non-eternal self is not even transformable. But by the time we see this mistake it is too late, though the work we have done on our superficial selves is probably for the better anyway.

I now had the sense of a new self and the beginning of a new life, but how was this new life different? Prior to coming to the unitive state my life had been unknowingly geared to coming to it; now, however, the previous goals and many of the practices were no longer a means of growth or helpful to transformation. Nor were they in any way necessary to maintain the unitive condition. I knew I could not go any deeper within or interiorly; having come to the divine Center, there was no possibility of going deeper. Thus the interior journey, the movement inward to the deepest Center, was over, finished. This unitive Center is the living flame of love, an enormous expansive love that continuously goes outward. Here I saw that once we come to the unitive state the journey turns around and begins to move outward, an expansive movement of love, a love engendered solely by God. So once the interior movement of the journey is over, the outward movement of the journey begins.

At this turning point, when pondering this new direction, I saw this point as similar to the one at which Christ deliberately "put off his divinity" and fully accepted the human phenomenal self in order to reveal God to man and show him the way home. Christ, of course, never put off his divinity; what he could put off, however, was his heavenly state or experience. In my case this meant forfeiting my divine experiences—which were at an all-time high. They were over and beyond the simple unitive experience. I saw that to do as Christ did, I might sacrifice all my divine experiences, and, out of sheer love for God, wholly accept this impermanent phenomenal self and put it to God's service. Though forfeiting or giving up my experiences of God cannot be compared to Christ's forfeiting the Godhead's heavenly condition, I now understood how this worked and wished to follow Christ in this matter. Unlike Christ, however, I wished to do this in order to love God with nothing in it for myself, whereas Christ did this out of love for man. I must say it never occurred to me to forfeit my experiences of God out of love for other people. I knew that only God could "save" us and transform us, and only God could give grace. Thus in matters that were of the essence to man, I could really help no one. But what, then, was my particular mission? I seemed to have none, none but to live the unitive life to the fullest extent of its potential. What this meant, I would not know until I had lived it.

Regarding the experiences to be forfeited, once we come to the unitive state it is possible to come upon a state in which there is no phenomenal self at all. The ability to sink into this state whenever we are not busy with the world (and sometimes even when we are) seems to be an inherent potential at this stage of the journey. We cannot, of course, forfeit the unitive state; this is an irreversible condition and one that needs no maintenance—such as time for prayer or meditation, silence and so on. No worldly concern or work affects the unitive state; it is everything we are. But once we come this far, if the opportunity permits we can sink into a state that is void of any phenomenal self-experience—a state in which there is no self. This ability is almost a given if we truly understand the unitive condition. Some of these experiences are true glimpses or foretastes of our final beatific state beyond this world—where no self-experience or self-knowing appears. For now, however, such a state seems incompatible with continued earthly existence where, of necessity it seems, the phenomenal self-experience has to arise if we are to get anything done in life. Apart from death, I saw no way out of this fact. Thus because I was not about to die (I was in my early twenties) and since there was no point in this heavenly state this side of the grave, I decided to give up these experiences and whole-heartedly embrace the phenomenal self-experience and all aspects of its mundane existence. But once again, the desire here was to love God with nothing in it for self—no heavenly experiences or graces. As John of the Cross put it, we desire to give to God and no longer receive from God—give without receiving a thing in return, that is.

Now I did not know ahead of time if I could get rid of my beatific experiences, but by going to the marketplace at least I would find out. By marketplace I basically mean being busy about everything but the spiritual or interior life—which no longer needs to be a concern. For about a year there was no appreciable change; the pull to sink in or drop out (I do not know how to put it) was much the same. My efforts to avoid this pull made no real headway. But after a year I suddenly knew that God was about to accept my forfeiture and to make it happen. I learned on this journey that it is one thing to offer something to God, and quite another for God to accept it. Our offering does not change a thing; it is God's accepting that changes everything. As soon as I saw that God was about to accept my offer, however, I began to have doubts about it; I was not sure if this was really a backward or a forward step. It would be many years down the road before I saw this forfeiture as a vital and necessary step in the total movement of the journey. At the time, however, it had been only a rather heroic gesture made from the heights of love, a willing forfeiture of all experiences in order to serve God in naked faith without any compensation.

This cut-off was a milestone with two parts. The first part was reminiscent of two previous "disappearances" of God, but with a great difference. At this time the divine Center was like an open vision more obvious than the hand before my face. Things had been this way for a number of years, but here now, looking straight into this interior vision, it gradually began to fade. For a few moments I did not breath. I was not sure if I should feel anxious about this or not; I waited to find out. At a certain level of dimness the fading stopped, and there it would stay. With this I knew that the extraordinary experiences would no longer be available. The impression was that God was going "underground" or becoming less visible so that I could live and work for God without any self-gratification. As long as God is our compensation, there is still self in it, which means this dimming was not really a dimming of God but a dimming of self. As God increases, self decreases. As self decreases there is less delight in God for self. Although I intuited how this worked, I was not sure how things would go. I only knew that I had asked for it, and that God had done it.[7]

The second part of the milestone was this. Once the light had dimmed to its chosen level there came what I can only describe as a sudden flash or explosion of light. In simple terms, I saw that Christ was my deepest unknown self or "that" unknown mystery in or about me that was truly one with God. This seeing was not a subjective experience of Christ. I did not experience Christ as myself or myself as Christ. Rather, this was a seeing and a knowing that the essential mystery of my existence or being WAS Christ. Intellectually I could not get hold of this; the seeing was the sole certitude. At the same time I felt a burden had been imposed, like the weight of responsibility; it seemed impossible ever to live up to such a knowledge. But then I suddenly realized that my knowledge of Christ had always been of someone "other" and that I could not imagine what it would be like to be Christ. Such a reality can only be lived; it can never be imagined. Thus in the living I intuited this

---

[7]Recently an experienced contemplative suggested we call this (unitive) marketplace stage "The Night of Self" to follow the "The Night of the Spirit." In the latter Night God seems to disappear; in the former, self disappears—or gradually diminishes until it is finally gone.

reality without, however, being able to imagine it, experience it, or even understand it.

This whole event did not change my usual experience of the phenomenal self. What I knew for sure, however, was that "that" in me which loved God and was one with God (the living flame), "that" was Christ. Only Christ is one with God, not me, "I" or any phenomenal self. At bottom, then, Christ was the whole mystery of the unitive state, and thus oneness with God was Christ's experience and not my own. Later of course I would see the difference between "experience" and "Reality," see that while the experience had indeed been mine, the underlying Reality of oneness with God belonged only to Christ.

Between this milestone and the next was a period of twenty years. While I was always looking for an adequate outlet to express the inner flame, every attempt turned into a failure. Whatever the reason for this, the inner flame of love, union, the divine and true self, never found an adequate or satisfying expression to the outside. After a while it occurred to me that if I should ever find a satisfying outlet, there would be some self-satisfaction in this. In an egoless state this is not permitted, perhaps, not even possible. But, however this works, the inability to find an adequate expression for the interior flame always struck me as sad and bewildering. The unitive state is a beautiful, charitable and fearless state, one that should be capable of great, noble and heroic acts. To be doing nothing was in no way satisfying. Again and again I put it to myself, "Have you ever really helped a single soul?" Always the answer was a sad "No." In one way or the other, however, I was always trying, but I saw clearly that anything I could do was only temporary and superficial. I knew that what people needed was grace and a profound transforming change, but this I could not do. Thus anything I did was accompanied by the sad knowledge that it was only temporary and of no profound or lasting benefit to others.[8]

But this brings me to one of the most unusual phenomena I discovered on the journey. There were moments when I knew, and even saw, that in some unknowable way all sense of self was dying.

---

[8]In a way, this realization underlies the whole monastic purpose and belief—namely, that since only God's grace can save and transform man, the greatest thing we can DO with our lives is pray that God will give this grace to every human being. After all, what good is it if we give all kinds of material goods to our neighbor and they still lose their souls?

This sense of dying was not on the level of the phenomenal self, but on the deepest unitive level of "being" or "life." I have never tried to articulate this particular sense of dying because it is such a mystery I doubt that other people could grasp it even if I could articulate it. This experience can be understood only against the background of many years spent in the unitive state, which is a life not lived for the self but solely for God and the good of others. These are years of such egoless living and giving that we seem to lose the habit of considering ourselves at all; we are no longer mindful of having any experience of life to call our own. Thus when we suddenly try to have a concern for our self it will not work. It has become impossible; there is no self there anymore to BE concerned. It is as if the deepest sense of self had just gradually faded away before we knew it was gone. All that is left of us is basically what other people see. Also I noticed that at times when a situation arose that would have evoked some spontaneous interior response—an energy or feeling—there would be no such movement at all, no response forthcoming. It seems that after years of literally giving ourselves away, retaining nothing and not protecting ourselves, we come to a point where life can go right on without all those responses of the phenomenal self.

At first I was not sure if this were a backward or forward movement, but on one occasion I had a glimpse of how it worked. The divine flame was gradually consuming the self from the center outward, and with every major selfless act, a chunk of the deepest unknown self would fall away and disappear into this flame. Self then is not phased out from the outside-in, but rather from the inside-out. It is not the phenomenal or superficial self that diminishes but the deepest unknown self, and this gradual diminishing is solely a divine doing. We cannot bring this about ourselves; we cannot diminish a self we do not even know, or a self to which we have no access. To help account for this we might recall that when we entered the marketplace our life became out-going and no longer in-going. Having come to the unitive state there is no need to be concerned about our interior life, as God is an automatic given—the first given. And with God we have no need to be concerned for ourselves. Thus after years of no concern for self we find that life goes on much the same without any sense of self.

So by the end of this stage (which I did not know at the time was a stage), I knew that the whole self-experience was dying and fading away. But how life could go on without it I had no idea. Having come so far in the journey, however, and having trusted God through thick and thin for forty years, there was nothing left that could shake or move an unquestioned trust. As I see it, self is literally worn out in the living of it. Eventually the constant flow of life's problems and crises become like water on a duck's back, so that finally life can go on without all those usual responses of self, or without any response of self at all. But if we have not first experienced or lived all these responses, then of course we cannot live without them. We cannot go beyond anything we have not experienced or known in the first place. But when life's problems become nothing but sheer repetition, they no longer provide the slightest challenge, in which case it is time for the journey to move on.

The self that is dying is "that" mystery which only the divine flame can consume, a mystery not even accessible to the conscious self. I saw no way of holding this flame back, but I also had no idea what would happen if it went forward and consumed all. One lesson learned many times over was that what God intended to do, he would do; I had no say whatsoever. Although this knowledge was disconcerting, it was also a fact of life that I had to come to terms with even as a child. The mysterious experience of dying was actually a premonition or foreknowledge of something tremendous down the road: a life wherein there is no awareness or experience of self—be it the true self, an unknown self, a phenomenal self, or even a Christ self. No one can imagine such a condition ahead of time because that which imagines such a condition is self.

V
Falling Away of Union: No-Self

At the end of the marketplace stage the situation was this: there was experiential knowledge that the unitive flame was the oneness not of myself and God but of Christ and the Father, and that the overwhelming love between Christ and Father was not my love, but the Holy Spirit. Seeing it was not I who loved God (which love was beyond me anyway) or I who was one with God, obviously I was totally out of the picture; there is no place in the Trinity for me. Though I already knew the phenomenal self was dispensable, the question was, "How, without my own awareness of the divine, could there possibly be any awareness or experience of the divine?" In other words, if I should cease to exist, who or what would remain to be aware of God? While I knew God did not depend upon my awareness, I could not imagine any life without any awareness of life.

This mystery reminded me of the dilemma I had at fifteen when I saw the identity of God immanent and transcendent and that I was nothing to this identity—that I was dispensable in other words. The major difference was that at the beginning of the journey this was an upsetting insight: not to count or be included in the Godhead struck me as terrible beyond words. Now, however, the situation was almost the reverse: that I would no longer be counted was good news. The dilemma or mystery, however, was how there could be any awareness of God if there were no one left to be aware of God? Furthermore, if there is no awareness of self or God then how can there be awareness of anything at all? I did not see how one could get around in the world with no awareness. Despite the inability to imagine any life beyond self, years of living with God had not been for nothing. Right here I felt my entire life with God had finally been brought to bear on this single point or fine line between self and no-self. To flinch would have been a lack of trust and love; it could only be a movement toward self. If trust is perfect, however, there is no movement, and in this stillness our existence hangs in the balance. To exist or not to exist, the choice is not ours.

This situation brought me to what I call the "fine line," which is a line between the divine and the last vestige of self-awareness which, in the unitive state, is equally awareness of the divine. Never before had I been aware of this fine line or had any knowledge of its existence; the possibility of a permanent falling away of self--awareness this side of the grave is not in the books. Nor can anyone know ahead of time what lies beyond this line because the line is the boundary of consciousness beyond which consciousness cannot go. For this reason consciousness is incapable of imagining life beyond its own existence or non-existence, nor can consciousness of its own accord pass over the line or put an end to itself. Only the divine can do away with the human boundaries; man has no say whatsoever.

The moment the line dissolves is unknown; it happens in great stillness and is not an experience. No event could be less spectacular or more momentous. In the strict sense this event is not a milestone of the journey; instead, it is the true end or ending of the journey. The events beyond this line are not meant for this world and have nothing to do with it; no-self or no-consciousness is not the true human condition, nor is the dimension beyond self comparable to the unitive state. What characterizes the unitive state is the love, charity and compassion of egoless giving and living, but what characterizes the no-self condition is knowledge of ultimate Truth as it lies beyond all self; this is its sole purpose, revelation and concern.

If, following this event, the particular destiny is not to remain in this world, then man dies and moves directly to his ultimate destiny. But if one is destined to remain in this world, the senses must go through the ordeal of staying awake to this world without self or consciousness. Few people realize what a difficult feat it is for the senses to stay awake without consciousness or without the experience of a functioning mind and experience of self. This is a choiceless feat, a happening beyond the efforts and choice of any consciousness or self. For this reason the dimension beyond self has about it the air of the miraculous. But the dissolution of the fine line (self-awareness), or the suspension of the reflexive mechanism of the mind, is only the first of two steps in the no-self experience. Another step is needed if the condition is to become permanent. Initially the suspension of the reflexive mechanism of the mind is similar to ecstasy, which is a temporary suspension of the entire self-experience. But ecstasy is not a permanent state; it is purely relative to the self-experience, and thus as a relative experience there is always a return to the former condition. This means that for the no-self condition to become permanent, a more definitive ending is required, another step which, paradoxically, is also the ending of the ecstatic state. (Once the ecstatic state becomes permanent there is no longer the possibility or potential for ecstasy.) But here is the second step.

About a week after the line dissolved, when the mind deliberately tried to look within, instantly the divine Center (the living flame) quietly exploded and vanished. The sensation was a sudden "drop." After this it is never again possible to look within; not only will the mind no longer function in this reflexive manner, but without a Center there is no "within" anymore. And without a "within" there is no vessel to experience any emptiness; simply put, there is nothing left to BE empty. It should be remembered that the divine Center was the experience of "life," "being," "existence" which, in the unitive state, is equally the experience of our own existence and God's existence. Without this unitive Center there is no experience of life, being or existence, nor any of the movements and feelings to which this Center gives rise. Obviously this Center had only been the unconscious "Self" responsible for all experiences of interiority— the whole psyche and its spiritual life—along with its various experiences of energy, emotions, feelings and so on. From now on the eyes (sensory eyes) can look only outward because without consciousness there is no ability to look inward anymore. Without consciousness there are no interior experiences, divine or phenomenal, no within or without—no psychic life at all. It is all over, finished.

The divine and self fall away as one because they are one in experience. Without the divine there can be no self; without self there can be no divine to be one with self. Some people have the notion that after self falls away, self is suddenly discovered to be divine or that some different divine self appears. Either everything we can call "self" including a "divine self" falls away or it does not; it cannot exist and not exist at the same time. (If, however, we think self is divine, all the more reason to understand the falling away of self as the death of God.) But on the other side of the line there is no self, no one and nothing left to BE divine. The divine is not self, has no self, and is not even aware of itself; the divine is beyond all man calls "awareness" or "consciousness." Divine knowing is something else entirely; it cannot be known or grasped by a mind, and it is not an experience.

Prior to coming to the fine line, I already knew that it was not I who was one with God; rather, it was Christ alone who was one with God. Thus the falling away of the unitive experience and awareness of oneness was not "my" death, but Christ's death—the death of God. In other words, Jesus' awareness of the Father IS self or consciousness' experience of God, but the Trinitarian mystery of the divine is beyond this, a mystery in which the divine is not even aware of itself. So although Christ's death is the death of self or consciousness along with its awareness of oneness with the Father, beyond this purely human experience of oneness lies the divine Christ and the Trinitarian Oneness. Thus Christ reveals two types of oneness: that of man with God and the divine Oneness of the Trinity. The difference is that in the case of humanity God is seen by way of self or consciousness, whereas in the divinity there is no self or consciousness to BE God. God is ultimately beyond our notions and experiences of union and identity.

VI
Resurrection

Initially life with the senses-only is spectacular and indescribable; it might be compared to seeing the universe in ecstasy. Everything glows with the brilliance and marvel of God; everything gives way to this indescribable divine. Though the sensory eyes see what everyone normally sees, the eye that beholds this vision is not of the senses, mind or consciousness; rather, this "eye" was over the top of my head and outside the body completely. As a child I once saw a picture of Pentecost where, over the heads of the apostles, there stood a brilliant little flame. This picture is an accurate description of this present phenomenon. This type of seeing lasted for a full nine months when, abruptly, one day the light over the head disappeared. The picture now, was of a dead, lifeless, almost stony universe, virtually a universe void of God. To this point in my life I had never made a judgment one way or the other regarding the existence of hell. As a child I figured that since I could not possibly exist without God, then God would have to be with me even in hell. At the time, this did not strike me as too bad. But here now, in this void of voids, I knew first hand that a condition does indeed exist that matches our notions of "hell" as a possible human predicament, one totally void of the divine. Where the night of the spirit had only been a purgatory, a virtual burning out of the self-center (ego) with the feeling of being empty or void of God, this present void of voids is of a different nature altogether. Purgatory is a self-experience, a drama that takes place within self or consciousness, whereas the void of voids is without self and beyond any and all consciousness. There is no way self or consciousness can ever get hold of this void of voids; it has no way of ever experiencing or imagining it. What obviously bears this predicament is just the body and the senses; how they stay alive is a mystery because they, too, are completely void.

This void of voids endured for about four months. There is almost a gradual acclimation to the predicament, in that ordinary life must somehow go on, though its going on is extremely difficult. There is no self here to pick itself up and go on, no self to employ all those efforts and ruses to help itself. There is no self to feel frightened, anxious, or even trusting and hopeful; there is nothing around but a complete void of voids. Naturally I did not know what to make of such a predicament. It did not bring to mind a single comparison or anything I had ever heard of before. Yet one day, while I was out walking, as if from above the trees Christ suddenly came to mind, as it were. Though I really could not "think" or use my mind, I knew without question that Christ had also come upon this same predicament. Despite all his love and trust in the Father, the whole thing had come to nothing; his journey had ended in the void of voids with no Father at all. He had been wrong about it all, just as I had been wrong; yet the fact I had gone all the way with him and come to his same end was strangely comforting. It may be difficult to believe, but here in the void of voids I knew a greater identity with Christ than at any time to this point in my life. An identity, however, of having given all for nothing—absolute nothing. This was nothing to be sad about because there was nothing else we could do. I took no hope from this identity; the void of voids is the end of the line. There is no "beyond" it. If there is anything "beyond," then this is not really "the void of voids."

The day of dawning was so simple as to be unbelievable. The void of voids is absolute because there is nothing beyond it, nothing above it, nothing behind it, and nothing emerging from it. The void of voids is the only thing that exists. It is relative to nothing, and here it dawns—the void of voids IS Absolute; it IS all that exists. Although this may sound like a purely intellectual deduction or conclusion, this is not the way it comes about.

To understand how it comes about, one must understand that without self or consciousness the major question is the true nature of "that" which remains or exists when there is no self or consciousness. The body and senses that remained were void; in fact, the body as experienced by consciousness had long ceased to BE an experience. Part of the acclimation to the no-self condition is getting around without a bodily experience, or experience of a body. But obviously some type of form remained, a form that was as void as all the forms beheld by the senses. The wrong notion of the void of voids is that it means form is void of the divine or empty of the divine; this is false. The void of voids means that form itself IS void or is THE void. Form is not other than the void; it is not something that can be full or empty of anything. It does not emerge from something or give way to something; there is nothing beyond, above or behind it. There is nothing besides it. Form then IS void and this void IS form; there is no distinction possible. If there is any distinction possible, then we have not gone far enough because the void would only be relative to something else or other. The day of dawning was the simple recognition that all form, or the void of voids, that remains beyond all self or consciousness, that form IS Christ. This dawning came about in what I have called a "smile of recognition," which, unfortunately, is not an apt description. There comes a point when anything we say is NOT it, because anything we say fails to convey absolute Truth. Absolute Truth can never be revealed TO someone or to an individual; rather, absolute Truth IS the revealed. So too, Christ is not the revelation of Truth to anyone; Christ IS this Truth—Truth beyond its revelation to others. As absolute Form, Christ existed before there was anyone around, any "who" or self. This knowing or seeing lies on the other side of the void of voids when there is no mind, no consciousness, no self or anyone around to grasp or understand it.

The revelation, then, is that the divine or Trinitarian Christ IS Eternal Form. This Form, however, is not what the ordinary senses see as form, or what the mind knows as form (including Platonic form or an idea in the divine mind), or what consciousness experiences as form. Rather, Eternal Form is concrete, material, physical, the underlying substance of all matter. Without it there would be no universe and no one to see it. So Eternal Form is not apart from what we see, yet it is also not what we see. In order to come upon Eternal Form, all form must first be an absolute void where nothing can possibly be relative to it; it is only from this position that Eternal Form can be revealed. By definition the divine or Absolute is "that" which is non-relative, and the only thing that can be non-relative is a void of voids. This void of voids or absolute nothing IS Christ.

What I inappropriately called the "smile of recognition" is also what I call "the resurrection." This is because it is the recognition of the true nature of the body or "that" which remains beyond all self. The ultimate nature of the body is Eternal Form or Christ; it is the true nature of the divine Manifest or Trinitarian Christ. Form and the Formless, Father and Christ, are one from all eternity. We say God made all things from nothing or that all things arose from the void of voids, but this nothing or void IS Eternal Form or Christ. In other words, whatever we are made of —we do not know its essence, which is forever beyond the scientific mind—IS Christ. The resurrection, then, is the revelation of the true nature of the body, its eternal nature. The body (and all form) is Eternal Form; it is the divine Christ and all that is manifest of the unmanifest Father. The unmanifest void (Father) is not Eternal Form (Christ); at the same time neither are they separate. As One they constitute the eternal Godhead of the Trinity.

As I know it, then, the true nature of Christ's death is the falling away of self or consciousness, followed by the "descent into hell," the void of voids. From this void Christ rises to reveal the divine nature of the body, Eternal Form or mystical body of God. It is not just Christ's single historical body that is revealed, but the ultimate nature of all bodies or form. Eternal Form is the All and Everywhere of the divine, which means we cannot point to any single form and say "There is the divine," or point to any person and say "He or she is the divine," nor can we refer to any experience and say "This is the divine." Even when we point to the historical Christ we cannot point to his divinity, only to his humanity. Consciousness had been responsible for experientially focusing on God or pinpointing the divine as this or that experience or individual. But beyond consciousness God as Eternal Form is Everywhere, neither the singular (he, she or it) nor the multiple (an additive of "all together"), but rather One Absolute Eternal Form. This is Christ, the eternal Form of the Formless.

The truth of the body, then, is the revelation that Christ is all that is manifest of God or all that is manifest of the unmanifest Father. Self or consciousness does not reveal this and cannot know it. In the "smile" there was no knower or one who smiles, nor was there anyone or anything to smile at or to know; there was just the smile, the "knowing" that is beyond knower and known. The wrong interpretation of the absence of knower and known is that in the Godhead knower and known are identical. But the identity of knower and known is only true of consciousness, which is self knowing itself. But the Godhead transcends this identity—it is void of knower or known. The "knowing" that remains beyond self or consciousness cannot be accounted for in any terms of knower or known. The truest thing that could be said is that the "body knows."

After the smile-of-recognition, the void of voids lifted and was never encountered again. By this time it was almost eighteen months after the initial falling away of self. Altogether, however, it took two to three years to finally acclimate to the no-self condition or dimension of living. This acclimation consists of the senses having to stay awake and remain functional without any self or consciousness. The tendency was for the senses to continually fall into the Great Silence—close down or drop out—which would have resulted in death. At one point in particular, this was indeed an imminent possibility. Without consciousness or the senses, all that is left is the vegetative body, which, without man-made (not God-made) support, moves into the divine. For the senses to stay awake without consciousness is so enormously difficult that I know without doubt that this resurrected condition is not meant for this world. The resurrected state is not the true human condition, nor is it man's final estate. While the unitive state is indeed man's true mature state in this world, the no-self condition is not compatible or even integrable with the human condition. That which was integrable—self or consciousness—is gone. The resurrected condition is incapable of true involvement in this world; as said before, its sole purpose is to affirm ultimate Truth. In Christ's case the resurrection revealed Truth, but for those who follow, the resurrection affirms Christ's Truth—a Truth that every human being will come upon some day.

About six months after the above events, I wrote *The Experience of No-Self* and basically considered the journey finished. At this point it never occurred to me that there was more down the road or that there was yet more to Christ's revelation. But after another year or so—perhaps three or four years after the falling away of self—there occurred a further disclosure of Christ.

VII
Ascension

After communion one morning the body seemingly began to inhale (though it did not come from the outside) what I can only describe as a type of odorless anesthetic (reminiscent of ether) that instantly spread from the lungs to the entire body. It was as if every atom or cell of the body had given way or was disclosed as a kind of elemental gas or "divine air." While there is no possible description for this divine air, it would not be entirely improper (based on the experience alone) to affirm that "God is a gas." It was as if every cell or element of which the body was composed WAS this "divine air," and that every element of the body dwelled in this indescribably divine and glorious state of existence. It was as if the body had dissolved into this "divine air," or better put, that the true body (Eternal Form or Christ's mystical body) dwelled eternally in this glorious divine estate. A few seconds into this phenomenon of the body dissolving into "divine air," there was instant recognition of the ascension experience. No mind, intellect or self is needed for this recognition; all that is needed is a physical body. We might compare this knowing to the mysterious "wisdom of the body" that we take so lightly throughout our lives, a wisdom beyond all self or consciousness. This condition, however, is incompatible with continued sensory existence or bodily functioning. Like an anesthetic, it closes down the senses; at one point the air became so heavy and condensed that continued breathing was all but impossible. If, at this moment, the air had not thinned, there would be no body remaining to give this account.

As for a description of this "divine air" no word enters the mind; it simply puts an end to the mind. About all that can be said is that if we put together man's loftiest experiences of ecstasy, bliss, love and all things ineffable, they fall as short of the divine condition as the size of an ant falls short of that of an elephant. Consciousness' most lofty heavenly experiences of the divine are but a palest shadow of the ultimate divine condition or "heaven." While I do not like calling this heavenly estate a "condition," I do so to differentiate it from a passing state or stage as well as from "experience," which is always and everywhere a temporary non-eternal phenomenon. The final estate has no description because it never reaches the mind—"eye hath not seen nor the ear heard, nor has it ever entered into the mind of man".....heaven or "the kingdom of God is not of this world."

Because consciousness or the mind cannot form any notion of the ascension, I wish to make clear that this particular experience is not a dissolving or disappearance of the body; it is not an out-of-the-body experience or the experience of a soul leaving the body. It was not an experience of bodilessness or the discovery of some other body and so on. Rather, it is the clear disclosure that the unknown substance of the physical body (Eternal Form or Christ's mystical body) dwells in a divine (heavenly or glorious) condition, which condition IS the unmanifest divine or Father. Thus where the resurrection reveals Christ as Eternal Form, the ascension reveals the unmanifest or Formless Father as the glorious condition in which Eternal Form dwells or exists. In itself a heavenly condition cannot be manifest, concretized or materialized; for this reason it always remains unmanifest. But the unmanifest is not all there IS to the divine; rather the unmanifest is eternally one with the manifest, which is why we say Christ is all that is manifest of the unmanifest. Too often we think that Christ was only "manifest" at the time of the incarnation, but the incarnation was only the revelation of the manifest divine. The divine manifest Christ is from all eternity; the incarnation was only the revelation of this Truth to man.

The historical Christ never verbalized this great Truth (which nobody would have understood anyway), but silently demonstrated it with his resurrection and ascension. As we know, Christ's body dissolved into air, became invisible to the mind and senses, but what is this "air" into which Christ disappeared? This "air" is not only Christ's Eternal Form but the unmanifest condition (the Father) in which this Form eternally dwells. Like the resurrection the ascension reveals the inseparability of spirit and matter, the Formless and Form, which means that what man or consciousness does not know about spirit IS matter, and what he does not know about matter IS spirit; one is the mystery of the other.

This ascension experience was not a mere passing glimpse of truth. For about six weeks the divine air varied in intensity just enough to allow a minimum of mundane existence. On one occasion, at a point of highest intensity, it seemed that the senses were going to permanently "drop" away—the expression "drop" describes a particular physical sensation that accompanied the falling away of consciousness and will accompany the eventual falling away of the senses. I can only compare this situation to having both feet in heaven, but without the door of earthly existence permanently closing behind us. After this there was a gradually lessening of the "divine air" and the senses slowly came back to their more ordinary functioning—their functioning in the resurrected condition, that is.

VIII
Incarnation

The next disclosure followed as a result of the ascension experience. With the lessening of the "divine air" (the unmanifest's divine condition) there was a gradual return to the former resurrected state. This return was a reversal of the ascension experience. Where the ascension had been a dissolution into the divine, here now, there was a coming out of the divine and a re-adjustment to full sensory perception (staying wide awake to the world, that is) which took between six and nine months. This was actually the second time there had to be an acclimation to the resurrected state; only this time, from a different side of the resurrection. Where the first adjustment followed the falling away of self, the second adjustment is the return from the ascension with its near falling away of the senses. Anything I can say about this return or adjustment is but a shadow of its reality; let me just say that it was so difficult and terrible that, in comparison, the void of voids was easy going.

Having to leave the divine condition and come back to the sensory or resurrected state can only be described as GOD-AW-FUL; it is an inhuman predicament, even an inhuman feat. This is more, however, than just a return to a previous state; it was a waking up to a sensory terrain and human condition that, compared to the divine condition, could only be described as "hell." (It was not even a living hell because none of it was seen as true life.) In contrast to the divine, the human condition is so terrible and devastating that even the worst of descriptions could never do it justice. I am not referring here to sin, evil or suffering, but rather to bare human existence itself—and the whole natural world included. What we usually think is so beautiful in this world is actually monstrous and unbearable to look at, but only in contrast to the divine.

Compared to this ordeal of entering the human condition, all our notions and experiences of suffering are as nothing. It was as if the divine were undergoing a terrible ordeal trying to stay awake to this world without falling back into the divine condition—because this world was so ugly and void. Again it was as if the divine were going against itself and its own nature because of its determined will to be in this world as a human being. Despite this terrible predicament, there was about this acclimation a knowledge that a mysterious divine feat was taking place. At one point I understood that this reversal of the ascension experience was not like any other return; rather, this coming down or out of the divine was akin to the "incarnation experience."

No one can understand this particular view of the world and the human condition unless he has first known the ultimate divine estate (heaven) and then returned (or originally come out of it as in the case of the incarnate Christ) to this world's condition. Those who believe man can have both heaven and this world at the same time are very much mistaken; such a notion is a total underestimation of God's utter transcendence, as well as heaven or man's final estate. Compared to the divine estate there is no beauty or happiness in this world; thus man cannot afford to have a glimpse or taste of the final estate and still expect to find this world acceptable. The ultimate estate is not of this world; it is not even compatible with it—which is why there is death. For this reason it is good that man does not see the reality of the divine beyond consciousness, for if he did he could not endure this world. What man does not know, he does not miss, and what he does not know is how utterly transcendent the divine really is. Thus man can settle for the world and the divine he knows, because this is all he knows. This is the way things were made to be. God fashioned consciousness, which is why it has no place else to go, or comes to no other end than in the divine.

Where full acclimation to the resurrected state had been difficult, after the ascension it seemed impossible. Until this point the journey had been an irreversible forward movement, but here the movement had reversed itself. Thus for God to take on consciousness it was necessary to forfeit the ultimate beatific condition, since to dwell in both conditions (beatific and human) at the same time is impossible. In moving from the divine to the human condition, Christ had to undergo the GOD-AWFUL forfeiture of the ultimate divine condition in order to take on consciousness directly from the divine condition. Man never goes through this GOD-AWFUL experience when coming into this world. Man comes from the manifest, the void of voids or out of darkness, whereas the incarnate Christ came from the unmanifest (divine heavenly condition) or out of Light and into our darkness.

So the movement of the incarnation is this: Christ moves down from the ultimate divine condition into the ascension experience; from here he moves down to the resurrected condition (sensory); and from here he moves further down into consciousness and into the unitive or egoless state in which he was born. Thus Christ came down the way man goes up; they are reverse passages. At his birth, however, Christ begins his return home, and in the return takes all men with him. We generally think of the revelation of Truth as a marvelous thing, but what no one realizes is that ultimate Truth is basically unbearable to man—to the senses, the mind, consciousness, the whole body in fact. In the end the fullness of Truth is virtually the death of man. Solely on an intellectual level, when man comes upon this Truth he usually takes it for an error. He does so out of ignorance because final Truth is unbelievable. This is why naked faith is the only way to make the passage.

Although the incarnation experience is devastating in its GOD-AWFULNESS, nowhere else in the journey is the Reality and Truth of Christ more obvious or absolute than in this ordeal. It should be remembered, however, this world is only GOD-AWFUL for someone who is not of this world or who is coming into this world directly from the divine condition. It is the sheer contrast between the divine condition and the purely sensory or resurrected state that is responsible for the GOD-AWFULNESS of the incarnation experience. No human being could ever see the world or human existence this way; in fact, even God does not ordinarily see it this way. It is only in the incarnation when the divine takes on the human condition and has to forego or preclude the divine condition that the divine undergoes such a terrible ordeal. For this reason I regard the incarnation as Christ's true "saving" act; compared to this his death is a blessed release, a glorious ascent back to his divine condition.

Altogether it took about nine months to fully acclimate once again to the resurrected condition. But after the experience of ascension and incarnation, the resurrected state was altered; it was not the same as before. The only way it is the same is that it is livable, and for all practical purposes this is probably all that matters. It is different because, having come upon the final divine estate, there can never again be any real acclimation to this world. By itself the resurrected state is enough to preclude this possibility, but after the ascension it is forever impossible. All that is left now is the Eucharist; everything else is sheer burden. While I regard the initial no-self condition as the resurrected state, after the ascension and incarnation, what remains is only the "Eucharistic state." Eucharist is the final word on Christ.

In the End

As someone who began the journey as a child not honestly able to believe that Christ was God, this journey went beyond anything I ever thought possible—and not only for myself, but above all for Christ. I never suspected the extent of his mystery or Truth. Evidently this Truth had to be learned the hard way because I was never able to believe in the same manner that many other people are privileged to believe. The one thing I can say, however, is that everything I know of Christ is solely through living experience. It did not come by way of intellectual belief, concepts, symbols, or passing insights. Although it was a very prolonged and difficult journey, it was all within ordinary daily living and not due to any extraordinary circumstance, opportunity or position in life. What was extraordinary was not the person or the life, but the grace; it more than stretched the human limits.

But what was this journey all about? Well, I only have one view of it, the only view I can really have—it was a gradual revelation of the truth of Christ. The revelation of God, the divine or Absolute, never provided the challenge or mystery that kept the journey going; if my only concern had been the experience of the Absolute, the journey could have been over before it had begun. But Christ is a further revelation of the Absolute, a revelation that challenges us to penetrate not only the nature of the Absolute, but our human nature as well. Although every Christian is on a journey, as to why there are different journeys within a single tradition I can only say that it may have to do with different levels of belief or faith. Though I did not start from disbelief or a refusal to believe, I had to start from no-belief or the inability to believe, and perhaps this was why my journey was so difficult. Christ said, "Blessed are those who believe and do not see." Obviously I was not one of those so blessed. Yet even without believing I did eventually see. And what this means to me is that in the end, whether man believes in Christ or not, he WILL SEE. This I know absolutely.

After the seeing or realization I call the resurrection, for a moment there crossed my mind that after a lifetime of "becoming" a Christian, now at last I had finally become one. But the thought no sooner came than it went, because now there was no one left to BE a Christian. For a moment this was as bewildering as having a hard won ribbon snatched away. But suddenly there was Christ—who was never a Christian! As the divine underlying everyone's reality, Christ belongs to no one, not even to himself. In the end, then, there is just Christ, and no one to be a Christian.

APPENDIX I
HOW IS CHRIST DIFFERENT FROM OURSELVES OR ONE OF A KIND AMONG MEN?

Introduction

Intellect alone cannot prove the existence of God or the Absolute, and neither can it prove the divinity of Christ. For most people, however, the intuition of an ultimate Absolute is not a problem, while belief that Christ IS the Absolute is not such an easy intuition, and for some it is a problem. Belief that Christ was a holy man who attained mystical awareness of oneness with God is not a problem, but then it is also not the truth of Christ. The question Christ poses is how the one eternal Absolute could possibly incarnate itself as a human being. The question of whether or not it has happened is secondary to its very possibility. Although the problem of God is equally the problem of Christ, Christ extends the problem by raising the question of what the Absolute can or cannot do. That the Absolute can incarnate itself confronts us with a step in belief that may never satisfy the intellect or lend itself to simple intuition. But this possibility is the mystery of Christ, a mystery that not only boggles the mind, but may even bother it.

Though faced with this dilemma from my earliest years, I was nevertheless able to go forward with the Christian contemplative journey. What made this possible, however, was the Eucharistic Christ, not the biblical personality of the historical Jesus. Because of the Eucharist I knew there was more to the mystery of the incarnate Christ than the passing historical figure.[9] To the end of the journey, however, the incarnation remained problematic, a question mark in my mind—sometimes, even, a thorn in my side. When the journey was completed, however, this problem dissolved; finally it was possible to see how it all worked. It is one thing,

---

[9]The difference between the purely historical Christ and the incarnate Christ reminds me of the difference between Peter and Paul. Where Peter had walked and talked with Christ, Paul, having heard of Christ solely by hearsay, set out to persecute those who believed in him. Paul's eventual first hand encounter with Christ was on a different plane than that of Peter, a plane beyond that of the purely historical figure and personality. Hearing the gospel stories obviously did not bring about Paul's conversion or convince him of anything.

however, to convey Truth in simple statements, but quite another to articulate "how it works." Where simple statements of Truth leave everyone to his own private perspective or way of seeing, describing "how it works" is a hazardous employment because it rarely matches or satisfies other people's perspective and way of seeing. For this reason any description of "how it works"—the incarnation that is—may be met with little agreement and much criticism. So why try to say anything?

There are two reasons. First, I know I am not the only one who has had a problem with the incarnate Christ; thus my desire to be of help to others represents the help I would like to have received. Whether anything I can say will help or not, this at least is the intention. Second, I never had the impression that the spiritual journey was made solely for myself. From the beginning, the major insights, graces and breakthroughs were quite beyond "me" and anything going on in my private life; in fact, "who" I was never seemed to be of concern to God. The journey, then, was not a "private affair" between "me" and God nor was it ever separate from the journey of other human beings. Since nothing in life is more important than our life with God, it is difficult to understand any reticence in talking about this fact or in describing the help we received and what we learned for having made the journey. For these reasons there is no reluctance on my part to address the present subject or to write about any aspect of this journey with God and to God.

Two Sides of the Incarnation

Although it is true that we cannot prove Christ's divinity, it occurred to me that there may be another way of pointing up the divinity of Christ. Instead of questioning how the human Christ could also be God, we might question, instead, why man is not also God, or question how it is that the incarnate Christ is different from ourselves. We do not ask this question because we think we are God, but because we question why only the incarnate Christ is God. Thus the question "How is Christ different than ourselves?" is the same question as "How is the incarnate Christ God?" But it is from the other side of the coin, as it were. Where one side affirms Christ's equality as God, the other side affirms his equality as man. But where we are asked to consider only our human equality with Christ, we are never asked to consider any divine equality with Christ. For this reason we usually consider only one side of the coin and ignore the other side. But to ignore either side fails to take in the whole of Christ and his revelation. Our question, therefore, has to do with the divine side of the coin; instead of asking how only the incarnate Christ is divine, we ask how man is not also divine. It goes without saying that the question of human divinity does not refer to any personal self or individual me, myself or I, or to any purely passing historical personality; the question goes beyond this to the ultimate nature of man or the clay out of which he was made, so to speak. How, then, is it that everyman is not like Christ or is not an incarnation of the divine?

On this level the question of the incarnate Christ is equally a question of the ultimate nature of our humanity, our existential link to God and our ultimate destiny. As we know, Christ's revelation had two sides: one, the revelation of the Trinitarian nature of God; the other, the true nature of man. In bridging the gap or void between the two, Christ's divine nature and human nature come together. If there is any problem with this, it is that the dichotomy between Christ as God *before* his incarnation and Christ as the man-God *after* his incarnation is a dichotomy we do not keep in balance. Thus we rarely give consideration to the Trinitarian nature of Christ before his incarnation. No doubt this is because, prior to the incarnation, we did not know the Trinitarian nature of God and therefore did not know any Christ. But this is why our view of Christ cannot seem to get past the incarnation or Christ's humanity —and consequently our own. Yet the fact that we can only consider the Trinity in terms of the human incarnate Christ does not give us the full story on the Trinity or on the divine Christ before the incarnation. If Christ were just another name for God (or the name we give God in human experience), or if Christ were just the human ideal of a God-realized man, understanding Christ would be easy. But as it stands, this is not the way it goes; the Christian belief is that the incarnate Christ had two distinct natures. As the one God, Christ is the sole human incarnation of God and God's definitive revelation to all men. Nothing short of this can rightly be called "Christ," "Christian" or "Christianity." The marvel of this, perhaps, is that there are any believers at all.

For the most part we tend to take for granted that while the divine nature is incomprehensible, human nature is somehow comprehensible or easily known. While I hold that the essence of man IS self or consciousness, man, however, consists of more than consciousness. Thus man is made up of the senses, the vegetative body, the elements, atoms, and after this? Nothing? If man came from nothing, then it follows that Christ's humanity also came from nothing, and how it is possible to get the divine and nothing together in an eternal hypostatic union (Christ) boggles the mind.

It boggles the mind because the mind is incapable of getting hold of "nothing"; it is impossible. And this impossibility brings us full circle, back to the impossibility of getting hold of the divine nature.

It seems that we can no more get hold of man's true nature than we can get hold of the divine's true nature. Beyond our intellects and consciousness, the divine is nothing to the mind and this same nothing is also man's beginning. Man does not know or understand his beginning anymore than he knows or understands God's non-beginning; in this, at least, they are alike. Man's origin from nothing leaves him no choice but to consider his beginnings from a purely scientific view; while the divine, of course, must only be considered from a non-scientific view. But this unbridgeable dichotomy does not address itself too well to the incarnation where a non-material divine becomes wholly one and inseparable with a wholly material human being—man and the material universe. Obviously the incarnation is telling us something—or rather revealing something. Its revelation is that the material and non-material are inseparably one, and that the true nature of this inseparability IS Christ. If we truly knew Christ, then, we could penetrate this mystery of inseparable oneness of spirit and matter, God and man. And if God can be inseparably one with a single human being, then God can be inseparably one with all human beings. As said initially, the question that the incarnation actually happened is secondary to its very possibility. What is not possible can never happen, but when something happens then we know it is possible. Thus the very fact that God COULD become man is an explosive revelation in its own right—and basically beyond the purely historical Christ who revealed this fact.

The incarnation reveals that some unknowable bridge exists between God and man, spirit and matter, the created and uncreated, and that the true nature of this bridge is everything we call "Christ." Prior to the incarnation we knew nothing about such a bridge; thus, for example, in Hinduism this world is an illusion or dream in the mind of the unmanifest Brahman; there is no bridge. In Judaism the divine is totally separate from man and the universe; so here, too, there is no bridge. The notion of a bridge is that of bringing together or uniting two otherwise separate dimensions of existence —the created and Uncreated. It does not mean that one side is the other side or that one dimension IS the other—in which case there would be no bridge. It does not mean the human dimension is the divine dimension or that the created "becomes" the Uncreated or that man "becomes" divine; rather, it means that so long as the created exists, in some mysterious way it is inseparable from the

Uncreated. To discover this mysterious link or bridge between God and man, spirit and matter, created and uncreated is the discovery of the true nature of the divine Christ.

Before going further I wish to make a clear distinction between what I call the ultimate nature of man and the essence of man or what makes man unique in the universe. The essence of the human dimension or human nature is self or consciousness, a purely created function over and beyond that of the senses, the purely vegetative body and so on. To know our own essence or human nature is to know ourselves. The deepest dimension of this self-knowledge, however, is not only to know that we (self or consciousness) are one with the divine, but this knowledge is also our deepest experience of life and being. Thus we cannot apprehend our own deepest experience of life and being without also apprehending the divine. But take away created consciousness or self and all its experiences, and then take away the senses and the physical body it knows, and now what is man? Is there anything left? Whatever is left is what I call the ultimate nature of man (not human nature) or "that" from which man was created in the first place; "that" of course is the divine Christ. Man did not arise from the unmanifest Godhead, but from the eternal manifest Godhead or Christ. Although man and the universe did not exist from all eternity, their eventual creation is not separable from the manifest divine or Christ; it would be impossible. As I see it, this good news IS the revelation of the incarnate Christ. This revelation not only reveals the Trinitarian nature of God (the manifest, unmanifest and their manifesting as One), but reveals the existential link between God and man as well as man's ultimate destiny. So the question posed by the manifest divine (Christ) is not how the divine could take on created consciousness or the impermanent human dimension, but how is it that every human being is not also an incarnation of the divine Christ? In other words, in what way was the incarnate Christ different from any other human being? How is the incarnate Christ one of a kind?

Any easy answer to this question means that we have not really grasped the question or the perspective from which it is being asked. This is not a question of Christ's divinity or the question of his humanity, but rather the question of the divine's sole singular incarnation in this world or among men. As said before, even if we were to see how this works or how the incarnate Christ is different from ourselves (all human beings, that is), this is not easy to convey in a way understandable to others. This is because the ordinary mind does not have a true or adequate perspective on the divine

Christ in the first place. And if we do not have the right perspective or understanding of the divine Christ, we are not in the right position to understand the difference between our own coming into this world and Christ's coming into this world. Nor can we understand the difference inherent in our human lack of the unmanifest or Trinitarian nature and the fullness of the incarnate Christ's Trinitarian nature. Since Christ's divine nature is the link between the unmanifest and all that could possibly be created, the divine side of the incarnate Christ is inseparable from the whole Trinity or Godhead. But the human side, or strictly our own human nature, goes no further than its link to the manifest divine—Christ. We are not the incarnation of the whole Trinity or Godhead; rather, we are only the incarnations of Christ.

We might visualize the difference this way. The Trinity or Godhead is a circle with the unmanifest on the inside and Christ, the line that forms the circle. Everything created comes from this line or manifest divine; nothing created has access to the unmanifest except the manifest divine. It is through the manifest that we eventually have this access. Again, if Christ is the uncreated clay or dust from which we are made, nothing made from this has access to the unmanifest; only the uncreated clay or dust has, or is, this access. Thus if we take away the created, the Uncreated divine Christ remains.

Obviously any analogy of the divine and "how it works" must, of necessity, fall short of its Reality. I would like to offer, instead, a few simply statements to articulate an insight into the incarnate Christ. Though the following insights may appear to be pure speculation, such was not their origin. While it seems that I begin with the usual Christian assumptions regarding Christ, it should be understood that these assumptions were not my beginning. Anything I know or learned of Christ derives from the end of the journey, not from the beginning.

THREE DISTINCTIONS

Regarding Christ's uniqueness among men, I offer the following three distinctions:

I. Where the uncreated divine Christ is the eternal Godhead or Trinity, man is *once removed* from the Godhead.

II. As the incarnate or historical man, Christ entered human existence by a *reverse process* than that of other men.

III.   The incarnate Christ *manifested* what man can only experience.

ONCE REMOVED

In simple terms "once removed" means that the wholly divine Christ as eternal Godhead is *all* that is manifest of the unmanifest Godhead; while we (man and the universe) are, in turn, the manifestations of the eternally manifest Christ. In other words, Christ is the eternal manifestation of the unmanifest Godhead; while we are manifestations of the eternally manifest Christ. Thus man is "once removed" from the manifest Godhead (Christ), whereas Christ IS the sole manifestation of the unmanifest Godhead.

Here are several ways of speaking of "once removed:"

1.   Man is once removed from the eternal manifest (Christ) in that man is an incarnation of Christ; man is NOT the incarnation of the unmanifest Godhead. Man is once removed because he is a manifestation of the already manifest Christ.

2. If we think of the manifest Godhead as "once removed" from the unmanifest Godhead, then man would be "twice removed" from the unmanifest Godhead. While I do not regard the eternal manifest as "once removed" from the unmanifest, yet if we think of it this way then we would have to say that man is "once removed" from the manifest, and "twice removed" from the unmanifest.

3. In terms of the Trinitarian nature we can say that the Father is the unmanifest, the Son is the eternal manifest, and the Holy Spirit is the manifesting creative power of the Godhead. There is no time when the unmanifest stands alone and then decides to manifest itself. The manifest Son or Godhead is eternal; it has always existed, and thus there was no time when the unmanifest Father brought forth an eternal manifest Son. But there was a time when the unmanifest Father, manifest Son, and manifesting Spirit (the Trinity) brought forth the universe and man—and the incarnate Christ. Man and the universe are not eternal; they have not always existed.

4. Regarding the incarnation, on his divine side Christ is the eternal manifest; on his human side Christ is similar to ourselves— that is, "once removed" or the incarnation of the already eternal manifest or Christ. Thus where we are Christ's incarnations, Christ is his own incarnation. Where we are manifestations of the eternal Christ, only the incarnate Christ is his own manifestation.

5. Since man was fashioned from the eternal manifest Christ, this means no man can come upon the unmanifest unless he first comes

upon the manifest divine—which is Christ's meaning, "No man comes to the Father but by me." It is only when man returns to the manifest divine (Christ) that there comes the "knowing" (not a good word) of the true unmanifest divine. Prior to this man can only theorize about an unmanifest divine because the divine revealed to consciousness is obviously the manifest divine.

Man often mistakes his realizations or experiences of the divine for the unmanifest divine. What has obviously touched him, however, is the manifest divine. The reason for this mistake is that the divine "stillpoint" *seems* to be unmoved and unmanifest compared to the continuous movement of self or consciousness. Thus our view or experience of the "stillpoint" as the unmanifest is purely a relative experience. Beyond consciousness, however, what we thought was the unmoved and unmanifest turns out to be the eternal movement of the divine. What this means is that self or consciousness (man's unique medium of knowing and experiencing) never experiences the unmanifest divine; indeed, it would be a contradiction to believe it did because the unmanifest is just that— UNmanifest. It is only beyond consciousness, or upon the return to the manifest divine that the unmanifest is known, or the true Trinitarian nature of the divine is revealed.[10]

In summary, man is "once removed" from the manifest Absolute or Christ. With the dissolution of man—as well as the universe— all that remains is the manifest Absolute or Christ, eternally one with the unmanifest Absolute or Father, and one with the eternal manifesting creating Spirit.

REVERSE PROCESS

1. The first meaning of "reverse process" has specific reference to the historical Christ and his journey from the divine to us (his incarnation) and back again to the divine (his ascension). Christ's coming down into the human condition, or his taking on humanity, was the reverse of his going back to his ultimate divine condition. In other words, the incarnation is the reverse of the ascension.

---

[10]In experience, the unmanifest divine would be no experience. We only experience God because of the manifest divine. Beyond consciousness, however, or without its mediumship, the unmanifest is what I call the "eternal divine condition"—akin to a beatific or experiential state. The eternal manifest or Christ always dwells in this condition of the unmanifest (or Father.)

This does not imply any change in the eternal essence of the manifest, but it does mean the forfeiture of what we might call the divine's "beatific" condition—actually there is no term suitable for the state in which the divine dwells. The most we can say, perhaps, is that whatever this divine condition is, it is incompatible with earthly human existence. If it were not incompatible, there would be no reason for death, and if death is not a gain for man, it is his loss. The whole problem with the human condition is the fact that it is *not* in the ultimate divine condition; we make our human journey or passage through consciousness in order to come, eventually, to this ultimate divine condition.

In order to become human Christ had to forfeit or move out of his divine "beatific" condition, which movement or event was the true nature of his incarnation. Thus we say that Christ put off this divine (beatific) condition, but did not put off his divine essence or divinity. (Again, there is a problem with any term used to describe the state in which the divine dwells. Terms like "heavenly" or "beatific" could mean any exalted human experience. The best I can do is refer to this as the "ultimate divine condition," meaning it is the very condition of the unmanifest divine. Christ put off this divine condition in order to enter the human condition.)

The ascension experience was the opposite or reverse of the incarnation experience. Here Christ leaves behind his human condition and returns to his former ultimate divine condition. This means that the essence of Christ's humanity as self or consciousness was temporary and impermanent—and so too is our own. At the resurrection Christ was beyond consciousness and yet his body was intact. We refer to this as Christ's "glorified body" to distinguish it from his body before he died. The way consciousness knows and experiences the body is totally different from the Reality of the body without consciousness. Indeed it is this Reality of the body as Eternal Form that IS the revelation of the resurrection. Although we may define man as consciousness, it is obvious that man is *more* than consciousness, more than anything we can truly define.

2. A second meaning of "reverse process" refers to the difference between Christ and ourselves. Quite simply it means that Christ came down where man goes up, or where Christ began his descent from the divine, we end our ascent to the divine. Or again, it means that the point at which man ends his human journey is the same point at which Christ begins his human journey. Thus we can say that our ending is Christ's beginning.

For a moment let us take a look at our human journey. We begin (at birth) in darkness and unknowing; gradually we wake up to the world and take our place in this limited human field of consciousness and its particular way of knowing and experiencing. At the same time, however, the divine reveals itself to everybody, and those who follow up this revelation (insight, or whatever the variety of experience) will begin to see a new dimension in life, which opening might be compared to the ability to see in the dark. Through the increasing ability to see in the dark, man makes his way back to his origin—to the light, to the divine. The way consciousness sees God is like a match in a dark room—but as the light goes up in the room, the match outgrows its usage and is no longer needed. Consciousness falls away because we do not need a match to see the sun; the moment we look directly at the Sun we are blind to this world. Thus we begin in darkness and end in light; we leave the divine unknowingly and return knowingly—there is a great difference.

To be human Christ had to take on consciousness, which means the incarnation experience was the movement out of the light and into darkness. Unlike our human passage through consciousness, which is the movement from darkness to light, the first movement of Christ toward humanity was the movement from light to darkness. Thus the original movement of Christ's life was the "reverse process" of our own. Where man begins at the bottom of the ladder and goes up, Christ begins at the top and comes down.

No one can imagine the terrible ordeal of the incarnation. In full light and total knowing it was the gradual diminishing of, or pulling away from, the ultimate divine condition—the unmanifest beatific condition that is the Father. (Being "sent by the Father" means leaving the unmanifest Father.) No human being comes this way into the world; as a created being, man never knew the ultimate divine condition. While such may be man's destiny; such was not his original condition. The divine manifest began its descent from a position prior to all consciousness, prior to the senses and prior to this world. As far down as Christ came, however, was unitive or God-consciousness; he did not come down far enough to share with us the egoic dilemma. Although the ego-self need not sin or go contrary to the divine, yet its potential for sin was never in Christ. He did not develop or emerge from darkness or unknowing as we did. But if the absence or emptiness of an ego is one difference between Christ and ourselves (that is, our birth into egoic consciousness and Christ's into unitive consciousness) this is not, however, the ultimate difference.

The event of Christ's incarnation was Christ's true redemptive or salvational act, an act that was a thousand times more horrible than his death.   In fact, Christ's death was a marvelous release from consciousness which began his ascent back to his original divine condition.   Thus the true salvational act was Christ's incarnation or the knowing forfeiture of his divine condition when he took on the bondage, darkness and ignorance of consciousness—our human condition.   I call this act or movement of the divine "God-Awful" because it was awful for God and far exceeded the human limits; it could not be endured by man.   The incarnation, then, is the "God Awful" act of God becoming man—awful for the divine, but a boon for man.

How this divine act of incarnation effected a change for all humanity is a subject we will not go into.   Let us just say that this was the beginning of a new order, virtually an order of grace and one that is still in the process of being realized.   Since the advent of Christ, man's realization of oneness with the divine has expanded in depth (the psyche) as well as in width (numerically).   Union is no longer a realization limited to a few rare, privileged souls.   Thus before the incarnation, man's encounter with the divine was an outstanding supernatural event, but now, after the incarnation, everyone can get into the act.   It might be said that when the realization of oneness with the divine has become "natural" to man and not something ecstatically extraordinary, humanity will have caught up with the incarnate Christ.   Beyond this, however, only the divine or Trinitarian Christ can take us.

But here, now, is the movement of the incarnation event. (1)   From the ultimate divine condition or unmanifest Father, Christ moves into the ascension condition or experience and begins to take on bodily form.   (2)   From here he comes down into the resurrected condition which is a wholly physical, but purely sensory condition. (3)   He then moves through the great void (that separates resurrection and death) and into consciousness.   (4)   He is born into unitive or God-consciousness which was his state until the time of his death.   At the point where the incarnation experience *ends* (unitive consciousness at birth), the whole movement then reverses itself, and Christ begins to move back toward the divine the same way he came from it—a "reverse process."

Man's journey is the reverse of Christ's.   From the manifest divine or void of voids (not from the unmanifest divine) man is created directly into consciousness and comes forth in darkness and unknowingness.   Man did not forfeit the divine condition or unmanifest to come into this world; in fact, man did not exist before he came into this world, and thus he had nothing to forfeit.   Only the manifest divine had something to forfeit in becoming human because only the eternal manifest knows or is one with the unmanifest. The incarnate Christ, then, did not have the same beginning as man, nor did he enter this world by the same route; Christ came down by the reverse route or path that man goes up.

Christ as The Way

What Christ revealed was everyman's passage through consciousness along with the milestones that all men must pass in their journey to the divine. This revelation was not anything Christ said, but what he *was* and what he silently *manifested*. The revelation of this passage is also the revelation of consciousness or man. Consciousness is the true movement of our life, and how this movement went for Christ is how it goes for all of us. The first imperative of this movement is to realize our human oneness with the divine because Christ IS the reality of this oneness beyond our experience of it.

This unitive consciousness, however, is not man's final condition; rather, it is only the point where we meet up with Christ's consciousness and follow him into the marketplace. When Christ had fulfilled this unitive consciousness and could go no further with its potential, he died. After descending to the void of voids ("descended into hell") he rose to a totally new condition or dimension of existence, one that was beyond all consciousness. After verifying the divine nature of the body in the resurrection, he ascended or returned to his eternal divine condition—the Father. Christ's ascension seemed to be a dissolution or disappearance of his body, as if it had evaporated into a "cloud," or perhaps divine air. We say Christ "ascended to his Father," but where is the Father? As we know, much like air, the divine is Everywhere, the Trinitarian Christ is Everywhere. What this tells us is that Christ's divine body is not what appears to the senses, intellect or consciousness—his mystical body is beyond all this. But there is a further Truth or dimension of Christ beyond even that of the ascension, and this is the Eucharist or the incarnate Christ who remains with us still—"I go that I might come." As the Eucharist, Christ remains among us until every human being has been gathered into the divine. As the All and Everywhere, we do not know where Christ is not, but as the incarnate Christ we know where Christ IS, and this is the Eucharist.

EXPERIENCE AND MANIFESTATION: THE DIFFERENCE

Besides "once removed" and "reverse process" there is another way in which Christ is unique among men or one of a kind. This is the difference between "experience" and "manifestation," meaning that *Christ manifested what others can only experience.* Where we experience oneness with the divine, Christ IS this oneness. Where we experience death and resurrection, Christ IS death and resurrection. He manifested them physically. Where we experience the ascension or dissolution in the divine, Christ physically disappeared —in a cloud. Where we may know incarnation through experience, Christ was physically incarnate. In short, all our divine experiences and enlightenments are shadows of the Reality of Christ who manifested what we can only experience.

Although experience may have accompanied Christ's manifestation, his manifestation was a physical materialization and change over and above mere experience. In some ways manifestation is akin to a miracle in that a miracle stands independent of any experience that may or may not accompany this phenomenon. Manifestation cannot be reduced to an experience, a behavior, or to mere words; thus we cannot call an experience a "manifestation"— not at least in the sense I am using the term. Man comes upon the divine or truth through experience, whereas the incarnate Christ is a manifestation beyond experience. Christ IS the manifest divine that is revealed to us; he is the truth which we only discover, intuit, or experience because of his manifestation. If the divine were not first manifest, we could not speak of experiencing it.

Where saints, seers, and prophets tell us of their divine experiences and revelations, Christ said nothing at all about the "experience" of incarnation, death, resurrection and ascension. He simply DID it. Obviously, the nature of manifestation is beyond description and mere experience. In fact, the reason we can describe our divine experiences is that they are NOT manifestations. Then, too, if there is any proof of ultimate Truth, it would have to be its manifestation and not merely its experience. Sometimes I think this is why man seems to have more faith in "nature" as the divine's manifestation than he does in his own passing experiences. In the long run experience tends to prove nothing; it is not really a valid basis for belief. This does not mean, however, that experience has no value. Certain experiences are pure grace and may be likened to an "experiential" manifestation of the divine in ourselves. But where experience is always limited to an individual realization, manifestation is prior to anyone's realization or experience. In this sense, manifestation is universal, whereas experience is always and everywhere limited to the individual.

The fact that man only experiences what the divine manifests does not deprecate human experience, personal enlightenment or revelation. There is no question that man can experience what Christ manifested; yet this experience still falls short of manifestation. Thus where manifestation can give rise to experience, experience cannot give rise to manifestation. One is not the other; experience and manifestation are of two different orders. Another term for manifestation might be "Reality." Where man takes his reality from his experiences, underlying his experiences is Reality. Thus while we experience Reality, the experience itself is not Reality in itself or as it stands independent of our experiences. In short, experience is once removed from Reality or manifestation.

Again, by manifestation I mean *Truth* itself and not just the realization or experience of Truth. As the sole manifestation of the divine, the revealing or manifest events of Christ's historical life were not mere experiences. As said, Christ did not merely "experience" incarnation, death, resurrection and so on; rather, he DID it, manifested it, *was* it.

There is a way, however, in which it can be said that the entire universe—everyman included—manifests the divine. In this sense of the term, the historical Christ as a manifestation of the divine is no different from anything else; indeed, in this sense even a rock and a flower is the manifestation of the divine. Without question a rock and a flower may be a medium of divine inspiration and insight— divine's revelation, after all, is not limited to human mediumship. But while the flower and the saint are beautiful manifestations of the divine, neither the flower or the saint IS the divine. Whatever the medium may be, it has no power of its own; thus neither the medium or the experience it effects in us is divine; *the divine cannot be a medium.* Thus while the physical form of the historical Christ may be seen and experienced as a medium like anything else in the universe, this still falls short of Christ's *being* the manifest divine and not merely a medium of the divine.

So there are a number of ways we can use the term "manifest."

1. All creation, all form manifests the divine, but only eternal form from which all is created is the Absolute manifest—Christ. Thus Christ is prior to creation and to his historical incarnation or manifestation. In this sense *manifestation* refers to Christ's Godhead as all that is manifest of the divine.

2. As we have tried to point out, the incarnate Christ is a singular unique manifestation of a different order than that of other human beings. Christ did not merely manifest the divine as the flower or the saint; rather, Christ *is* this manifestation, his own cause and effect, the uncreated and created. No human being brings himself into the world or is his own cause. Where we experience

and know the divine's manifestation in various and sundry ways, Christ was this manifest embodiment. Thus what we experience and know through enlightenment, Christ IS. Manifestation, then, is the Reality underlying our experiences, while experience itself is not Reality or true manifestation.

3. Within man the divine manifests itself in the form of grace. Because this (grace) is divine life in us, it is prior to all experience. Though we may sometimes experience grace or God's immediate manifestation in us, few graces are experiential, and not every experience that we think is divine is grace. Relying on experience can be deceptive, and any clinging to experiences is the surest way to delusions. In this sense, *manifestation* refers to grace or the divine's true manifestation in us, which means Christ is manifest in us as grace and not as experience.

4. Though the incarnate Christ and a sage or seer may reveal the same truth to us, the manner of this revelation is the difference between "experience" and "manifestation." In total silence and without a word of description Christ manifests what the sage only experiences, discovers or comes upon. While the sage verbalizes and describes the truth he has discovered, Christ manifests this truth in silence. The truth or event of the incarnation, for example, does not rest on any intellectual proof, experiential verification, description, or a single word. If it had not been God's incarnation, nothing would have come of it.

Saying that Christ manifested what others only experience or discover, does not deprecate our personal experiences or deny that they may shed light on the truths that Christ manifested. Though "manifest truth" belongs to the divine and "experiential truth" belongs to man, in some ways one is not more humanly meaningful than the other. We cannot manifest truth, but we give our whole lives to see, know and understand it, even to experience it.

SUMMARY

We have pointed out three ways in which the incarnate Christ is different from ourselves or is unique among all men. First, as the one Absolute, Christ is the eternal manifest prior to creation, prior to the advent of man and prior even to the incarnation. Where Christ is the eternal manifest of the unmanifest Father, man is solely the manifestation of Christ. Thus only the eternal manifest can be an incarnation of the unmanifest; while man can only be a manifestation (or incarnation) of the eternal manifest. Man then is "once removed" from the eternal Christ and "twice removed" from the unmanifest.

Second, at the incarnation Christ took on human existence in the "reverse order" of man's coming into this world and man's going out of this world. Christ began his journey into this world at the "point" where man's journey comes to a definitive end; thus we say that in Christ's beginning is our ending. Where man comes forth in darkness and makes his way to unitive consciousness, then to death, resurrection, and ascension, Christ begins in the ultimate divine condition and comes down as far as unitive consciousness. At this point Christ's journey turns around and begins its return to the Father or ultimate divine condition, and, in doing so, takes all men with him. Christ's whole journey was the "reverse process" of everyman's journey.

Third, Christ as the eternal divine is all that is manifest of the unmanifest divine. Only the eternal manifest can be a true incarnation of the divine because only the manifest can forfeit the unmanifest condition (heaven) and take on the human condition. To enter this world, no human being forfeits the unmanifest condition because he neither knew it nor had it in the first place. Prior to coming into this world man did not even exist. As the manifest divine and its sole incarnation, Christ is the manifestation that man only experiences. While this manifestation is revealed in our experiences, our experiences are not the Reality or Actuality of the manifestation: this alone IS Christ.

POSTSCRIPT

After reading these pages on how Christ is different or one of a kind among men, a friend asked why God could only be incarnated once—why not many times? Her tradition was Hinduism, where it seems the belief is that "avatars" are Brahman's periodic incarnations, the purpose of which is to reveal Truth anew or to reaffirm it. Apart from the fact that the concept of "Brahman" is not the same as the concept of God and that the Hindu and Christian notion of "salvation" are very different, for most Christians, perhaps, the immediate response would be that a single incarnation of God was all that was needed to save or redeem all men for all time. If this were not sufficient, God would not be God. In other words, God would be deficient if he could not save man in a single stroke —or needed to hit the rock many times before water came out, so to speak. But my first response to the question is that since the incarnate Eucharistic Christ is still with us, how could there be another incarnation? You cannot reincarnate the divine that is still incarnate; this would make no sense. Those who do not know the Eucharist, of course, would not understand this. That at the end of time the Eucharistic Christ will be revealed to every human being is not, however, another incarnation, but rather, the open revelation of the divine Christ that is already here, Christ still with us.

DATE DUE

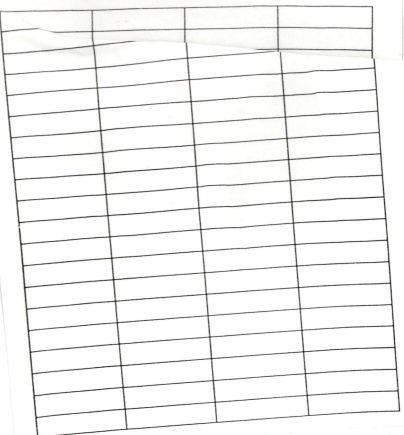